Willey Francis Gates

Anecdotes of Great Musicians

three hundred anecdotes and biographical sketches of famous composers and

performers

Willey Francis Gates

Anecdotes of Great Musicians
three hundred anecdotes and biographical sketches of famous composers and performers

ISBN/EAN: 9783337014032

Printed in Europe, USA, Canada, Australia, Japan

Cover: Foto ©Thomas Meinert / pixelio.de

More available books at **www.hansebooks.com**

ANECDOTES

OF

GREAT MUSICIANS.

ANECDOTES

OF

GREAT MUSICIANS.

THREE HUNDRED ANECDOTES AND BIOGRAPHICAL SKETCHES
OF FAMOUS COMPOSERS AND PERFORMERS.

BY

W. FRANCIS GATES,

AUTHOR OF "MUSICAL MOSAICS," "PIPE AND STRINGS," ETC.

LONDON:
WEEKES & CO.,
14, Hanover Street, Regent Street, W.
1896.

INTRODUCTORY.

In the search for what this volume comprises, much material has been examined. Had the intention been to make it include all the anecdotes that are related of various musicians, three times the present space would have been necessary. But many of the narratives of past and current literature will not stand the test of probability, and in some cases the humor or reason for relation is hard to find.

I have attempted to cull from the mass of material that came to my notice such anecdotes as have two features,—that of being characteristic of the person referred to, and that of possessing sufficient interest; and in this re-narration I have incorporated such bits of musical information, along biographical and historical lines, as came to mind at the time of writing, but letting this feature be secondary to the main idea of the work. Thus it is hoped that while my readers may find interesting anecdote, they may also incidentally find that which is of more permanent value.

This work may be regarded as a companion volume to my "MUSICAL MOSAICS," supplementing the thoughts of the great musicians there expressed with incidents giving somewhat of a clue to their personality.

It would be in vain for me to attempt to acknowledge

all the sources from which these anecdotes have been gleaned, owing to the extent of the field covered. The majority of the matter appears in this volume for the first time in its present form, although in a few cases there are partial quotations.

No classification has been made in the body of the work, thus avoiding monotony in a consecutive reading. The indexes furnish ample references.

If these narrations awaken a more general interest in musical biography, one purpose of my labor will have been accomplished.

W. FRANCIS GATES.

CONTENTS.

NO.		PAGE
88.	A Basso's Wit,	86
254.	A Bold Pupil,	249
40.	A Boy's Memory,	43
211.	A Burial Place Denied,	207
291.	A Charitable Trio,	290
229.	A Comical Revenge,	226
30.	A Concert Preacher,	35
232.	A Compliment from Haydn,	228
96.	A Composer's Chagrin,	92
206.	A Costly Fiddle,	204
19.	A Critical Composition,	26
190.	A Deserved Chastisement,	187
144.	A Double Dose of Brahms,	145
255.	A Dressing-room War,	260
63.	A Fiddler's Trick,	64
98.	A Frightened Desdemona,	95
224.	A Great German Songstress,	220
183.	A Great Thief,	180
153.	A Gentle Critic,	154
227.	A Gory Drumstick,	223
135.	A Great Quartet,	135
75.	A Hatful of Pearls,	74
186.	A Kind Act,	185
249.	A Little Trick of Paganini's,	245
197.	A Long Encore Number,	195
37.	A Musical Priest,	41
217.	A Musical Tragedy,	213
193.	A Narrow Escape,	190
233.	A Particular Prima Donna,	229
114.	A Patient Pupil,	111
72.	A Patti Reception that She Didn't Receive,	72
105.	A Peculiar Genius,	101
288.	A Peculiar Visiting Card,	285
260.	A Prima Donna's Pets,	255
50.	A Queen's Regard for her Music Teacher,	53
92.	A Second Napoleon,	89
146.	A Sharp Rejoinder,	147

CONTENTS.

NO.		PAGE
93.	A Singer's Sense,	90
225.	A Sight for the Boys,	222
61.	A Song for Forty,	62
13.	A Sudden Cure,	21
10.	A Test of Precocity,	18
194.	A Pyrotechnic Violoncello,	191
142.	A Violin for Eighteen Pence,	143
52.	A Witty Songstress,	55
117.	Absent Minded,	115
159.	An Absent-minded Conductor,	159
36.	An Army, a Cow, and a Prima Donna,	40
51.	An Earnest Student,	54
78.	An Episode in the Life of an Artist,	76
257.	An Erratic Prima Donna,	252
178.	An Even Distribution of Honors,	176
110.	An Eventful Career,	106
215.	An Exciting Musical Duel,	211
58.	An Ignorant Tenor,	59
157.	An Interrupted Concert,	157
216.	An Interrupted Strain,	213
172.	An Interrupted Opera,	170
222.	An Obese Basso,	219
256.	An Opera Sacrificed,	251
25.	An Uncringing Reply,	31
46.	An Unorthodox Creed,	48
22.	An Untalented Royal Pupil,	28
69.	Another Way,	69
42.	Artistic Aversion to Empty Honors,	45
266.	Aristocratic Patronage—Haydn's Farewell,	261
243.	Arrested for Treason,	238
154.	Art Before Business,	155
280.	Artistic Pride,	276
207.	Bach's Great Works. How Enjoyed by Some,	204
6.	Balfe's Strange Room Mate,	14
44.	Baton Waving.—Lully Losing a Limb,	46
202.	Beethoven *a la* Cupid,	199
271.	Beethoven, Brain-owner,	267
150.	Beethoven's First Triumph,	151
292.	Beethoven's Forgetfulness,	291
281.	Beethoven's Friends,	276
218.	Beethoven's Gratitude,	215
34.	Beethoven's Kiss,	39
173.	Beethoven Punished,	171
7.	Berlioz and Paganini,	15
156.	Bülow's Bits,	156
231.	But One Seat Left,	228

CONTENTS. ix

NO.		PAGE
235.	Campanini as a Soldier,	231
28.	Catalani and Goethe,	33
138.	Cherubini as a Revolutionary Fiddler,	139
219.	Choleric Händel,	216
125.	Chopin's Technic,	125
101.	Clementi's Economy,	98
113.	Clerical Wit,	110
139.	Conscientious Acting and Singing,	140
158.	Coöperative Composition,	158
160.	Costly Admiration,	159
297.	Cuzzoni—Bordoni,	295
251.	Delayed Appreciation,	247
5.	Discovering a Nightingale,	13
85.	Disposing of an Audience,	84
79.	Earning a Violin Easily,	78
198.	"Englyshe Meetre,"	195
264.	Fallible,	259
115.	Field Fooled,	113
49.	Forewarned is Forearmed,	51
277.	Fortunes in Fiddles,	272
167.	French Wit,	165
180.	Friends,	178
131.	From Humble Origin to Wealth and Fame,	131
276.	Fugues and Chess,	272
188.	Fun on the Stage,	186
132.	Gallant Haydn,	133
247.	Genius Discovered by Punishment,	243
4.	Glimpses of Cherubini,	12
296.	Gluck—Piccinni,	294
262.	Goat Hair for Hero Worshipers,	257
24.	Good English in Song,	29
176.	Gounod's Faust,	173
228.	Great Musical Memories,	224
295.	Händel—Buononcini,	293
151.	Händel's Duel,	152
74.	Händel's Escape,	74
23.	Händel's Persuasiveness,	29
87.	Händel's Successful Scheme,	85
141.	Händel's Youth,	142
94.	Haydn's Noble English Pupil,	91
286.	Haydn's Last Appearance,	283
181.	Haydn's Reception by Prince Esterhazy,	178

CONTENTS.

NO.		PAGE
18.	He Didn't Purchase,	25
39.	High Art,	43
8.	History Repeats Itself,	16
274.	Honest Opinions,	269
82.	How Berlioz Fooled the Critics,	80
122.	How Paganini Secured his Favorite Fiddle,	121
68.	How to Make a Singer Sing,	68
60.	How to Secure a Successful Début,	61
285.	Humor in Composition,	280
191.	Il Trovatore,	188
169.	Imagination a Factor in Hearing Music,	167
200.	Impositions on Musicians,	197
128.	In Bülow's Class-Room,	128
11.	Irish Enthusiasm,	19
54.	Jealousy in the Family,	56
270.	Jenny Lind's Generosity,	266
104.	Keeping at It,	101
20.	Keep in with the Accompanist,	27
95.	Lablache and Tom Thumb,	92
67.	Leoncavallo's Whimsical Opinion of his "Clowns,"	67
149.	Lind's First Engagement,	150
242.	Liszt as an Advertiser,	238
250.	Liszt's Completion of the Beethoven Monument,	246
123.	Liszt on Mendelssohn,	122
130.	Liszt's Playing and his Generosity,	130
103.	Liszt's Precocity,	99
269.	Liszt's Reply to Louis Philippe,	265
299.	Liszt—Thalberg,	298
134.	Lives of Labor,	134
241.	Longevity of Musicians,	235
71.	Manuscript for Kettles,	71
81.	Malibran's Generosity,	79
124.	Mara's Revenge,	124
76.	Mendelssohn Composing for Fun,	75
35.	Mendelssohn's Dislike of Meyerbeer,	39
234.	Mendelssohn's Kindness,	230
143.	Mendelssohn at Work,	144
195.	Misdirected and Repressed Talent,	192
109.	Modulations,	105
53.	Moscheles' Blunder,	55
65.	Mozart's Acknowledgment,	66
170.	Musical and Non-Musical Accent,	168

NO.		PAGE
38.	Musical Criticism,	42
279.	Musical Cooks,	275
56.	Musical Gratitude,	57
283.	Music for the Eye,	279
83.	Music Hath Charms,	81
43.	Music and Madness,	46
102.	Music at So Much per Note,	99
192.	Music *vs.* Commerce,	189
220.	Music *vs.* Conversation,	217
111.	Napoleon Outwitted by a Songtress,	108
253.	Nasal,	249
108.	Nilsson and the Shah of Persia,	103
213.	Not at First Sight,	210
239.	Not the Geese that Saved Rome,	234
17.	Ole Bull as a Duelist,	25
14.	Ole Bull at "Rouge-et-Noir,"	22
89.	Old Words to New Tunes,	87
278.	One Kind of Criticism,	274
66.	Operatic Sore Throat,	66
209.	Original Tapestry,	206
289.	Origin of the Name "Kreutzer Sonata,"	286
273.	Our Musical Advancement,	268
15.	Outspoken Admiration,	23
252.	Overfed Composers,	248
152.	Paganini's Generous Deed,	153
226.	Paganini in Court Dress,	222
261.	Paganini's Method of Study,	256
177.	Patti, Madame,	174
100.	Patti's Vanity,	97
208.	Peculiar English,	205
64.	Personal Appearance,	64
12.	Playing like "Zwei Gotts,"	21
86.	Playing on a Shoe,	85
175.	Pot-boilers,	172
55.	Prejudice,	56
223.	Preserving Identity,	220
45.	Prima Donnas Come High,	48
282.	Prolific Composers,	278
182.	Proving Identity,	179
187.	Public Criticism,	185
179.	Rapid Composition,	176
27.	Rather a Hard Opponent to Conquer,	33
136.	Rec'd in Full of A/c,	137

CONTENTS.

NO.		PAGE
214.	Restoring an Organ,	210
99.	Retentive Memories,	96
248.	Richard Wagner and the Number "13,"	244
163.	Royal Honors to a Singer,	162
290.	Royal Musicians,	286
133.	Rossini and the Italian School,	133
293.	Rossini's Arrogance,	291
70.	Rossini Hearing the Impossible,	70
244.	Rothschild's Music,	240
259.	Sarcasm,	254
116.	Saving a Fiddle,	114
230.	Scherzo,	227
162.	Schubert's "Erl-King,"	161
272.	Schubert's Modesty,	268
80.	Schubert's Serenade,	78
246.	Schumann's Failure,	242
284.	Schumann's Madness,	279
127.	Securing Music under Difficulties,	127
106.	Shaking all Over,	102
41.	Slippers at a Premium,	44
121.	Some Liberal Musicians,	120
298.	Sontag—Malibran,	297
91.	Sontag's Revenge,	88
26.	Southern Passion,	32
126.	Spohr as a Horn Player,	126
263.	Stage Censorship,	258
112.	Stubborn Composers,	109
240.	That Patti Kiss,	235
2.	The Bach Revival,	10
90.	The Composer's Debt to Nature,	88
164.	The Deaf Beethoven,	163
155.	The "Dear Saxon,"	155
196.	The Discovery of a Tenor,	193
199.	"The Devil on Two Sticks,"	197
47.	The Devil's Trill,	49
73.	The Encore Fiend,	73
300.	The Financial Circumstances of the Great Composers,	300
97.	The Friends, Mozart and Haydn,	93
57.	The Greater the Composer the Greater the Student,	58
9.	The Greatest Musical Prodigy,	17
1.	The Gregorian Chant,	9
201.	The Hallelujah Chorus,	199
119.	The "Harmonious Blacksmith,"	117
267.	The Hebrew in Music,	263
287.	The Heroic in Music,	283

NO.		PAGE
165.	The History of a Violin,	163
210.	The Manual Labor of Composition,	207
275.	The Modern Tendency,	271
29.	The Music but Not the Face,	35
107.	The "Ox" Minuet,	103
140.	The Peculiarities of Genius,	141
118.	The Prima Donna of the Eighteenth Century,	116
245.	The "Prison Josephs,"	241
77.	The Right Kind of a Patron,	76
268.	The Story of Mozart's Requiem,	264
62.	The Temple Organ,	63
189.	The Thirty-three Variations,	187
120.	The Ups and Downs of a Singer's Life,	118
221.	The World's Reward to Genius,	217
21.	The Youthful Beethoven's Trick on a Singer,	27
185.	Their Favorite Surroundings for Composition,	182
59.	Three Classes of Players,	60
294.	To a Pauper's Grave,	292
236.	To Make a Player Play,	231
168.	Too Literal,	166
31.	Traveling in State,	36
237.	True Kindliness,	232
32.	Tuning Up,	37
147.	Two Kinds of Bills,	147
145.	Unfailing Sight Reading an Impossibility,	146
48.	Unlucky Manuscripts,	50
174.	Violin Collectors,	172
238.	Viotti's Independence,	233
129.	Viotti's Tin Fiddle,	129
33.	Voice Against Trumpet,	38
148.	Von Bülow as a Political Speaker,	149
184.	Von Bülow's Memory,	182
212.	Von Bülow's Peculiarities,	209
171.	Von Weber to a Bawling Choir,	169
166.	"Vorts" vs. Music,	164
204.	Vox Populi,	201
255.	Wagner's Activity,	250
203.	Wagner and the Beggars,	200
84.	Wagner's Melodies and Chords,	83
137.	Wagner's Working Costume,	137
205.	What's in a Name,	202
258.	When They Began,	253
16.	Whims of Composers,	24
3.	Why We Should Sing,	11
161.	Wine and Music,	160

ANECDOTES
OF
GREAT MUSICIANS.

1.—THE GREGORIAN CHANT.

There have been musical antagonisms in all ages of the world. Church and State have joined in them as well as individuals. But not all of them had as judicious an arbiter as had the dispute between the French and Roman singers on the occasion of a visit of Charlemagne to Rome to celebrate Holy Week, about the year 803, A.D. This most Catholic magnate had taken with him his choir; and the Gallic singers soon started a controversy with the choristers of the Roman Church, claiming to sing better and more agreeably than the Italians.

But the Roman choristers knew that their style of music was in direct descent from St. Gregory, and accused the Gauls of corrupting and disfiguring the true ecclesiastical style.

Finally this dispute between the singers of the good King Charles and those of Pope Adrian waxed so warm that the King thought it time to take a hand and end the hostilities. He called his singers before him and asked them whether they thought the water of a fountain would be purest at its source, or after it had run a good distance and been mixed with other streams. Of course, they answered that the nearer to the source the purer the water. The King then exclaimed, "Mount ye then up to the pure fountain of St. Gregory, whose chant ye have manifestly corrupted."

On his return to France, Charlemagne took with him, at his request and by the appointment of Pope Adrian, two singers learned in the true ecclesiastical mode. He stationed one at Metz and the other at Soissons. The Pope also sent choral books which had been written by Gregory, so that these teachers, who had themselves studied under him, could correct the French books. The King ordered all singing masters in the kingdom to be taught by these Roman monks and to conform their books and teaching to the Gregorian antiphonal.

2.—THE BACH REVIVAL.

One of Mendelssohn's ardent friends in his youthful days was Edward Devrient, a thorough musician and an excellent singer. These friends used to delve into the music of "Old Bach" and revel in the learning displayed there. One day they resolved to take up the old cantor's "Passion Music," which had not been heard for a hundred years and which was, even to such good musicians as they, known by name only.

They became enchanted with the beauties of this lofty masterpiece, and Devrient enthusiastically declared it ought to be given in public. Mendelssohn at first ridiculed the suggestion, saying the public would not give it a cordial reception and that it was sure to be a failure. But after talking it over, Mendelssohn became as enthusiastic on the subject as was his friend. So the two young fellows—for Mendelssohn was then only eighteen—went to see Zelter, Mendelssohn's teacher, the most influential musician in Berlin.

After considerable argument, they convinced Zelter of the feasibility of their plan, and, securing his promise of co-operation, went home to begin the arduous labors that such a performance entails on manager and conductor. They had to secure the soloists, the double chorus, and the double orchestra demanded by the score. Devrient himself sang the part allotted to "Christ," and Mendelssohn conducted.

It is needless to say that the performance (given in 1829) was a success. A repetition was demanded; and not Berlin alone, but the whole musical world began to realize that in Sebastian Bach's great works there was a mine of wealth that would be unexhausted for ages. And it was to these young men, Mendelssohn especially, that we owe our knowledge and appreciation of the Leipzig cantor's masterwork of sacred music.

But Mendelssohn did not stop with this. Through his efforts there was erected a fine monument to Bach's memory, which perpetuates the face and figure of this fountain head of modern music. It was erected in 1842, in front of the "Thomas Schule" in which Bach taught, and facing the windows of his study.

3.—WHY WE SHOULD SING.

It is generally admitted that there is a beneficial physiological side to the matter of singing as well as that of entertainment and musical pleasure. Long and learned articles on this subject come from erudite pens; but we venture that it would be hard to find anything more unique in this line than the "Reasons briefely set downe by th' auctor, to perswade euery one to learne to sing," given in William Byrd's "Psalmes, Sonets, and songs of Sadnes and Pietie," published in England in 1588.

These reasons that are "briefely set downe" are as follows:—

First, It is a knowledge easily taught, and quickly learned, when there is a good Master and an apt Scoller.

2. The exercise of singing is delightfull to nature, and good to preserue the health of Man.

3. It doth strengthen all parts of the brest, and doth open the pipes.

4. It is a singuler good remedie for a stutting and stamering in the speech.

5. It is the best means to procure a perfect pronunciation, and to make a good Orator.

6. It is the only way to know when Nature hath bestowed the benefit of a good Voyce which guift is so rare, as there is not one among a thousand, that hath it; and in many, that excellent guift is lost, because they want Art to expresse Nature.

7. There is not any Musicke of Instruments whatsoeuer, comparable to that which is made of the Voyces of Men, where the voyces are good, and the same well sorted and ordered.

8. The better the voyce is, the meeter it is to honor and serue God therewith; and the voyce of man is chiefly to be employed to that ende.

> Since singing is so good a thing
> I wish all men would learne to singe.

4.—GLIMPSES OF CHERUBINI.

Cherubini was a gruff old fellow, but occasionally a bit of kindness or humor came to the surface, and then he showed the better side of his nature. He was one day met, at the Paris *Conservatoire*, of which he was the head, by a father who came bringing his talented son to gain admission to the institution. Cherubini exclaimed, when the man had told his errand, "What do you want? I do not take infants to nurse!"

The father was about to give up his attempt, but was told to take the boy to a certain room and have him play whatever he could think of, and not to stop when Cherubini came into the room. Soon the Director came in. Hearing the boy play, he was astonished at the talent and youth of the performer, and proceeded to question him on the principles of music. The result was that he at once admitted the boy to the *Conservatoire*. Cherubini afterward, in telling others about the affair, said, "I had to be very careful about pushing the questions too far; for the baby was beginning to prove to me that he knew more about music than I do myself."

When Berlioz was a student in the *Conservatoire*, he was generally at sword's points with the crusty director. Once, on examination day, Cherubini was running over a piece which Berlioz had submitted, when he came upon a complete rest of two measures.

"What is that?" he asked, in his usual ill-natured tone.

"Mr. Director," said the pupil, "I wish to produce an effect which I thought could best be produced by silence."

"Ah, you thought it would produce a good effect upon the audience if you suppressed two measures?"

"Yes, sir."

"Very good. Suppress the rest; the effect will be better still!"

As an instance of Cherubini's curt wit, the following little conversation is cited:—

One day a friend handed a score to Cherubini, saying it was by Mehul. After looking it over he exclaimed:—

"It is not Mehul's; it is too bad to be his."

"Then will you believe me if I tell you it is mine?" said the visitor, and Cherubini replied:—

"No! It is too good to be yours."

5.—DISCOVERING A NIGHTINGALE.

Many years ago, in 1827, there lived in an almshouse in the old city of Stockholm a little six-year-old girl, who had been put in charge of an old woman who, by the way, was none too kind to the orphan in her care. When her guardian went out to earn her daily pittance, this little maid was locked in the house to prevent her wandering about; and so the lonesome little Johanne was deprived of the bright sunshine and the sight of the beautiful trees and flowers so beloved by every Swedish heart.

One day she had worked over the little tasks assigned her until she was tired, and oh! how she longed to get out into the open air. But no, the door was locked. No wonder she poured out her childish grief in tears. Soon her sole companion caught her eye, and, taking up her half-starved pussy, she rocked her pet until they both fell asleep. When she awoke the sun had gone well down. Fearing the scolding she was sure to get when the old dame came home, the child caught up her work and began to sing in a sweet voice that seemed far too old for a girl of her age.

While she went on with her singing it happened that a lady of high rank was passing the house; and so struck was she by the clear, sweet tones, that she stopped her carriage to listen. On caroled the little songstress, perfectly unconscious of her audience, till she was startled by a knock at the door. She could not open it, but some kind neighbor told the fair visitor about the little prisoner. The kind-hearted lady came back afterward and secured the child admission to a school and later to the Royal Theater classes. As the girl grew older her talent developed, until as the "Swedish Nightingale" she was known the world over. Do you recognize in her—Jenny Lind?

6.—BALFE'S STRANGE ROOM MATE.

The composer of the popular "Bohemian Girl" once had an experience that he did not care to duplicate. Landladies are not supposed to be very sentimental beings, at least toward their lodgers, but have the reputation of being business-like and matter-of-fact; but the one who caused this peculiar occurrence, in which Balfe was an interested party, certainly stood at the head of the procession in her delight in silver rather than sentiment.

Balfe and other musicians were engaged for a short

time in some musical doings on the outskirts of London, and rather than go back and forth from the city each day, they decided to take rooms for the time in that neighborhood. But apartments were scarce, and the genial Irishman was compelled to take what offered at a house not any too prepossessing in its external appearance. It was quite late. The landlady was uncertain whether there were any spare rooms or not, but left him standing in the hall-way while she went to see if she could arrange a room for him. Finally she returned and told him in a confused way that his apartment was ready.

Tired by the day's labor, he soon fell asleep without examining the room, but early the next morning proceeded to make a tour of his apartment. He had not gone far before he discovered in a closet opening from his room—a corpse, which had evidently been put in its cramped quarters in great haste.

Balfe stopped not on the order of his going, but took his departure, thankful, however, that he had not made the discovery in the moonlight of the night before. The old lady had evidently been unable to withstand the temptation to make a little ready cash, and summarily deprived the body of her deceased relative of its temporary resting place, and Balfe had calmly stepped in and taken its place. He used to joke over the landlady's eye to business, but that experience so impressed him that he never occupied a strange room without making an examination prior to sleeping in it.

7.—BERLIOZ AND PAGANINI.

Berlioz was no exception to the majority of composers in the matter of finances. In fact, it was a continual struggle for him to keep the pot boiling, and he could only do so by his literary work. But his genius and need were recognized in other quarters. He gave a concert in which he conducted his great " Childe

Harold" Symphony and achieved much success. After the concert, when the composer had sat down to rest, there came to him a tall, dark man, thin as a skeleton, and, kneeling down before the whole orchestra, he kissed Berlioz's hand. It was Paganini!

The next morning Paganini's son brought to Berlioz a letter, saying, " Papa wants you not to read this letter until you are alone," and then the little fellow vanished. When Berlioz opened the letter he found it to be from Paganini, saying that, Beethoven being dead, Berlioz alone could revive him, and asked Berlioz to accept the enclosure as Paganini's homage to his greatness. The enclosure was an order on the firm of Rothschild for 20,000 francs. Berlioz was delighted with this princely gift, and wrote and tore up four letters before he could get one that would sufficiently express his thanks. The eight hundred pounds served him a good turn, even if he never found out that it was not out of Paganini's pocket-book. He had the money and the violinist the credit of giving it.

8.—HISTORY REPEATS ITSELF.

This old saying is particularly true of musical anecdote and story. Of course, it must be that history really does repeat itself, for certainly no one could be so heartless as to charge the enterprising manager or the penny-a-liner, sadly in need of copy, with hunting among old tales for one to apply to modern favorites. *Munsey's Magazine* for December ('93) gives the following incident:—

"A touching incident is recorded among the experiences of Madame Melba (now singing in New York) last year at Palermo. It was during a performance of 'Lucia.' The diva was changing her costume between the acts, when a lady appeared in her dressing-room. After complimenting her on her singing, the stranger took up in one hand some strands of Madame Melba's hair, which was flowing loose over her shoulders, and asked :—

"'Is this all your own?'

"Upon being satisfied on this point the visitor continued:—

"'Allow me, Madame Melba, since I have no wreath of flowers to offer you, to twine you one with your own beautiful tresses.'

"This she did, trilling a bar or two of music meanwhile, for the visitor was none other than Christine Nilsson."

It seemed to me that the above incident had about it the flavor of antiquity, and turning to an English work published several years ago, I find the following: "On the occasion of her second visit to Naples in 1835, an incident occurred which afforded Madame Persiani deep gratification. During the representation of 'Lucia' she was one evening changing her costume between the acts, when a lady entered her dressing-room, and after a few general compliments on her singing, took in her hands the long, fair tresses which floated in wild profusion over the shoulders of the *cantatrice*, asking if they were really her own.

"Madame Persiani laughingly invited her to satisfy herself on this point, when the visitor said with a smile, 'Allow me, Signora, since I have no wreath of flowers to offer you, to twine you one with your own beautiful tresses,' and she did so.

"Madame Persiani's heart beat with pride and joy, for it was Malibran, 'the greatest singer of the day,' who spoke."

9.—THE GREATEST MUSICAL PRODIGY.

The receipt from London of a musical work edited many years ago by Dr. William Crotch calls to mind the fact that nowhere do we find record of a more remarkable exhibition of musical genius in a mere baby than in the case of this same person in his early years. He was born in 1775, and when but two years of age showed a great enjoyment in music, and could pick out on the organ keys such tunes as "God Save the King." He would also play little melodies of his own, supplying them with a simple but correct harmony.

He played before the King, royal family, and other titled personages of England, and was greeted with admiring wonder wherever his talents were displayed by his proud parents. At the age of four years he had frequently appeared in public. He could name any tone heard by him, and took great delight in pleasant harmonies, though he could not hear a discord without expressing disgust. Mozart was, in his youth, a great prodigy, but his genius was not of so early development as that of little William Crotch. Mozart became one of the greatest composers; but Crotch, though he was granted the degree of Doctor of Music in 1799 by Oxford University, and though regarded as a great musician in his day, is now almost unknown to the musical world.

10.—A TEST OF PRECOCITY.

The youthful Mozart was not the greatest prodigy known to history, but he was one of the few whose early precocity did not lead to expectations which were disappointed in later life. His musical life was a continual growth. Great stories were told of his marvelous abilities, and some of them were doubtless exaggerated. But every claim that was put forth by himself or by the parents of this wonder-child he could fulfill.

The Archbishop of Salzburg had it in his power to benefit the art of all succeeding time by granting proper patronage to Mozart, but this the churlish old fellow declined to do. He even declared that the boy Mozart was a fraud, and in the interests of art and religion he would unmask him. His plan was to confine the young genius in a closed room, give him pens, ink, paper and the necessary words, and to hold him prisoner there until he should have composed a mass. The Mozarts, father and son, consented to the trial, knowing it was entirely within the boy's powers. For more than a week did he stay in that room, seeing no one save the servant who brought his meals: At the end of this time he sent to the bishop his composition, which, after trial by the court band, the bishop ordered to be placed in the repertoire of the cathedral choir. But even after this display of genius the prelate was lacking in that appreciation of art which would have led him to become a beneficent patron.

11.—IRISH ENTHUSIASM.

On the last night of her series of performances at Dublin, in 1868, Mdlle. Titiens was the recipient of such an ovation as is seldom given even to those petted beings, operatic *prime donne.*

At the close of the aria, "Ocean, Thou Mighty Monster," in Weber's "Oberon," the audience rose *en masse*, some calling for a repetition and others for favorite Irish songs. The uproar continued for ten or fifteen minutes before quiet could be restored, and then the *diva* decided to sing the favorite, "Last Rose of Summer." But the orchestra had no music for the song and a further delay ensued. Finally, Signor Bettini was seen pushing a small piano out on the stage, and meanwhile Titiens assisted the conductor to climb up out of the orchestra. In turning the piano around the slant of the stage caused it to tip over. Now, behind the wings were the rest of the company waiting to go on with the next scene. Among them were several attired as demons. On the upsetting of the piano out rushed half a dozen devils to set things straight—an unusual occupation for the satanic brood.

Again silence was secured, and this time Titiens finished her song. At its close the uproarious applause was again indulged in.

But after the opera came the climax. The crowd of students who had filled the gallery hastened to the stage entrance, cut the traces of her carriage, and tied in their places two long ropes. These were grasped by two files of shouting students. The *prima donna* entered her carriage and was in this way escorted down the street, the crowd continually being augmented by new arrivals. Several had supplied themselves with fireworks, and the whole thing had the effect of a triumphal procession.

When the strings of volunteer horses arrived at a corner, owing to there being no agreement concerning the route, one set turned one way, and the other in an opposite direction. The result was that the carriage containing Titiens, and her escorts came to a sudden and forcible stop against a building. But after some parley both teams agreed to unite on the same direction.

When, finally, they arrived at her hotel the enthusiastic students threw their coats on the pavement from the carriage to the doorway, over which the *diva* passed to her rooms. The crowd remained around the hotel for over an hour, making continual calls for a song, and their numbers were so great that the police were unable to disperse them.

Though Titiens darkened her rooms to give the impression that she had gone to bed, still they remained.

Finally a police official came up and said that unless Madame would assist in dispersing the crowd the consequences might be disastrous. So Titiens consented to try. She went to her window and motioned for silence. Then, addressing the crowd, she said:—

"I will sing you the 'Last Rose of Summer' providing you will promise to go home at once and be as quiet as mice."

Then, a second time for that evening, did she sing the old song; and, to the surprise of the people in the hotel, the mob melted away like magic, without another sound.

The police official declared that if ever a mob broke

out in Ireland he should send for Mdlle. Titiens as the person who would most probably be successful in quelling it. The manager, Colonel Mapleson, and the *prima donna* had to pay well for the enthusiasm of their admirers, for the jolly Irishmen forgot to return the horses they took from the carriage, and the owner sent the bill to the manager.

12.—PLAYING LIKE "ZWEI GOTTS."

De Pachmann, the pianist, is so full of whimsicalities, of grimaces and odd doings, and withal is such a superb player, that he has been characterized by one epigrammatic writer as "having the soul of an angel in the body of an ape," and by another as "a combination of specialized wisdom and undifferentiated dam-foolism."

An instance of this latter element of his character took place after a recent recital of his in New York. A pianist of some note went on the stage to congratulate him on his brilliant performance. He found De Pachmann pacing up and down the stage exclaiming in fury:—

"Ach Gott! Dese Ameri*ken* beeples, how dey do—dey know not mus*eek*! I vill go back to my Jerman*ie*. Here dey know notings. I blay like von Gott and vat dey do?"

Taking his hand, the visitor tried to assuage his wrath by saying, "Yes, yes, Mr. Pachmann, you did play like a god."

Whereupon the irrepressible combination of egotism and genius burst forth:—

"Blay like *von* gott! I blay like *zwei* gotts, and dey do notings!"

13.—A SUDDEN CURE.

He who undertakes to manage an opera troupe chooses a road beset by thorns. Opera singers, especially if their salaries be high and they feel they can afford to follow their own sweet wills, generally do about the exact opposite of what a sensible person would predict. The manager must be ready for any emergency and be surprised at nothing.

Some years ago when Mme. Gerster was billed to sing in St. Louis, she suddenly sent word to the manager that she was ill and unable to sing her part in "Lucia," which must be given that evening. He suspected the indisposition to be not very serious, but requested a medical certificate to put before the public to satisfy them for the non-appearance of the songstress. Gerster declined to be seen by a physician, saying her word was as good as her bond, and that when she said she was ill, that settled it.

The manager insisted upon calling in a physician, who asked to see her tongue. So, as she was leaving the room, she derisively stuck out her tongue at him, with the exclamation, "There!" The doctor at once wrote out a certificate, saying that the epiglottis was irritated, the uvula contracted, and the tonsils inflamed.

When Gerster was shown this certificate she grew quite angry, and insisted upon singing that night, "just to show what an ass that doctor was."

All the same, the doctor sent in his bill for $60.

14.—OLE BULL AT "ROUGE-ET-NOIR."

Ole Bull first visited Paris in 1831. He was then twenty-one years of age, and had left his native country to make his journey to the French capital on foot, feeling that he must get a hearing, if possible, in some of the musical centers if he was to be successful in his musical life. He arrived tired, with little money and no letters of introduction. In a few days his clothes and his violin were stolen. In his despair, he was ready to seek relief in the Seine; and had it not been for a chance acquaintance who suggested a plan by which he might better his fortunes, he might have come to the same end which has overtaken so many discouraged artists in Paris. The stranger, who turned out to be Vidocq, the great detective, directed Ole to go to a gambling establishment where they played "rouge-et-noir," and to continually place his money on the *rouge*. The young fellow did so, placing his last francs on the red. He won. He played again. Again he was winner. And he continued until a large sum of money was before him.

Fearing to lose what he had won, he retired from the table and watched the play for a few moments, just long enough to see that, had he continued playing the red, he would have won a fortune. But though he was on the verge of starvation, the money thus obtained was not without its sting. He wrote a friend, "What a hideous joy I felt—what a horrible pleasure it was to have saved one's own soul by the spoil of others."

The young Norwegian soon purchased another violin, and, being invited to play at a private concert, succeeded in attracting attention to himself in spite of the fact that all Paris was then worshiping Paganini.

15.—OUTSPOKEN ADMIRATION.

Here is a case of admiration of one artist for another that deserves mention. When the English musician, Rosengrave, was in Italy, at an evening company, a quiet and unassuming young man, who was present, was asked to play. "When he began," writes Rosengrave, "I thought ten hundred devils were at the instrument, for never had I heard such passages and effects before. So far did he surpass my own playing that had I but had a knife within my reach I would have cut off my fingers. So ashamed was I, that I declare I could not touch an instrument for a month afterward."

The quiet young Italian was Scarlatti, the celebrated Italian composer and performer.

16.—WHIMS OF COMPOSERS.

Composers get peculiar ideas into their heads as to the circumstances under which they must work, or the surroundings that must be at hand if they are to get the best results in composition. No doubt after the habit is once formed, the regular accompaniments to composition are necessary. But the question is as to the necessity of forming the habit.

Haydn thought he could not compose unless he had on the ring which Frederick the Great sent him; and, besides this, the paper on which he wrote must be white and of the best quality. Glück wrote best when seated out in the middle of a field. Rossini was most productive of good music when "lined within with good sack wine;" and he and Paesiello both enjoyed composing while in bed.

Sacchini enjoyed having a pretty woman by his side —by the way, several of the great composers had no aversion to such an accompaniment, whether composing or not—and his pet cats must be playing around him. Mozart could compose beautiful music while playing billiards or bowls. Zingarelli prepared himself for writing music by reading the Scriptures or some classic author, and Sarti liked best a funereal gloom lighted only by a single taper.

Beethoven could compose best during or after a brisk walk in the woods and fields, and many of his greatest works were inspired by the beauties of nature.

Cimarosa and Mehul were opposites in this matter. The former wished to be surrounded by a dozen gabbling friends. The light conversation and flow of spirits (probably of two kinds) seemed to inspire his music. On the other hand, Mehul once went to the Chief of Police of Paris and asked to be imprisoned in the Bastile. That personage in surprise inquired the reason. Mehul said he desired to get away from the noise and bustle of the city, and to escape from the good graces of his friends for a time, that he might give his whole mind uninterruptedly to composition. It is needless to say that his wish was not granted. Few would wish to be surrounded by the walls of the Bastile unless it were to write a tragic overture or a funeral anthem.

Wagner thought he must be clothed in the costume of the age and place in which was laid the plot that he was then working on. He also desired a perfectly quiet and uninterrupted time in which to write. His family was denied admission to his study and he would not even see any letters that came for him; his meals were passed in to him through a trap door.

17.—OLE BULL AS A DUELIST.

Händel was not the only great musician to fight a duel, although he was the greatest composer who took a part in that exciting pastime. Ole Bull once had an adventure similar to Händel's, but from all accounts the Norwegian violinist must have been a better swordsman than the "Dear Saxon." In his student days in Germany, Bull once fell in with a party of carousing students and was persuaded by them to take the part of their violinist (who had become more than "half seas over") in a concert they were about to give. He accepted the position and played so well that the drunken fiddler whom he succeeded was jealous of his success and challenged him to a duel. Now, Ole could handle a sword as well as a fiddle bow and soon had disabled his opponent. This made things so warm for him in that neighborhood that he had to take his departure to Norway.

18.—HE DIDN'T PURCHASE.

Perfect command of one's instrument does not necessarily imply complete control of one's tongue. This was the case with Lindley, an English 'cellist of the first half of this century. Though he gained great fame as a player, he never succeeded in controlling the unruly member,—it would stutter in spite of him.

One day, in his rambles through the streets of London, he came across a shop where there was a parrot hung up for sale in the window. He and his friends were quite interested in the bird, and finally Lindley called out the shopkeeper saying, as he pointed to the polly, "C-c-ca-can h-he t-t-t-talk?"

"Yes," was the answer from the dealer, who thought he could see that it was mere curiosity that prompted the question, and not a desire to purchase. "Yes,—and a d—d sight better than you can, or I'd wring his blanked neck!"

19.—A CRITICAL COMPOSITION.

Musical progress depended largely at one time on the effect produced by one composition. It came about in this way: In the middle of the sixteenth century the music used in the Mass of the Catholic church had become so light and trivial that Pope Marcellus concluded he would discontinue the use of music in the service. But the great composer of that day, Palestrina (who, by the way, was generally known by the name of his native place), believing that could the Pope and cardinals hear a mass written in what he believed to be the true ecclesiastical style they would reverse their decision, begged them not to put the order into execution until they had given his music a hearing. The request was granted, and on Easter, 1555, this mass, called "Missa Papæ Marcelli," *i. e.*, Mass of Pope Marcellus, was performed before the highest dignitaries of the church.

It was an entire change from the trivial church music of the time; so refined, elevating and appropriate was it to the sacred office for which it was intended, that the Pope and cardinals were delighted, and had no further thought of banishing music from the service. Another result was that Palestrina was appointed chapelmaster to the Pope, and exercised a most beneficial influence in church and other styles of composition for many years. He is now regarded as a landmark in musical history, and when we remember that the Catholic church was in those times the main conservator of musical art, we realize that even at this day we owe him a debt of gratitude.

20.—KEEP IN WITH THE ACCOMPANIST.

It is good policy for a singer to keep "on the good side of" his accompanist. A really fine accompanist is a *rara avis*. Besides the technical skill necessary to a soloist, an accompanist must have the finest musical feeling and discrimination, and at the same time sacrifice himself to the interests of the singer.

And oftentimes the accompanist has to shoulder the sins of the singer. It is an easy way to relieve one's self from the blame of a "bad break" by charging the fault to the accompanist. A singer once tried this with Händel, and declared that if Händel didn't accompany him better he should jump over onto the harpsichord where the player sat, and smash it. Said Händel:

"Let me know ven you vill do dot, and I vill adverdise id. I am sure more beoble will come to see you shump as vill come to hear you sing."

He didn't jump.

21.—THE YOUTHFUL BEETHOVEN'S TRICK ON A SINGER.

Another incident of the necessity of a good understanding with the accompanist is found in the life of Beethoven. He, as a mere boy, held the responsible position of organist in the Electoral Chapel at Bonn. In the choir was a smart singer, who declared he could sing anything, and no accompanist could disconcert him.

Beethoven made a wager with him that he could succeed in "putting him out." So, in a service in holy week, by an adroit modulation in his accompaniment of this coxcomb, the latter was landed in a key where all he could do was to break down. The singer at once complained to the Elector, who heard the case and reprimanded them both. But we can hardly blame Beethoven; for a boy of fifteen, Beethoven's age at that time, could hardly withstand the temptation to try his skill under such provocation.

22.—AN UNTALENTED ROYAL PUPIL.

Louis XII was endowed with more love for music than talent or voice for singing. On his attempting to sing, it was only courtesy or policy that caused the unfortunates who happened to be present to remain. In his attempts to read music he succeeded no better. At last, in despair of singing the ordinary music of the day, he ordered the conductor of his chapel music, the *Maitre de Chapelle*, Josquin by name, to write a piece of music that he could succeed in singing. So in a few days the king was presented with a piece for four voices, two of which were in canon form; the other two accompanied, simply furnishing the harmony.

Of these latter voices, the upper had but one pitch to sing throughout the whole piece, and the lower but two, the tonic and dominant, sung alternately. After careful drill the king was able to take his, the upper part, and later acquired sufficient skill to sing the lower part with tolerable accuracy.

This may illustrate to the non-musical public one, at least, of the difficulties that beset the path of a singing teacher; for some people that the Lord never intended to sing, will persist in singing, and are not content to sing music fitted to their capacity.

23.—HÄNDEL'S PERSUASIVENESS.

There was a day when players and singers so ruled directors and composers that the latter hardly knew whether they could call their lives their own. But that day is past, and Händel was one who prominently assisted in bringing about the new order of things. Two instances will serve to show how he controlled his unruly singers.

When Carestini was given the beautiful aria "*Verdi prati*," in "Alcina," he sent it back to Händel saying it was too trivial for him to sing in public. Händel rushed off to the singer's rooms and, foaming with rage, yelled to the astonished Italian:

"You tog! Don't I know bedder ash yourself vat ish best for you do sing? If you do nod sing all de song vat I gifs you, I will not pay you ein stiver!"

Nor could this choleric composer be bullied by the weaker sex. At a rehearsal of one of his operas, the great soprano, Cuzzoni gave him great trouble by her impudence. Finally she refused to sing a certain aria. Händel concluded the time had come to see who was master; so he rushed onto the stage, and, catching the astonished *prima donna* around the waist, he dragged her to an open window, crying: "I always knew you was a very teufel, but I vill show you I am Beelzebub, de prince of de teufels!" Then he threatened to throw her out headlong unless she promised to sing the song. Cuzzoni was frightened half to death, and begged to be released, promising to do anything he might require.

24.—GOOD ENGLISH IN SONG.

In the eyes of many singers and in the minds of much of the public, the words used when singing are of no particular value. This may be true of a goodly number of popular songs that live for a day. But in the strict sense of the word, and speaking of good music, the mission of the music is to give the sentiment a proper setting. A perverted idea has, with one class of opera and song writers, brought music to the place of prime importance, it is true, but this is an unnatural arrangement of things. Music, as separate from all else, has its true place in the instrumental field.

When words are set to music they should be good enough to merit a hearing. And the singer who slights his words and leaves you in doubt as to the language he happened to be using, is just that far from being a finished singer.

It is claimed that English is a hard language to sing. So it is, for those that will not give it the necessary study and practice.

It is likewise claimed that Italian is easy to sing. So it is, for an Italian. But an Italian might be as much in doubt about the American student's Italian words as the American auditor is forced to be concerning the student's English words.

It is well known that many a singer covers her inability to sing distinct English by a retreat into poor Italian, which she thinks will be "Greek" (if not Italian) to her audience.

Vocal teachers are coming to realize that the highest vocal art requires one to sing their own language perfectly, and that years of practice in mongrel Italian do not give ability to sing good English. The reason for this is that there are many difficult consonant and vowel combinations appearing frequently in the English that are unknown to the Italian.

That German or Italian are not good preparations for English singing is shown by the remarkable combinations of sounds that foreign singers will use when called on to sing an English song. This is all right if we follow the doctrine that words are of no importance. But that doctrine does not obtain among artists. Why should we have to listen to that grand solo from the

Messiah tortured into "Ze keens hof ze hurt rees hoop?" Who could be expected to know from hearing this sort of continental English that "The kings of the earth rise up?"

Then, when some celebrated Italian *prima donna* is called on to sing our national hymn, how patriotic we must feel to hear

>" Mi coontray tees oof thee
> Swet Landa of Leeberta,
> Oof The Ih seeng;
> Landa wer mifa ters dida,
> Landa oof de peelgreem's prida,
> Froma eefrey mon-tin sida,
> Leta fretum reeng."

25.—AN UNCRINGING REPLY.

Queen Elizabeth is sometimes pictured as possessed of a temper which, carrying with it the power of revenge, made it greatly feared. The "Virgin Queen" is also reported by some writers to have been a proficient musician. Probably both statements are true. Although it was hardly safe to speak of her temper during her life, it was the proper thing to flatter her musical attainments. One of her desires was to excel Mary Queen of Scots, as a performer. But Elizabeth's temper did not always cause her to wreak vengeance on those who spoke in an unbecoming manner to the queen. This is instanced in the case of Dr. Tye, who frequently performed on the organ in the royal chapel. On one occasion while he was playing some music more scientific than tuneful, she sent the verger to him with the message that he was playing out of tune. The doctor's quick reply was:—

"Tell the queen that her ears are out of tune."

The queen let the remark pass without rebuke.

26.—SOUTHERN PASSION.

We of the Northern nations often think of the mock tragedies of the operatic stage as being overdrawn and untrue to the life. Such incidents and plots are often said to be exaggerated and of the blood-and-thunder "stagey" sort.

But we must remember that blood flows much more rapidly through Southern veins than through Northern, and that we, with our cold calculating way of looking at things, do not take into consideration the fiery temperament of the Southern climes that makes such plots but representative of the real passions of the Italian and Spanish nations.

The plots of the Mascagni and Leoncavallo school may not be elevating or over refined, but they undoubtedly do picture one phase of life.

This is not saying, however, that it is well to dwell on that phase, or that it has in it much that can ennoble the listener. Passion and pain and the lower emotions need not be continually served up to the opera-goer simply because the method of representing them is artistic. There is enough that is good and beautiful in the world out of which to make our operatic plots, without descending to the slime and filth of life, however artistically it may be dressed up.

But the other, the lower side, exists, not only in opera plots, but in the real life. The little incident here given, if presented on the stage, would be classed as a mere bit of melo-dramatic Italian opera; yet it is one of many such things that continually happen.

Leonardo Vinci was one of the numerous talented composers of the old school. In the midst of his successful career at Rome, he made the acquaintance of a noble Italian lady who was possessed of great beauty, and who conceived quite a passion for this distinguished musician. The admiration was mutual. All went well until the lady granted the composer some particular favors, and he (with an absence of discretion unusual to musicians) boasted to his friends of his good fortune in securing the lady's regard.

His words coming to the ears of the fair damsel, and disliking to have her private affairs made public talk (she would never have made a modern opera songstress), she determined to be revenged for his gossiping about her, and gave him his quietus, not with a bare bodkin, but in a cup of poisoned chocolate!

This summary method will doubtless commend itself to all who suffer from indiscreet friends.

27.—RATHER A HARD OPPONENT TO CONQUER.

It is not always safe to deride one whose abilities seem to be less than our own. This lesson was painfully learned by a young violinist of Berlin at an evening party, to which he had been invited. He played several pieces, not with great applause, however. Afterwards another young man was invited to play, but his playing was worse than that of his predecessor; in fact his style and execution were wretched. So our young professor again came forward and showed his superior abilities in a very pretentious way, as if to utterly crush the strange musician. But when it again became the stranger's turn to play, his performance was given with such expression and brilliancy of execution as to utterly vanquish the young upstart, who disappeared and was seen no more that evening. He had been contending with Paganini.

28.—CATALANI AND GOETHE.

Angelica Catalani was a singer who held sway in Europe for thirty years in the last century, as the peer of all *prime donne*. It has been said that never has the public been so carried away by the voice of any songstress as by hers. One writer calls her the " Paganini of Song," and from the accounts that have come down to us of her flights of vocalization the title must have been well bestowed. Going on to the stage at the age of sixteen, this musically gifted person was ignorant in all matters but her art; and besides this she was of an excitable temperament, vivacious and talkative.

Her ignorance of people and things often led her into making amusing blunders. One writer relates a ludicrous scene which took place between her and the great poet Goethe.

They were at Weimar; and at a court dinner she was seated next to Goethe, who was the most distinguished guest. Goethe and his works were utterly unknown to her; but seeing that he seemed to be a man of consequence and that much attention was paid to him, she inquired of the gentleman on the other side of her who this personage was. Thereupon the following conversation took place:

"He is the celebrated Goethe, madam."

"Oh, he is! And on what instrument does he play?"

"He is not a musician, madam; he is the celebrated author of 'Werter.'"

"Oh, yes, I remember." Then turning to the venerable poet she declared:

"Ah, sir, what an admirer I am of 'Werter!'" The poet bowed low in acknowledgment of the compliment.

"I never," continued she, "read anything half so laughable in all my life. What a farce it is to be sure!"

Goethe looked aghast at this remark, but managed to exclaim:

"The 'Sorrows of Werter' a farce, madam?"

"Oh, yes; there never was anything so exquisitely ridiculous," declared the talkative lady, laughing heartily at the remembrance.

It was found out afterwards that she had once seen in Paris a parody on Goethe's "Werter," which had ridiculed the original most unmercifully. But parody and original were all the same to her.

29.—THE MUSIC BUT NOT THE FACE.

While the great composers have, as a general thing, had remarkably retentive memories for musical matters, some of them were not so good at remembering other things. Rossini was one of these. He had a remarkably poor memory for names but could remember faces. On one occasion he met Bishop, the English composer, and, recognizing him, started to greet him with:

"Oh! my dear Mr. ——," but he could get no farther. The name was gone. But to show Bishop that he remembered the man, if not the name, he began to whistle Bishop's chorus, "When the Wind Blows." This was a compliment that the "English Mozart," as Bishop has been called, was not slow to recognize.

30.—A CONCERT PREACHER.

Hans von Bülow, was considered by the political authorities of Berlin and Leipzig as a great nuisance as well as a great musician. This arose from the fact that he persisted in interpolating in the speeches he frequently made at his concerts, remarks of a political nature, and often they were of a decided incendiary cast.

In the latter city this "concert preacher" as he was called, was compelled by the police to sign a promise not to speak a word at his concerts, not even to announce the date of his next appearance. And this was not two hundred years ago, either, as one might suppose from the denial of the right of speech, but was in our own times, in a supposable free country.

But it was in Berlin that he had a still greater difficulty with the powers that be. Having conceived a strong dislike for the government intendant, that official which had control of the operatic performances, who in this case happened to be Count von Hulsen, he referred to him in one of his impromptu concert speeches in a derogatory way, and to the opera as "the circus that von Hulsen runs." As von Hulsen was a court officer, this brought on Bülow's head the wrath of the court, and he was deposed from his rank as court pianist, and stripped of his medals.

Shortly after, von Hulsen died, and at a commemoration concert his successor gave orders to the ushers that they were not to admit Doctor von Bülow, and furnished them photographs of him that there should be no mistake. So when Herr Doctor arrived he was spotted and summarily ejected.

But the pianist had his revenge. The next night, on his appearance at a concert, when he sat down at the instrument be began to improvise on a theme from Mozart's "Figaro," and immediately the audience broke into laughter and applause. The theme he had chosen was in the opera, set to the words "Will the Count venture on a little dance?"

31.—TRAVELING IN STATE.

The great singers of the olden time, even of the first half of this century, would stand aghast at the splendor that surrounds the *prima donna* of to-day. The most regal elegance is thought none too good for her who has the public at her feet.

The *prima donna* of "ye olden tyme" traveled in a lumbering stage coach; the most favored one of to-day, in a private car costing some £11,600—for that was the cost of Patti's conveyance. In this beautiful coach the walls and ceiling were covered with gilded tapestry, the curtains were of silk damask, and the furniture was upholstered in the same material. The drawing-room was fitted in white and gold, with paintings by celebrated artists. The lamps were made of gold and the woodwork of sandalwood. The same wood was used in the piano, which alone cost £400.

These are some of the main points in the construction

and adornment of this car, which might well have been built for royalty. But at the day Patti was thus accommodated, no king or emperor on earth enjoyed such luxurious traveling accommodations; for in no country in the world had there been built such a sumptuous coach.

32.—TUNING UP.

An audience which listens to an amateur orchestra, and, unfortunately, the same is true of some which are professional, frequently has to go through the aural agony of hearing the instruments "tune up." This process, when conducted in a haphazard way, is most excruciating, and the effect is to give sensitive nerves an unpleasant shock at the very beginning of a concert, which it takes some very good playing to counteract.

This is also true of some solo players. I have in mind quite a good Teutonic violinist, of Boston, who arouses his hearers' musical wrath in this way for several minutes before he succeeds in satisfying his exacting ear. Perhaps the process is prolonged to show the delicate adjustment of that organ. Who knows?

But there is, ordinarily, no necessity for such a scratching and blowing prelude. The tuning might and should be done before the audience assembles, and if there is any "touching up" to be done afterward, it should be in the most *pianissimo* manner possible.

The Boston Symphony Orchestra sets a good example in this matter, as in many others musical. In the days of the old Music Hall there was set in continual vibration by electricity a large tuning fork, which, when desired, sounded an uninterrupted "A." Each man as he entered tuned his instrument to this fork, and the result was that when the orchestra gathered on the stage every man was ready to go to work without an agonizing process of pitch adjustment to inflict on his hearers.

Händel realized the necessity of a preliminary "tuning

up" period, and used to have all things ready before the concert. But on one occasion some practical joker did not neglect the opportunity offered to him, and the result was an opening chord not as harmonious as the music of the spheres.

Each instrument had been tuned at the close of the rehearsal. The orchestra returned for the performance, had taken their seats, and pompous Mr. Händel had stepped to the conductor's desk and lifted his *baton;* at the proper instant the opening *fortissimo* chord was played. But such a chord! It was discord itself! Every instrument had been thrown out of tune by some person intent more on provoking mirth than music. Händel raved. He jumped from his stand, and, after upsetting the drums and a double-bass, rushed across the stage, losing his wig on the way, and snorting with rage and vowing vengeance on the one "vat take such vicked liberty!"

33.—VOICE AGAINST TRUMPET.

It seems strange to read of the human voice exceeding wind instruments in length and loudness of tone; but there are some remarkable instances on record of great endurance on the part of singers. Lablache, the great basso, was noted for his power of tone, his voice being so strong as to dominate over the whole orchestra and chorus combined.

Farinelli, a famous tenor, in a contest with a trumpet player at Rome, not only excelled him in brilliant passages, in force and ornamentations, but when the trumpeter was out of breath and exhausted, Farinelli went on with increased brilliancy and power, apparently with the same breath, until he was silenced by the plaudits of the crowd.

On one occasion when Mrs. Billington, a favorite English singer, was holding forth in London, she was accompanied by a trumpet *obligato* in part of her solo.

As the trumpeter did not play his part with sufficient tone, the leader called to him to play louder. But even then the quantity of tone was not great enough to suit his conductor or to balance Mrs. Billington's voice; so he called out again: "Louder! louder! confound you, play louder!" The enraged foreigner, at what he considered an insult to his instrument, threw down his trumpet, exclaiming: "Loudere, loudere be ver easy do say; but, by gar! I say *ver is de vint?*"

34.—BEETHOVEN'S KISS.

When Liszt was but twelve years of age (in 1823) he was advertised to give a concert; and upon the solicitation of Schindler, Beethoven went to hear and encourage this youthful prodigy. When the little Liszt came out on the platform, he saw Beethoven sitting in the front row. Instead of being unnerved by the great man's presence, it was an inspiration to him and he played with great fire and abandon. In the storm of applause which followed, the great master was seen to step up on the platform and catch up the little fellow in his arms and kiss him on both cheeks. Liszt never forgot this incident and used to repeat it with great pride, for he felt that the master had set the seal of greatness upon him in that kiss.

35.—MENDELSSOHN'S DISLIKE OF MEYERBEER.

Mendelssohn had a great aversion for the music of Meyerbeer. Mendelssohn's music was polished, elegant, scholarly, devoid of clap-trap or effects attempted for mere show. Meyerbeer's music, on the contrary, while containing much that was good and being especially effective in instrumentation, had much that was blatant, and that savored largely of the sensational. Both men had several points of personal resemblance. Both were of Jewish descent and inherited a Hebrew cast of countenance; both were of slender build, and they were accustomed to dress the hair in the same fashion.

The aversion held by Mendelssohn for Meyerbeer's music extended somewhat to Meyerbeer himself; and great was Mendelssohn's disgust if some one of his friends teased him on his resemblance to the detested composer. On one occasion, in Paris, after having been subject to some good-natured jokes about the similarity of his personal appearance to that of Meyerbeer, the composer of "St. Paul" and "Elijah" rushed off to the barber and had his hair clipped short to dispel the likeness. This, of course, only made him subject to a fresh lot of jokes on the hated resemblance.

36.—AN ARMY, A COW, AND A PRIMA DONNA.

It is not often that an army does the bidding of a *prima donna*, but a story comes to us from the siege of Hamburg, many years ago, which intimates as much. It is said that during the bombardment of this city the opera continued as usual, and the beleagured officers and soldiers took great pleasure in hearing Madame Fodor, the *prima donna* of the occasion. Now all great singers have some favorite stimulant, from beer down to beefsteak, without which they think they cannot make a success of their singing. Madam Fodor's favorite beverage happened to be fresh milk, a very harmless drink, to be sure, but one not so easily obtainable when a town is in a state of siege and the last cow has been slaughtered for food.

Learning that their favorite was thus deprived of her customary beverage, the officers determined at all hazards to supply the deficiency, and the soldiers made a gallant sortie from out the city walls and, capturing—not the enemy, but a cow, returned in triumph. The cow was escorted by the officers to the theater and publicly presented to the fair songstress. It was then installed in a property room on the stage, and from that time on

Madam Fodor could regale herself at will with the lacteal extract.

37.—A MUSICAL PRIEST.

All priests are not musical, and, queer as it may seem, all musicians are not religious! The writer once interviewed a priest as to the musical characters in the antiphonal and breviary and found him entirely ignorant as to the note values, pitch indications, and musical characters generally. On showing him a breviary dated 1692 we found the notation virtually the same as in the service book of to-day. The C clef appeared somewhat like a double square note or two notes joined together. But the good father, oblivious to the mission or use of a clef sign, said it did bother him to see how they could expect a man to sing two notes at once!

Another kind of priest was Antonio Vivaldi. He was a good violinist and, in his way, quite a composer. Once, when officiating at Mass, a musical idea occurred to him, and not wishing to lose it, he left the altar and, going to the vestry, jotted it down for future use, and then returned to his place in the church and resumed the service.

This was so out of the usual order of things that his superiors forbade his continuance in the priestly service. However, the bishop in charge of the diocese, evidently having a weak spot in his heart for the musical art and its followers, although put to it to find an excuse for the breach of duty, restored Vivaldi to his post, on the ground that, " being a musician, he could not have been in his right mind," a conclusion more flattering to the good bishop's kindness of heart than to musicians generally. But of such one-sided material are the clergy occasionally made.

38.—MUSICAL CRITICISM.

If variety of expression and a frequent change of complimentary phrase was necessary to the average reporter of musical affairs in the columns of the daily press, we fear many a quill-shover would be incapacitated for further duty in this line. Outside of the large city papers the reporter of musical affairs is not required to have a knowledge of music, and his weekly repetitions of stock phrases amounts to "Miss A. played beautifully," "Miss B. sang in a very sweet way," "Mrs. C. shows the result of careful practice," "Mr. D. sang in his customary pleasing manner," "Miss E.'s performance was very nice," *et cætera ad nauseam.*

We know of one fellow who gets around it all by saying, "Miss F.'s playing was a good example of her teacher's method," and afterward explains to his friends that the said teacher's method was abominable.

Musical criticism is not so flowery in the present day as it was formerly. Just read this sample, *æt.* two hundred years. It was written by Pepys, that old gossip who persisted in writing a diary which people since have persisted in publishing. It was concerning a performance of a tragedy in which music was used. He writes: "But that which did please me beyond anything in the whole world, was the wind-musique when the angel comes down; which is so sweet that it ravished me, and indeed, in a word, did wrap up my soul so that it made me really sick, just as I had formerly been when in love with my wife; that neither then, nor all the evening going home, and at home, I was able to think of anything, but remained all night transported, so as I could not believe that ever any music hath that real command over the soul of a man as it did upon me; and makes me resolve to practice wind-musique, and to make my wife do the like."

39.—HIGH ART.

Even theatrical people, accustomed, as they are, to good acting and to artificial feeling well expressed, are sometimes moved by the force or feeling which an actor or singer brings to his part. Perhaps as prominent an instance of this as can be found was in the singing of Pacchierotti, a vocalist of the last century.

When singing at Rome in a certain opera, he sang with so much beauty of tone and true feeling that, at a certain place where a solo passage was followed by a short orchestral symphony, the orchestra was so moved by his singing as to forget to go on with their playing. Pacchierotti turned to the conductor, saying, "What are you about?"

The leader started as if from a dream, and could only say, "Pray forgive me." The whole orchestra were sitting with tears in their eyes, oblivious of their duties.

40.—A BOY'S MEMORY.

Part of the service used in the Pope's chapel at Rome is sacredly guarded and kept with great care in the archives of the chapel. Any singer found tampering with this *Miserere* of Allegri, or giving a note of it to an outsider, would be visited by excommunication. Only three copies of this service have ever been sent out. One was for the Emperor Leopold, another to the King of Portugal, and the third to the celebrated musician, Padre Martini.

But there was one copy that was made without the Pope's orders, and not by a member of the choir either. When Mozart was taken to Rome in his youth, by his father, he went to the service at St. Peter's and heard the service in all its impressiveness. Mozart, senior, could hardly arouse the lad from his fascination with the music, when the time came to leave the cathedral. That night after they had retired and the father slept, the boy stealthily arose and by the bright light of the Italian moon, wrote out the whole of that sacredly guarded "*Miserere.*" The Pope's locks, bars, and excommunications gave no safety against a memory like Mozart's.

41.—SLIPPERS AT A PREMIUM.

No more excellent or generous lady has ever graced the operatic stage than Madame Malibran. Pure in life, beautiful in character, generous in heart, she made friends of all who knew her.

When she arrived in Venice on one of her continental tours, Malibran found the manager of a theater which had just been built, to be on the verge of bankruptcy. The great expense of completing his building had brought him to this point, but he had hoped to have the edifice graced by the presence of the King on the opening night, and that would secure him a large attendance and an overflowing treasury. But, unfortunately, the King died. The manager was in despair.

Hearing of Malibran's arrival he besought her to sing on the opening night and save him from ruin. She consented; but owing to his financial difficulties she declined the sum which he offered for her services.

The manager was not mistaken in the drawing power of the artiste; when it became known that Malibran was to sing in "Somnambula," every seat was taken.

In the course of the opera, Malibran slipped on a leaf from a bouquet that had been thrown her and but for one of the singers would have fallen into the orchestra. That singer was Balfe, who afterward became famous as a composer. As it happened, in the effort to recover her balance, one of Malibran's slippers came off and dropped from the stage into what was then called the "pit." The occupants of that part of the house at once entered on a struggle for the possession of this prized relic. Malibran was much amused at their efforts and, taking off the other slipper, threw it to those in the rear of the house. Both slippers were finally torn in pieces and the fragments carried away by the enthusiastic Italians as mementos of the occasion.

At the close of this incident Malibran was led forward by the happy manager; he explained the circumstances of her appearance at his theater and added that, in view of her saving his credit, he should name his theater after the generous *prima donna*. And to-day the "Teatro Malibran" stands as a monument to her kindness of heart.

42.—ARTISTIC AVERSION TO EMPTY HONORS.

Many of the great musicians as well as great *litterateurs* and scientists have scorned the honors and decorations of courts and kings. As a general thing, an institution that honors a really great man with a degree, honors itself more than it does the man. This was the case when Oxford University granted Haydn the title of Doctor of Music. We might imagine how Beethoven would have received the proffer of such a title. His spirit of contempt for orders and decorations was well shown when the Prussian Ambassador at Vienna gave him his choice between fifty ducats, or to be decorated with the insignia of a certain high order. The answer was what we might expect from Beethoven, viz.: "Give me the ducats." Not every one would choose ducats in preference to decorations.

Rameau, one of the great French composers, was equally careless as to honorary distinction. Louis XV bestowed on him the order of St. Michael. Learning that Rameau had not registered it with the proper official, and supposing it was because of his inability to defray the necessary expenses, the King offered to pay the charges.

"I thank your Majesty," Rameau responded, "but let me have the money; I can find a much better use for it."

Mozart was another who would have chosen money rather than orders, rings, and gold snuff-boxes, had he been given a choice. He was overwhelmed with such things, but had hardly enough income to support his family in proper comfort. But those days are past; the artist and composer now receives more money and less snuff-box.

43.—MUSIC AND MADNESS.

There are many stories told of the benefits of music in cases of sickness and insanity, and some of them tax heavily our credulity. Here is one that may be taken for what it is worth.

A friend of Madame Camporese, when that lady was once singing in Milan, told her there was a man in the hospital that was a musical fanatic, and had gone mad from the failure of one of his operas. Hearing of her arrival he demanded to see her, and this being denied, he became so furious that they had to fasten him to his bed.

When this was told her, although she was preparing for an evening party, she at once gave that up and went to the hospital. In an adjoining room to the maniac she sang a melody of Haydn's. He soon became quiet and finally burst into tears. She then went to his bedside and sang again. After she had finished the song the now quieted man pulled from underneath his pillow a melody he had composed, and asked her to sing it for him. She did so, and at his request repeated it. When she left the building the poor musician was gentle and docile, all produced by the kindness of heart of the good Camporese.

44.—BATON WAVING.—LULLY LOSING A LIMB.

Did you ever notice the peculiarities shown by different chorus and orchestra leaders in the way they handle the *baton?* The direction of the motion made by the leader is supposed to indicate to his singers or players the part of the measure then in progress, and the amplitude, extent or vigor of the motion may give some idea as to the quantity of tone desired. It is, in many cases, past comprehension how the singer is to perceive the leader's intention, owing to carelessness on his part or to mannerisms which obscure his meaning.

One conductor describes a circle through the air and expects his choristers to sing in correct common time; another has a beat that transforms everything into down-up-down-up, until one wonders why an automatic pump-handle couldn't fill his place. One leader will be cool and collected; and another will fly all to pieces, keeping one on the verge of expectancy, as one is when awaiting an explosion of some piece of fireworks.

We may see one conductor flapping his hands at his singers to indicate something (the singers are supposed to know what, but the audience do not), while another meekly raises his hands as if to give his benediction to all before him. One will hold his *baton* as gingerly between thumb and first finger as though it were made of straw; another will let it rest against the side of his hand as though it were a pen with which he was inscribing on the vibrating air his ideas as to the effect he would make on the ears of his auditors; still another will grasp his stick firmly and securely, as though he were master of his forces and knew it.

In too many cases the motions of the conductor cease to have any particular meaning and become, as Mark Twain says, mere "ornamental beckoning." We have seen conductors hit themselves on the head in their frantic efforts to "mark time," but such a mishap is small compared with that which befell a celebrated French composer.

Lully, in conducting a *Te Deum* before Louis XIV, in celebration of that monarch's recovery from a severe illness, found that his orchestra was getting a little uncertain as to the time; he became excited, and in making large motions with his *baton* accidentally struck his foot, producing a slight blister. It must be remembered that the *baton* of that day was a violin bow, considerably heavier than the bow of the present century. Inflammation set in, and on the advice of his physicians he had a toe taken off. Still later it became necessary to remove the foot and, finally, the whole limb.

The moral is obvious. Let conductors beware!

45.—PRIMA DONNAS COME HIGH.

Gabriella was a singer who, like Jenny Lind, could be generosity personified when occasion offered; nevertheless she appreciated her own worth as an artiste, and on occasion could demand what she considered her value. At one time she was summoned by the Empress Catherine the Second, of Russia, to sing before her Majesty. Shortly after her arrival at St. Petersburg, Gabriella was asked by the Empress her terms for amusing her royal audience. It seems that no amount had previously been stipulated. She determined that a royal patron should pay a royal price and answered: "Five thousand ducats."

"Five thousand ducats!" exclaimed the queen. "Why, not one of my field-marshals is paid so much!"

"Then your Majesty had better get one of your field-marshals to sing," answered the quick-witted *diva*.

46.—AN UNORTHODOX CREED.

It is frequently the case in church music that some serious or sacred words are used as a mere peg on which to hang a display of musical ability. In some cases the value of the musical composition causes us to forget the absurdity of the continued repetition of the same word or words. This is the case in the "Amen" chorus in the "Messiah." Händel has here given a fine contrapuntal display on the word "Amen," and evolved a long fugal chorus.

In other cases where the musical talent is not so great, continual repetition can hardly be forgiven.

It frequently occurs in the Latin service that parts of sentences must be repeated; and in order that the sense may be preserved the composer must have a good knowledge of the Latin. Otherwise he is liable to make some such blunder as did Porpora, Haydn's teacher, who once, in setting the Latin creed to music, arranged his words thus: "*Credo, non credo, non credo in Deum.*" The church authorities were scandalized by such a sentiment expressed in a church service, and it was only by his explaining that he was ignorant of the Latin and did not mean to say he did not trust in God, that he saved himself from the terrors of the inquisition.

He was not the only composer that has set unorthodox words to his music. Many lesser lights in our own days are grinding out church music that is said to "combine poor poetry, bad music, and worse theology."

47.—THE DEVIL'S TRILL.

Tartini was one of the greatest violinists of the last century. He was born at Pirano, in 1692. His parents were determined that he should enter the priesthood, but being unsuccessful in turning the lad that way, persuaded him to study law.

His secret marriage with a beautiful girl being discovered, he had to take flight. Finding refuge in a monastery, he remained there for some time, till he was discovered by a former acquaintance. His whereabouts being reported to the irate parents and a reconciliation being effected, he returned to his young wife, and, making his home at Padua, took up the study of the violin. He became famous in the musical world, and was besought by other countries to visit them that they might hear his wonderful playing, but he could not be tempted to leave his native soil.

The following story, concerning the composition entitled "*Il Trillo del Diavolo,*" was told by Tartini himself:—

One night, in the year 1713, while Tartini was yet a young man, he had a most surprising and realistic dream. He dreamed he had made a compact with his satanic majesty, by the terms of which the gentleman with the cloven hoof was, contrary to the usual order of things, always to be at the service of the violinist. After some little time spent in getting acquainted, Tartini handed his violin to his new servant to find out what kind of a fiddler he was; when, to Tartini's utter astonishment, he heard a solo so beautiful, so bewitching, and played with such skill and taste, that it surpassed all the playing that he had ever heard in his life.

Just at this interesting point in the affair, Tartini awoke. Filled with the memory of the beautiful playing he had heard in his dream, he hastened to his instrument, and in his excitement and delight he tried to reproduce some of the strains that fell from the Mephistophelian bow. But, alas, the devil was to pay! for the devil was gone and his music with him.

Nevertheless, Tartini, inspired by the memory of the dream music, took pen and paper, and composed this sonata called "The Devil's Trill."

He declared it to be far inferior to what he heard in his dream; but be that as it may, it certainly excelled in value any other composition that he wrote in the sober moments of daylight, and uninspired by diabolical compact.

48.—UNLUCKY MANUSCRIPTS.

Some of the original manuscripts of valuable compositions have occasionally found strange resting places and been put to unforeseen uses. We have read of how Beethoven's cook used some of his precious leaves in kindling a fire and in wrapping up old pots and kettles; how the original pages of some priceless works of Bach were used by an ignorant gardener to tie round some young apple trees, thus to preserve them from harm; and how many of Schubert's beautiful melodies lay for years in garrets and in out-of-the-way corners, until resurrected by Schumann and other enthusiasts.

But perhaps the worst misfortune that ever happened to a composer in this line, fell upon Rinaldo di Capua, said to be the originator of the "recitative." Whether this honor justly belongs to him or not is, however, uncertain. Be that as it may, he was an excellent and industrious writer, and accumulated during his years of composition a goodly number of scores.

In his old age, feeling the need of the money they would bring from the publisher, he searched for them, but could find them nowhere. Further inquiries pointed to the probability that a profligate son, who had been the apple of the old man's eye, so to speak, had disposed of this valuable pile of manuscripts to a dealer in waste paper!

49.—FOREWARNED IS FOREARMED.

It is no infrequent thing in musical centers, especially in European cities, to find organized attempts to affect the appearance of some prominent singer, either favorably or the opposite.

Perhaps the manager of the opera may have some new star whom he wishes to bring to the notice of the public in the most flattering manner possible. Perhaps it is some singer unknown to that city whom he wants to give a flattering reception. If so, the machinery is at once set in motion.

Men and women are scattered through the house, and each one has his instructions to assist in the applause, the "*bravos*," the *encores*, and probably the flowers that are sent up to the stage. The favorite is brought before the curtain and a spontaneous (?) ovation is given her, and, of course, the public are informed of all this in double headlines. The first appearance has been successful and the *prima donna's* popularity is assured. But there is another side to the matter. There may be an opposing manager, or a rival singer, or a jealous company who wish to throw every possible obstacle in the path of the *cantatrice*. There may be a *claque* formed to make the initial performance a dismal failure. Scattered through the theater may be a body of people who have orders to hiss and jeer, and perhaps to create such a disturbance that an impartial hearing is impossible.

But sometimes even such a cabal meets its match.

Madame Alboni was a woman of much strength of character and possessed of much energy and decision. Such a *claque* was once formed against her, but with results rather unforeseen to the partakers in it.

Having an operatic engagement at Trieste, this noted singer went to that city; but on her arrival she found that a conspiracy had been formed against her, and that unless she took prompt action her success was endangered. So she disguised herself in male attire, and having a strong face, short hair, and solid build, this was not a hard matter to do.

Then hunting up the managers of the *claque*, she offered her services to assist in ruining the performance of the new *prima donna*.

"I am quite unknown to all of you," she said to the leader, "but if there's fun on hand, count on me."

"Very well," was the answer, "we are preparing to hiss off a new *cantatrice* this evening."

"Why," said the disguised singer, "what is the matter, what wrong has she done?"

"We know nothing of her save that she comes from Rome, and we wish to have no singers here whose reputation has not been gained amongst us."

"That is only fair. In what way can I help?"

"Each of us will carry a whistle like this one," producing a little black whistle. "Take this one, and at a signal which will be given after the air of Rosina, in

Rossini's opera, to-night, you have but to add to the uproar which will be raised."

"Very well," was the answer, "you may depend on my being there."

That night the theater was filled to overflowing to hear that popular opera of Rossini's, "The Barber of Seville." At first all seemed to go well. The singers who took the parts of Almavira and Figaro were warmly welcomed, for they were two native favorites.

But now Rosina comes on, and immediately several whistles are heard in various parts of the house, without waiting for the leader's signal. Madame Alboni advanced to the front of the stage, and, holding out her whistle, said:—

"Gentlemen, *we* must not hiss *me*, but the cavatina. You have commenced too soon."

The whole audience at once saw through the affair and broke into hearty applause, and before the close of the opera she had received a dozen recalls.

When the manager expressed his surprise at her knowledge of the conspiracy against her, she said: "My dear sir, it is here as in politics—you must lead the movement or else be swept away."

50.—A QUEEN'S REGARD FOR HER MUSIC TEACHER.

The following, told of Empress Catherine of Russia, shows that queens may be just, as well as quick-tempered or spiteful. It is said that at one time the music teacher of the Empress, Paesiello, a celebrated composer, was the cause of jealousy on the part of a certain marshal. Perhaps it was caused by many favors shown the musician by the queen, who appreciated his worth and talent. At any rate, the marshal became so angered as to give Paesiello a blow, which was returned with such good interest and vigor that the military officer was the surprised recipient of a sound drubbing.

Hastening off to the Empress he made complaint that

he had been struck by the musician, and to strike a marshal of the Russian empire was worthy of dire punishment. The Empress laughed at his complaint, saying, "Sir, you forgot your dignity in striking an unoffending man and a great artist; and as to rank, it is in my power to make fifty marshals, but not one Paesiello."

51.—AN EARNEST STUDENT.

At the time of the intense Gluck-Piccini rivalry in Paris, there came to that gay city from Belgium an awkward youth who had determined to gain a musical education at whatever hazard, although he had no money to speak of and no immediate prospect of obtaining any.

The rivalry between the two great composers, Gluck and Piccini, was every day growing more intense, and all artistic Paris was taking sides for or against the imported Italian composer, who was finally to be defeated by his more earnest and able rival, Gluck. Our young musician was an ardent disciple of Gluck, and was determined to see the representation of his opera "*Iphigenie en Tauride*," which was soon to occur.

By the assistance of a friend he managed to gain admittance into the theater where the final rehearsal was held. So enchanted was he by the beauty and nobility of the music that he resolved to hear the public performance as well; but alas! the wherewithal was not forthcoming; he had no money to purchase a ticket. As he sat listening to the rehearsal a happy thought occurred to him; he would hide in one of the boxes and remain there till the performance.

Unfortunately for his plan, he was discovered at the close of the rehearsal by the employees of the house, who proceeded to summarily eject him. But the young man's spirit was aroused and he resisted. Gluck, who had not left the house, heard the disturbance, and coming to investigate it, was told that a young man from the country was so anxious to hear his music as to take this method of securing the opportunity.

Pleased with the youth's eagerness for musical instruction and enjoyment, and perhaps somewhat flattered as well, Gluck ordered his release, gave him a ticket to the performance, and later sought to know more of his ardent admirer. This was the beginning of a lasting friendship between the two composers Gluck and Mehul, for the young man later achieved great prominence in the musical world. Mehul composed twenty-five operas and numerous other works, and was paid the highest honors the French nation could bestow. But through all of his successful career he never forgot the debt of gratitude he owed to Gluck for the interest taken in the crude young student, an interest which dated from the incident narrated above.

52.—A WITTY SONGSTRESS.

Sophie Arnould was noted for being one of the wittiest as well as one of the handsomest women in France, and withal could hardly be excelled as a vocalist. On one occasion, while out taking a constitutional, she met a friend, a physician, who was carrying a gun under his arm. In the course of his remarks he mentioned that he was on his way to see a patient. "Ah, doctor," said she, "so you are afraid of your ordinary treatment failing?"

53.—MOSCHELES' BLUNDER.

One of the most popular of the classical *virtuosi* was Ignaz Moscheles, whose seventy-six years of life was ended in 1870. A friend of Beethoven, a teacher of Mendelssohn, a great player, teacher, and composer, he exercised a most beneficial influence in the musical world with his strong personality. For twenty years or more, Moscheles made his home in England.

A remark of his made at a dinner table soon after his

arrival there illustrates the difficulty which foreigners have in conquering the English language. One evening, when the cloth had been removed and the hostess had asked him what fruit he preferred, he hastily referred to the knowledge of English he had secured by a study of the dictionary, and politely answered that he wished to be helped to "some sneers."

This answer produced a burst of laughter on the part of the guests, who could not contain their merriment at the dilemma in which the musician's ignorance of the language had placed him. Moscheles hastened to explain. It seemed that on searching for English sentences he had learned that the idiom "not to care a fig" was synonymous with the verb "to sneer," and so supposed that in asking for "sneers" he had the right word for fig. Turn about is fair play; we must have our laugh at the foreigners, as they have so much fun at our expense.

54.—JEALOUSY IN THE FAMILY.

A musical artist without any jealous feeling toward his brother musicians would be almost as rare as one who does not think himself perfect in his chosen art. But when jealousy enters a family, one might expect it to meet the fate of the "house divided against itself." An extreme case of this kind may be noted in a tenor named Ansari and his wife, who lived about a hundred years ago. These kindred spirits were so enraged, if perchance one secured more applause than the other, that they were known to employ men to hiss each other off the stage!

55.—PREJUDICE.

We hate to be convinced that our preconceived opinions and hastily uttered statements are not in accord with the facts of the case. Musicians and musical critics (the two terms are not always synonymous) are like the rest of the world in this. Few of us like to reform our ideas and retract our dogmatic statements even in the face of overwhelming proof that we are wrong.

An amusing incident illustrating this peculiarity of the human race occurred during the rivalry that existed between Sontag and Malibran. The former lady was a German. It was a favorite idea of the friends of her rival that only Italians, or those of the Italian school, could do any singing worthy of the name; hence, Sontag could not sing.

So great was the prejudice against German singers in their own country that Frederick the Great, when asked to hear Mara sing, declared: "What! Hear a German singer! I should as soon expect to derive pleasure from the neighing of my horse!"

It is true that Germany has produced fewer great singers than other musical countries. While Germany boasts Devrient, Titiens, Lucca, Mara and Sontag, for every one of these we have a score of non-German singers of equal or greater worth.

An Italian critic who had not heard Sontag was, in spite of this prejudice against German singers, persuaded to go and hear her one night. After listening a short time, he rose from his seat and made preparations to leave the house.

"What, you are not going?" said his friend, who was an admirer of the German songstress. "Stay a little longer and you will be convinced that a German can sing."

"I know it," answered the Italian; "therefore I go!"

56.—MUSICAL GRATITUDE.

Liszt was not the only musician that took holy orders. Josquin de Pres, chapel master to Louis XII, of France, was also an officer of the Holy Church. It seems the king had promised him a position which gave an increased income, but had forgotten his promise. Josquin reminded the king of his lapse of memory in a peculiar way. He composed an anthem for the chapel service, using the words (from the 119th psalm) as his subject: " Oh, think upon Thy servant as concerning Thy word." His majesty took the hint and bestowed upon the quick-witted musician the promised appointment.

Josquin was equally good at expressing gratitude in a musical way, for soon after he produced, as an anthem of thanks to the king, a composition set to the words from the same psalm: " O Lord, Thou hast dealt graciously with Thy servant."

57.—THE GREATER THE COMPOSER THE GREATER THE STUDENT.

The greatest composers have been proud to acknowledge themselves the pupils of the masters with whom they studied. In fact, the only one among "the immortals" who did not have thorough drill in all departments of composition was Schubert; and his music shows this. For, while he has seldom been excelled in melodic inventiveness, his thematic treatment is weak, and he has not been able to make the most of the goods the gods gave him. Recognizing his lack of technical knowledge in the line of contrapuntal treatment, he made arrangements to study counterpoint with one of the best teachers of the day. But illness overtook him, and the grim reaper carried him off ere he could profit by his studies.

While this is true, while the greatest students of music that ever lived and those to whom most genius was given were eager and anxious to study as hard and as long as possible, we have, on the other hand, many who, relying on the mite of talent that has been given them, attempt to strike out for themselves, and who are so blind as not to see that with their untutored splashings they do not make the most dignified and successful progress in the tonal sea.

Every one who can conjure up a bit of melody thinks himself a full-fledged composer, though he may know naught of the spelling, grammar, or rhetoric of music. Others who have considerable talent consider that it supplies the place of study properly directed by competent teachers.

The writer was approached not long before penning this sketch by a man who claimed to have written symphonies, operas, string quartets, and dear knows what all else, and who wound up by boasting that he had never taken a single music lesson of any kind whatever. When his claim and list of compositions was made known we felt as though we might be standing in the presence of some unknown and unrecognized Beethoven; when the final statement as to taking no lessons was uttered, we felt as though we were standing in the presence of—a fool.

Perhaps it would be better if we could all be as conscientious as that honest old German teacher, who, when approached by his admiring pupils with the exclamation:—" Oh, Herr Teufelsberg, you know so much about music; why *don't* you compose; you could write such perfectly elegant pieces?"—exclaimed: "Nein, nein, I vill nod write mine mu*seek*. Mein Gott! dere ish genug bad mu*seek* in de vorlt, alreadish!"

58.—AN IGNORANT TENOR.

Campanini once made an enemy by the use of a title which a rival singer thought to be his own particular property. Fancelli, the rival, was a very ignorant man and could hardly read or write, but he deciphered the term *"Primo Tenore Assoluto"* on Campanini's baggage, and this aroused his wrath, as he considered the word *"Assoluto,"* (meaning absolute or unrivaled), should be applied exclusively to himself. So ignorant was Fancelli, who, by the way, had formerly been a baggage porter at Leghorn, that he had to hire one of the opera chorus to write the autographs he gave to admiring damsels. He was once asked to append his signature to the autograph album of the Liverpool Philharmonic Society. His scribe was not at hand, so he undertook the painful operation himself. He got along fairly well with the name, only omitting one "l" and a "c." Not content with that, he attempted to add his pet title, and succeeded, in his schoolboy hand, very well till he got to the final word, the most charming of them all, in his eyes. After he had written an "a" and three "s's," he managed to spread a huge blot of ink on the page which obliterated one of them, and to-day the signature stands,

Faneli Primo Tenore Ass———"

59.—THREE CLASSES OF PLAYERS.

Salomon, a London musician, had as pupil King George III. One day, when the king had not distinguished himself by great practice or skill in playing, the teacher gave him the following classification of fiddlers:—

"Fiddlers, your Majesty, may be divided into three classes: To the first belong those who cannot play at all; to the second those who play badly; and to the third those who play well. You, sire, have already reached the second class."

The majority of the players on all instruments reach only this second class. This feature of the matter is bad enough, but a worse feature is that the most of them are willing to stay there and are not willing to put forth the effort necessary for attaining the third. As to those who try to sing, comparatively few graduate from the first class, and as to those who do sing, only a small minority reach the third.

60.—HOW TO SECURE A SUCCESSFUL DÉBUT.

We have spoken in another sketch of the incident where Madame Alboni discovered a rascally cabal and averted threatened confusion on the occasion of her début in an Italian city; and also of the efforts of friends to make a singer's first appearance a great success, or of her enemies to make it a fiasco. The Alboni incident was an illustration of the latter. We relate below an illustration of the opposite kind.

Christine Nilsson was introduced to the English people under the auspices of Colonel Mapleson, perhaps the best known of modern opera managers. At that time she was almost unknown, but Mapleson knew that he had secured a jewel, and determined that her English career should be launched with becoming enthusiasm.

He also knew that should the thing be poorly done, should the hired applause be given at a wrong time, or, as has sometimes been the case, before the singer has had time to utter a note, failure instead of success would follow his well-meant plans.

So Mapleson hired some twenty-five boatmen from the Thames and gave them tickets to various parts of the house, with the understanding that they were not to applaud Nilsson,—the lady wearing a pink dress and who appeared in the first act; but, moreover, they were promised a shilling apiece every time they, by their applause, caused the curtain to go up after the first act.

By this arrangement disaster was averted and the rivermen took care to earn five or six shillings apiece that night. Mapleson knew that if he could once get the songstress a fair hearing, her own abilities would carry her through and make her reputation. But if the public did not realize her great talents on the first night, or if, rather, the lack of trumpet blowing in advance of her coming lost her an enthusiastic reception, it would be up-hill work to have her merits appreciated thereafter. But from this he was saved by his wit and the boatmen's horny hands.

61.—A SONG FOR FORTY.

Musical composition may be divided into epochs, each one of which is preparatory to those which follow. That period from 1750, stretching back some three hundred years, was a period of contrapuntal writing in which that composer was considered the best that could produce the best counterpoint,—could combine into a harmonious whole the largest number of independent melodies. In the latter part of the period, however, quantity of parts was not a *sine qua non* of greatness so much as the most thorough contrapuntal development of a few parts, as witnessed in Bach's and Händel's works.

One English composer, Thomas Tallis, who flourished some three hundred years ago, was a learned contrapuntist; and one of his compositions, written for forty voices, shows his skill at manufacturing music, for there could not have been much musical inspiration in such compositions. In this piece each one of the forty voices had an independent part differing from every one of the other thirty-nine. For 138 bars these forty people are supposed to go "every one to his own way," but not " like sheep," for these mild-mannered animals are supposed to follow one leader instead of forty.

But even this combination was exceeded by a composition in fugal style, written by Raimondi, an Italian composer living in the first half of the present century. This was arranged for sixteen choirs of four voices each, giving a total of sixty-four different parts. This style of composition has been called Gothic. Be that as it may, we may congratulate ourselves that we have passed the day of mathematical composition, and have come to the point where learning is the means, not the end, of a composer's work.

62.—THE TEMPLE ORGAN.

Cromwell and his soldiers played havoc with the organs of merry England. These "squeaking abominations," as the old Puritans called the organs, were everywhere torn down and their pipes melted into bullets. The soldiers would go through the streets blowing the pipes from some demolished organ, or perhaps pawned them for cups of ale. Very few organs escaped the fury of these zealots.

But after the restoration a different order of things set in. The Cathedral services were restored and it was a golden time for organ builders. The organ, by the way, had reached a great degree of perfection at that period.

In the reign of Charles the Second, the authorities of the Temple Church, in London, determined to build as fine an organ in their edifice as money would afford. There was a peculiar condition attached to the matter, to the effect that each builder who wished to contest for the honor should set up his organ in the church, and then all were to be given a fair trial.

Two builders, Schmidt and Harris, were the only ones to accede to this condition, but they were the best builders of their day. In nine months they were ready for the trial. Schmidt's organ was first tried, and in the hands of such performers as Purcell and Blow we may be assured it had a fair hearing. Harris secured the French musician, Lully, to show off his instrument, and his playing was on a par with that of the English performers. Trial after trial was held, but no decision could be secured, as the organs seemed to be so equal in value. The builders added new stop effects, but still no decision. Then they descended to malicious destruction. Each maker had his friends in the church and out, and soon pipes were removed and bellows cut, and anything was done that would injure the opponent's chances of success.

Finally, the matter was placed in the hands of Lord Chief Justice Jeffries, and he decided in favor of Schmidt's organ, and that is the one which still stands in London Temple.

63.—A FIDDLER'S TRICK.

Archangelo Corelli was once taken in by a little ruse of a certain German fiddler, named Strunck, who was traveling in Italy. The German called on the great Italian violinist, and after some conversation asked him to play. Corelli did so, and exerted himself to please his visitor. Then, after he had concluded, he asked his visitor if he did not play. Strunck said he did play some. So Corelli, to return the compliment, asked him to play in turn, and when he had finished, complimented him on his use of the bow, although the German had purposely played very carelessly. Corelli told him that he could, with practice become an excellent player.

Strunck smiled, and quietly put all of the strings of the violin out of tune, and then played with amazing brilliancy, correcting the false pitch of the strings by his skillful use of the fingers. Corelli, in amazement, cried out, "Sir, they call me Archangelo, but, by heaven, you must be an Archdiavolo!"

64.—PERSONAL APPEARANCE.

There is an individuality that shows itself in dress and personal appearance; though to form any concept of what a person may be, musically, by these indications would be work for an expert in reading character by outward manifestations.

The well-groomed and polished gentleman may have as strong a musical personality as the one who would proclaim his descent from Beethoven by his disorderly garments and flying hair. On the other hand, some genius of clumsy walk and slouchy appearance may have the soul of a Mozart or a Chopin.

We may well imagine that Bach was a methodical man, in dress as well as music, though, to tell the truth, those twenty children must have sensibly reduced the amount the irascible cantor could squander on dress. Both Haydn and Mozart were neat and tidy men in personal appearance, but one could not say the same for Beethoven and Schubert. The matter of externals was of little import to them. Perhaps the fact that they were confirmed bachelors made them less careful of their personal appearance.

Mendelssohn was a pronounced aristocrat in dress as well as music, and the same might be said of Liszt, though, of the two, Mendelssohn had perhaps the more refined appearance and the more elegant bearing. Liszt had less of delicate refinement in his appearance, and more of the mien of a commanding general.

Chopin, in the latter part of his life, must be ranked as a musical aristocrat, although in his earlier days music occupied his mind to the exclusion of matters of dress and appearance. Yet one who comes before the public must concede something to custom, and the manner in which Chopin steered between his indolence and fashion was, to say the least, peculiar. The way in which he reconciled his carelessness in respect to one matter of his toilet with regard for the feelings of his audiences, he tells in a letter sent to his parents from Vienna, in 1831. He says, in writing of some family friends: "When they saw me at Madame Schascheck's, their astonishment knew no bounds at my looking such a proper fellow. I have left my whiskers only on the right cheek. They grow very well there; and there is really no occasion to have them on my left cheek, as I always sit with my right toward the audience!"

65.—MOZART'S ACKNOWLEDGMENT.

True genius is not averse to taking a hint from whatever quarter it may come. An ordinary person may occasionally give a very gifted one a valuable point.

In Mozart's "*Nozze di Figaro*" one of the characters is a stuttering judge. Mozart desired Kelly, who was singing that part, to stutter all through the opera save in one number, a sextet, a favorite number with the composer. In that he feared to spoil the music. But Kelly protested that he should stutter in that piece also and thus preserve the unity of the character throughout. He apologized for presuming to set his judgment against Mozart's, but declared he would sing it that way or not at all. Finally, Mozart gave in. Kelly sang it as he promised, and the result was a tumult of applause, the Emperor himself crying "Bravo, bravo!"

Mozart rushed on the stage, and taking Kelly by the hand, said: "Young man, I feel obliged to you, and acknowledge you were right and I wrong."

This *amende honorable* was worthy of the true gentleman Mozart always showed himself to be.

66.—OPERATIC SORE THROAT.

Opera singers have the name of being capricious people. While, on the whole, they undoubtedly average up about the same as the rest of humanity in this regard, that still leaves a margin for a good deal of caprice and unaccountable ideas.

Impossible colds and suspicious illness on the part of his singers are some of the most perplexing features an operatic manager encounters. The following incident gives a fair example of one kind of "operatic cold."

Ronconi and his wife were singing in the same troupe, and when the lady was irritated by being cast to sing with some one she did not like, or by being entirely omitted from the cast, peculiar as it may seem, this circumstance had an immediate effect on Ronconi's throat, —it would be impossible for him to sing.

On one occasion the manager, after receiving a note to the effect that it would be impossible for the singer to appear, took a physician with him and called on the invalid. Ronconi expressed his regrets in a hollow whisper; but the *impresario*, knowing the tenor's consummate powers as an actor, doubted the genuineness of this whispering performance. So he simply expressed his sympathy and proceeded to converse on certain topics that he knew would interest the singer.

In a few moments Ronconi forgot his assumption of vocal inability, and was talking in his full natural voice. When his attention was called to the fact he ascribed his wonderful recovery to the mere presence of so excellent a physician. He sang that night and with more than usual energy.

67.—LEONCAVALLO'S WHIMSICAL OPINION CONCERNING HIS "CLOWNS."

Composers are not always keen to tell stories at their own expense or at that of their compositions, but the following related by Leoncavallo, the prominent young composer of the modern Italian school, he deemed too good to keep, though at the time it put him in the light of a first-class plagiarist.

Being one day in the town of Forli, he heard that his opera "Paggliacci," that work which has given him so much fame, was to be produced, and he decided to hear it *incognito*. That the rising young composer was in town, was not generally known.

At the opera his seat was beside a bright-eyed and enthusiastic young lady, who, when she saw the composer did not join in the general applause, but remained quiet, turned to him with the question:—

"Why do you not applaud? Does it not suit you?"

The composer, much amused, replied: "No, on the contrary, it displeases me. It is the work of a mere beginner, not to call him anything worse."

"Then you are ignorant of music," she said.

"Oh, no," replied the composer.

Then he proceeded to enlighten her on the subject, proving the music worthless and entirely without originality.

"See," said he, "this motive is ———," and he hummed lightly a short melody; "this aria is stolen from Bizet, and that is from Beethoven." In short, he tore the whole opera into pieces.

His neighbor sat in silence, but with an air of pity on her countenance. At the close, she turned to him and said: "Is what you have said to me your honest opinion?"

"Entirely so," was the reply.

"Good," said she, and with a malicious gleam in her eyes left the theater.

Next morning, glancing over the paper, his eye fell upon the heading, "Leoncavallo on his 'Paggliacci;'" and reading further, was somewhat startled to find the conversation of the evening before fully reported and accredited to the proper source. He had, unfortunately, played his little joke on a lady reporter, who had proved too smart for him.

Leoncavallo swore off from making disparaging remarks concerning his own works to vivacious young ladies, no matter how handsome or how enthusiastic they might be.

68.—HOW TO MAKE A SINGER SING.

There are various ways of making a stubborn singer exhibit his abilities. John Abell, a celebrated tenor of the time of Charles the Second, experienced one of these methods. Being a spendthrift by nature, he once took a journey through Europe to restore his depleted finances. On arrival at Warsaw, his fame having preceded him, he was ordered to appear before the king and sing for the enjoyment of his majesty and the court. Abell, blind to his own interests, refused.

The king then ordered him to appear the next day, under pain of imprisonment. The singer made a virtue of necessity and at the appointed time went to the Palace and was shown to a chair in the center of a large hall. By some mechanical contrivance, and without warning to Abell, the chair was drawn up quite a distance from the floor. In a short time the king and some of his courtiers came out into a gallery and simultaneously several bears were let loose in the room below. Our tenor was then given his choice; it was either sing or be lowered among the beasts. It is needless to add that Abell chose to sing, and to sing in a way that would have made his fortune had he a more kindly disposed audience.

69.—ANOTHER WAY.

Equally satisfactory in its results was the method of voice production applied by a band of Mexican freebooters to Garcia, another great tenor, but of modern times. One of the semi-annual revolutions taking place during Garcia's concert tour in Mexico, he was making his way toward the coast to sail for more peaceful climes. But before he could reach Vera Cruz he was attacked by a wandering band of Mexicans and relieved of his *impedimenta* even to the most of his wardrobe. The search for valuables in his baggage soon revealed a quantity of music, and it came to light that the captive was a singer.

Not satisfied with their tangible booty, the robbers demanded a song. Garcia respectfully declined. More demands, this time with fervor, *con spirito*, as it were. Garcia absolutely refused. But repeated encores being accompanied by threatening gestures, a knowledge that his audience would not hesitate to put their threats into execution led the great tenor to accede to their wishes. The brigands gave him an elevated position and gathered around ready to pass judgment on his performance. It is well known to musicians that a free audience always considers itself most free to criticize a performance. So it was in this case; each auditor had, as it were, a complimentary ticket.

Garcia, on first trial, was perhaps justified in feeling somewhat of stage fright, so much, in fact, that his song was an abject failure. Even these rough Mexicans hissed him. This was unusual treatment for the tenor. He was used to rapturous applause, not hisses. Spurred by the insult he burst forth in such a vocal effort as might have graced the best concert hall. Derision had conquered where threats had failed. Charmed by his voice and his use of it, the robbers not only returned money and clothing, but escorted him far on his journey that he might be saved a repetition of this experience.

70.—ROSSINI HEARING THE IMPOSSIBLE.

The modern flute as perfected by Böhm is a very different instrument from that used prior to 1835. The flute of former days, like the harp of olden time, was effective only in certain keys; but, while the harp could be tuned so as to reach other keys, the flute was more limited in this respect. In fact, there were some scales that were so difficult to play on the flute that they were practicably impossible to conquer. In certain other keys there were trills and other ornaments that no sane composer would have thought of writing, as they certainly would not have been played.

Böhm invented a system of keys and an arrangement of fingering which made all scales, trills, runs, and arpeggios possible, and not only possible, but brought them all to a practically equal degree of difficulty. Böhm made journeys to London and Paris to introduce his improvements; and it was at the latter place that he sought to obtain the patronage of Rossini, who was then one of the prominent figures of the musical world.

As Rossini was in his dressing-room shaving himself, Böhm was instructed to remain in an adjoining room. Thinking to predispose the master in favor of his instrument, he proceeded to play all manner of scales, arpeggios, trills, and roulades in various keys, with an agility which was almost unheard of; but not content with this he suddenly dashed into the key of D flat, in which key it had been impossible to play with such agility and brilliancy. Rossini could stand it no longer, but rushed out of his dressing room, wigless, and his face covered with lather, and cried in great excitement:—

"You cannot play that!"

"But I am playing it," responded the inventor calmly.

"I don't care if you are," retorted the composer furiously, "it is utterly impossible."

But Rossini was finally convinced, and the Böhm flute is the one now used by *virtuosi* the world over.

71.—MANUSCRIPT FOR KETTLES.

Beethoven had a hard time of it with his landladies and servants. Evidently these necessary personages were not easier to get along with in his day than in ours. One of the latter class caused him a deal of trouble once upon a time.

Beethoven was working upon the great mass in D. He began the work in 1819, and was to have had it ready for the celebration of the appointment of his friend, Archduke Rudolph, to the archbishopric of Olmutz, which was to take place the next year. But the mass grew in magnitude as Beethoven grew more interested in it, and when it was finally completed the celebration had been over for two years.

During its progress the composer missed certain sheets

of his manuscript. He searched high and low, but nowhere could he find them. He called in the servant, but she was as ignorant as he of their whereabouts. Finally, when he had given up the search and was about to sit down to rewrite the Kyrie, the missing part, some loose papers with notes on them were discovered in the kitchen. They were brought up to his room, and there, begrimed by soot and dust, was the missing music.

The servant had removed them from his room one day when "clearing up," and had used the precious sheets to wrap some superannuated pots and kettles! As to Beethoven's words on this interesting occasion, deponent sayeth not.

72.—A PATTI RECEPTION THAT SHE DIDN'T RECEIVE.

There was once a glorious reception for Adelina Patti which did not come off as per programme. She was expected to arrive in New York on a certain steamer, and her manager, in order to stir up public interest in her appearance, chartered sixteen huge tugboats. These, covered with bunting, were to range themselves on each side of her vessel as it steamed into the harbor, and by means of their steam whistles and military bands which they were to carry, such a racket was to be raised as to leave no one in doubt that Patti had arrived.

Besides this there was to be a salute of twenty-one guns at Sandy Hook, and the opera chorus was to sing a cantata which Arditi had written for the occasion.

But as luck would have it, owing to the fog, the ocean steamer was not perceived until it had arrived almost at its anchorage. Patti disembarked unobserved and took a cab for her hotel "as happy as though twenty boats had come down the bay to meet me," she said.

73.—THE ENCORE FIEND.

An English writer speaks as follows of the people who insist upon *encore* numbers being given at all times and places. We might remark, parenthetically, that this *genus* is not confined to Great Britain. We have some of him—and her—on this side of the water. But to quote his pertinent remarks:—

"There are two, if not more, ways of showing regard for those we admire and esteem, one which is agreeable and another which is disagreeable. Unfortunately, of these two the latter has by far the most patrons. In their zeal to show respect, three out of every four persons are obtrusive, not to say offensive.

"Thus the British public have a weakness for *encores* which at times almost approaches lunacy. They insist upon a concert singer giving three or four songs when he is paid for two—apart from the questions of the singer's own feelings in the matter and the state of his voice.

"Then again the *prima donna* of the opera is vociferously applauded in the most touching and thrilling scenes. She must acknowledge it all; so that not unfrequently we see such absurd sights as a mad lady suddenly becoming herself again for a few bouquets and some applause, only as quickly to be transformed back to her distracted state.

"Instrumentalists, too, suffer the same fate. After a magnificent performance of some *finale*, dashed off at a surprising speed and at the cost of much mental and nervous force to the performer, three-fourths of every audience have the 'nerve' to demand a repetition of it!

"If the popular enthusiasm does not take this form in the acknowledgment of an artist's merit, there are others equally unpleasant."

Few artists have the nerve to quell a superabundance of applause in the method used by Hans von Bülow.

On one occasion the *encore* was so persistent as to arouse his ire; and, vexed by the applause, which was loud and continuous, he came to the front of the stage and said sharply:—

"If you do not stop this applause I will play all of Bach's forty-eight Preludes and Fugues from beginning to end."

The audience knew that he was able to keep his word, and if he took the notion he would undertake the task; so they laughed, and did not insist on an *encore*.

74.—HÄNDEL'S ESCAPE.

In the early days Händel learned that the post of organist at Lübeck was vacant, and went on foot to that town to make application for the place. But he found an unusual stipulation attached to the vacancy. Whoever obtained the position was required to marry the deceased organist's daughter. Händel immediately retraced his steps without making application. Had the girl been prettier and Händel's pocketbook heavier, the result might have been different and his whole career changed—for the worse.

The musical world should be thankful that this young German musician was not attracted by the flaxen-haired daughter of that old organist. Had it been otherwise, Händel might have settled down to an honorable obscurity in that ancient German town and been diverted from that wonderful career of composition which has left the world so much his debtor.

75.—A HATFUL OF PEARLS.

Jenny Lind was the recipient of many handsome compliments, and none was more worthy of them than she. Some of her admirers were rather extravagant in their praise, and these she liked to joke when opportunity offered.

Lablache, the great bass singer, when he first heard her, could think of nothing more expressive of his admiration than to say "every note was a pearl."

Some time afterward, when they were both at a rehearsal, the young *prima donna* asked him to lend her his hat. He very politely did so, though not without secret wonder at her request.

She took it, and stepping to another part of the stage, placed the edge of the hat to her lips and sang several strains of melody; then returning to Lablache, she ordered him to fall on his knees and receive a royal present she had for him. He could do nothing but comply with the whim of the fair songstress.

She then told him that she was bestowing on him untold wealth, for, by his own saying, she was presenting him with a hatful of pearls.

76.—MENDELSSOHN COMPOSING FOR FUN.

There is a great deal of mechanical as well as mental labor about musical composition. But musicians who compose a great deal become as expert in the quick transfer of their ideas to paper as do those who deal in words rather than notes. When spurred by necessity, remarkable speed in composition has been developed. Mendelssohn once had his pride slightly wounded, and the result was the composition of an overture in two days' time.

He had expected to write a romance and an overture for a performance of "Ruy Blas," but owing to other duties had only completed the romance. The music was to be played for the benefit of a charitable society. After sending the committee the romance music they soon called on him to express their thanks, and said "it was a great pity he had not written the overture, though they understood it could not be done in a hurry, and next year, if they might be allowed, they would give him longer notice."

Mendelssohn felt the inference was that he could not write the overture without much time for consideration, and owned to being "rather nettled" by their remarks. But in two days he had completed the overture; and they were not two days of uninterrupted work on it, either, for in that time he had rehearsals to attend and a concert to give. But with all this he declared that the composition of this overture gave him more fun than anything he ever did.

77.—THE RIGHT KIND OF A PATRON.

Piccinni, that composer who came so near taking the palm from Gluck in the race the two ran for the favor of musical Paris, at the end of the last century, had a happy experience when, as a young man, he essayed to enter the arena of composition. He had presented his first opera to a manager just after he graduated from the Naples *Conservatoire*. Like many another first attempt, it was refused. Prince Vintimilla, learning this, called upon the manager and asked, "How much would you lose if you presented Piccinni's opera and it turned out a failure?"

"Fifteen hundred dollars," was the reply.

"Here it is. If the opera fails you may keep the money; if not, you can return it to me."

The opera was brought out and proved a great success. This brought Piccinni to the notice of the musical world and gave him a reputation which remained bright until he met his Waterloo in the competition with Gluck at Paris.

78.—AN EPISODE IN THE LIFE OF AN ARTIST.

Carl von Weber, after passing through many trials and hardships during his youthful years of theatrical wandering with his ill-tempered old father, finally settled down as private secretary to the brother of the king,

Frederic of Wirtemberg. Now, the Duke was considerable of a spendthrift, and when he got "hard up" it was Weber's duty as secretary to go to the king and try to secure the reckless Duke Ludwig another appropriation. Not a very enviable mission was this, as the king was a man of coarse manners and violent temper, of which the poor secretary got the full benefit.

One day, after some particularly insulting treatment at this unworthy monarch's hands, Weber left the room in a white heat, declaring he would never go back. As he went out into the passage way he met a dilapidated old woman who asked him to direct her to the royal washer-woman. Weber, still boiling with the rage which policy compelled him to conceal in the king's presence, pointed to the door of the king's private apartment, saying, "There."

So in walked the old dame; and, not recognizing the monarch, she told him the young man outside had said she would find the washer-woman there. This so enraged the king that he poured forth a torrent of abuse on her, and summoning an officer, ordered Weber thrown into prison.

In a short time he was released, but the king's wrath followed him. Some time afterward, just as Weber was about to bring out his opera of "St. Sylvana," and as he was on the eve of a gratifying success, this royal rascal had both Weber and his father imprisoned. After a farce of a trial at which the king presided, sentence of banishment was pronounced on them. Weber gladly left Wirtemberg, and after this unpleasant "episode in the life of an artist" gave himself up to composition and the production of those romantic operas which have made his name famous.

79.—EARNING A VIOLIN EASILY.

Paganini's exceedingly great perseverance and practice in his early life gave him such a command over his instrument in later years that he needed no practice other than his frequent concerts gave him. His knowledge of music was so great and his perceptions so quick, that he was reported to be able to play at sight any music written for his instrument.

There was once an artist at Parina who disbelieved these stories of Paganini's wonderful powers. He told the violinist one day that he was the owner of a fine Stradivarius violin, and he would make him a present of it, if Paganini could read at sight a concerto he had in manuscript. "Then prepare to part with your fiddle," said Paganini, and taking the music, he played it at once, and walked off the possessor of a "Strad" worth perhaps £700 or £800.

80.—SCHUBERT'S SERENADE.

Franz Schubert, like Beethoven, was accustomed to carry with him a note-book in which he could jot down musical ideas as they happened to occur to him. Many a beautiful theme would have been lost had it not been for this practical habit of these great composers. There are times when the muse is asleep, when the ideas will not come; then it is that such a note-book becomes valuable and the inspirations of other times may rouse the dormant muse.

Wherever Schubert happened to be, in the city or the fields, in the tavern or the beer garden, did a valuable idea occur to him, out came the note-book and it was hastily scratched down for further treatment. When he was seized by an idea it must go down on the first scrap of paper that came to hand. This was the manner in which that beautiful and well-known "Ständchen" first appeared, though it is also told of "Hark, the Lark."

One Sunday, during the summer of 1826, Schubert, with several friends, was strolling about among the suburban villages in the vicinity of Vienna. As was their custom, they stopped at a beer garden where they sat chatting and enjoying the good company they found. Schubert picked up a book of poetry one of his acquaintances had laid down, and, after turning over the leaves, suddenly stopped, and pointing out a poem exclaimed: "Such a delicious melody has just come into my head; if I but had a sheet of music paper with me!"

One of his companions hastily drew a few staves on the back of a bill of fare and passed it to him, and in the midst of the hubbub of a German beer garden Schubert wrote out that beautiful melody that has pleased such a multitude of music lovers since his day.

81.—MALIBRAN'S GENEROSITY.

That beautiful songstress, Maria Garcia, better known as Madame Malibran, had a varied experience. Her father, a man of fiery temper, was her instructor; after her childhood was passed, she was for some years on the stage with him. Neither her years of childhood nor the time she spent singing in opera with her father were particularly pleasant years, owing to his tyrannical exactions and their fluctuating fortunes. America was the scene of their operatic performances.

Later, when M. Malibran appeared on the scene and posed as a wealthy banker, Maria married him to escape the unpleasant scenes of her early years. But Malibran turned out to be a rascal, to have little money and to be dependent on his wife's exertions. So this great singer was followed by more misfortune. It was not until this marriage was annulled by a French court and she had some time later been married to the great violinist, De Beriot, that her life became one of peace and happiness.

The disposition of this great songstress was one heartily to be admired. Says one biographer: "Living among the sons and daughters of pleasure, her only luxury was the luxury of doing good, and in the midst of wealth her only profusion consisted in beneficence." It is a pleasure to find such words as these spoken concerning a *prima donna*. The records so many of them leave of their personality speak only of selfishness, avarice, sharp temper, and whimsicality, varied now and then by an ostentatious bit of charity.

As an illustration of Malibran's kind-heartedness we may cite the following incident: Only about a year before her death she was engaged by an Italian professor to sing at a concert he was giving, and at her regular terms of twenty guineas. For some reason the concert was a financial failure. The teacher called on her the next day to explain this, and to see if Malibran would be content with a smaller sum. But no, she declared she must have the full amount.

The Italian slowly counted out twenty pounds and then looked up and asked if that would do.

"No, another sovereign," she said, "my terms are twenty guineas, not pounds."

So he put down another pound, sighing to himself as he did so, "My poor wife and children." Then Malibran took up the money and pretended to depart, but turned around and put it all back in the hands of the astonished professor, saying:—

"I insisted on having the full amount that the sum might be all the larger for your acceptance."

82.—HOW BERLIOZ FOOLED THE CRITICS.

It is very easy to criticize, especially to make adverse criticism. A critic may tear to tatters in ten minutes a composition which represents a composer's best thought for ten years. Many of the so-called musical critics have not a tithe of the learning or natural ability of the men whose works they deride. This being the state of affairs, it behooves a composer to be able to defend himself with his pen as well as with a music score.

A few of the greater lights have been quite able to take their own part in an argument. Berlioz and Wagner were especially given to polemics. Berlioz was particularly caustic in his writings, and Wagner was well able to defend his position in the musical and even in the political world. It is not often that we find a great composer and a prominent critic and musical writer in the same person. But Berlioz was a critic and liked to make fun of the lesser critics, like a big fish would worry the smaller fry.

One of his plans to prove the incompetence of his brother critics was, to say the least, original. He wrote a work of much value and interest, called the "Flight into Egypt," and put it on a programme as the work of one "Pierre Ducre," who was stated to have lived in the seventeenth century. The composition was, of course, in the antique style of that day. The critics gave glowing articles concerning the valuable work Berlioz had unearthed, and went so far as to give historical details of the life of the composer and to speak of hunting up more works from his pen. When the admiration was at its height, Berlioz stepped in and claimed the work as his own composition and showed such a personage as Ducre to have existed only in imagination.

The critics could then hardly withdraw their unanimous approbation. So Berlioz had his work favorably criticized and brought prominently before the public, getting a share of public attention that it would not have received were it not for its supposed antiquity.

83.—MUSIC HATH CHARMS.

'Tis said that "music hath charms to soothe the savage breast." An instance of this we find in the Scriptures when the youthful player quieted the passionate king by his soothing music.

Another illustration is found in the influence of the

singing of Farinelli, the great tenor, on Philip V, of Spain. That monarch was affected by a mild kind of insanity and refused to be properly dressed, shaved, or to transact State affairs. Consequently, he presented a rather unkingly appearance and altogether was decidedly useless in his royal capacity. Numerous remedies and plans were tried, but without success. Finally, music was suggested, as the king was very susceptible to its charms, and a messenger was dispatched for the great tenor.

It was arranged that Farinelli should sing in a room adjoining the royal apartments. By the time he had finished the second song, the king appeared much moved by the beauty of his voice and ordered that the singer should be brought to him. When this was done the enraptured monarch overwhelmed him with compliments and offered to grant him anything he might ask.

Farinelli was modest in his demands, only asking that the king should allow himself to be properly cared for and should attend to his duties of State. To this the royal patient assented. So pleased was he with Farinelli's singing and its effects on his royal mind, that he engaged the singer to give him four songs every night and agreed to pay him the equivalent of £2,000 per year for life. It is unnecessary to say that Farinelli was wise enough to accept so good an offer.

The difference between the two kings in their treatment of their musicians was that one threw javelins at his humble servant, the other, ducats.

For ten years Farinelli stayed in King Philip's service, singing the same four songs to his Majesty every evening. Under Philip's successor, Ferdinand VI, Farinelli enjoyed the same position and, as this monarch was subject to the same infirmity as his father, had the same duties to perform. He was the king's prime favorite and acquired great power and riches; but under the next inheritor of the throne he was ordered to leave the kingdom.

84.—WAGNER'S MELODIES AND CHORDS.

Wagner's music has been much ridiculed for its close harmonies and mammoth combinations of tones. But even in the last twenty years ridicule has subsided and a degree of appreciation has come to prevail, which, although it is only partial, augurs well for our musical advancement and educational possibilities. Some have called Wagner's music tuneless, while the fact probably is that it is too tuneful for their ears, that is, it has, in some cases, too many melodies progressing at the same time,—is too polyphonic in character.

Liszt used to call Wagner's melodic combinations "seven-storied melodies." It is hard for a one-storied musical education to appreciate a seven-storied composition. These heavy harmonic combinations do not make things any easier for the singers in Wagner's operas. One cannot come from an Italian opera where everything is plain sailing and the orchestral accompaniment is a continual aid, and expect such a "calm sea and prosperous voyage" under the German composer. Northern weather is not so peaceful and serene as southern. So with the harmonic barometer.

At many times the singers and the orchestra seem to be pursuing each their own path, and the orchestral tones are not always a guide to what the singers' tones are to be. But from this seeming confusion the master's hand has evolved a higher harmony than the periwigged classicists ever dreamed of.

Whitney, the great bass singer, in speaking of Wagner's huge chords, said that composer generally used about seven notes of the scale on the opening chord, and all the singer had to do was to find the other note and "blaze away on that"—an interesting figure of speech, but with a decided tendency toward hyperbole.

85.—DISPOSING OF AN AUDIENCE.

It is a very interesting experience to see any good orchestral conductor drill his men, and especially so when the leader is an exacting drill-master. But add to this that he has a thousand peculiarities and a fiery temper, and the scene becomes well worth a good price of admission.

Such a conductor was Hans von Bülow. But with all his eccentricities and his manifestations of temper, he was one of the foremost orchestral leaders in the world. There was much curiosity among musicians to see him drill his orchestra, but Bülow had an aversion to spectators and generally managed to get rid of them one way or other.

Several ladies once obtained entrance to the hall when he was to conduct an orchestral rehearsal, and prepared themselves to hear quite a treat and to see quite a performance.

When Bülow arrived he saw them seated in the house and at once turned to the orchestra, saying: "We will have a rehearsal of the fagott parts first." Now the fagotts (*i. e.*, bassoons) had not a note until after thirty-two measures of rests, but he gravely beat the time for the thirty-two measures. The fagott players sounded a few notes and then came sixty-four measures of silence, Bülow all the while beating the time. Before the end of this passage of quietness rather than music, the audience had had enough, and taken its flight. When the whimsical conductor saw this he stopped practicing rests and set his orchestra to work.

After the experience of these ladies as a self-invited rehearsal audience had become noised abroad, Bülow was not frequently disturbed in that manner.

86.—PLAYING ON A SHOE.

The following story places Paganini in a better light than this musical miser was accustomed to appear. And really one is led to wonder which is the true Paganini— the miser or the kind artist giving his talent to assist a poor servant girl. One morning the maid who waited on him in Paris came to him, weeping, and told how her lover had been conscripted and sent away to the war, and she, of course, was too poor to buy a substitute for him.

Paganini resolved to aid the girl and took a unique way to do it. He procured a wooden shoe and so fashioned it that it could be strung up and played like a fiddle. Then he advertised that he would give a concert and play five pieces on the violin and five on a wooden shoe. Of course, this strange announcement drew a good house. The violinist had given the girl tickets to the concert, and after it was over he went to her, and pouring twenty thousand francs into her lap, he told her that she could now purchase a substitute for her sweetheart and with the remainder set up housekeeping. He also gave her the wooden shoe that had brought her such good fortune and told her to sell it. Of course, this curious instrument brought her a goodly sum, which she added to the amount which was to bring her domestic happiness.

87.—HÄNDEL'S SUCCESSFUL SCHEME.

Before Händel went to England he held the appointment of *Kapellmeister* to the elector of Hanover. But he became dissatisfied and quitted the service of his royal patron without leave or ceremony.

Not long after Händel had become well intrenched in the good graces of the English court and aristocracy, the elector of Hanover became King George I, of England, and the late Queen Anne's music master began to fear for his royal pension. Händel dare not appear personally at the court and ask that he be continued in the good graces of his former patron whom he had so discourteously deserted, for fear of the king's displeasure. But he had a friend at court who told him that on a certain day the king was to take a ride on the river Thames; so Händel set about to compose a series of pieces and had them played by a band of musicians on a boat which followed the royal barge.

Pleased at this attention, the king inquired who the author of the plan was; and learning that Händel was the composer of the music, he received the repentant musician at court. Händel was soon appointed the instructor of the princesses in the royal household and was granted a pension of £200 a year.

This was a piece of good fortune quite unexpected by the composer. The possession of the royal favor was of inestimable value to him, for as went the king so went the court and all the aristocracy, and the time came when Händel was in need of the support of all his aristocratic friends.

88.—A BASSO'S WIT.

That huge basso of stentorian voice, Lablache, was "a fellow of infinite jest" as well as occasionally one of poor memory. This was once shown in a laughable way, the occasion being his reception by the King of Naples. As Lablache was seated in the reception room awaiting his turn to pass into the king's presence, he noticed a draught from the open doors and begged to be allowed to keep his hat on to ward off any evil effects.

A few moments later his turn came for admittance, and as the usher beckoned him he hastily caught up a hat that was lying close by, and, forgetting that his own hat was on his head, carried the borrowed one with him into the king's presence. His Majesty greeted him with a hearty laugh, which soon brought Lablache to a realization of his ludicrous appearance at a royal reception. But not chagrined by the matter, he brought his ready wit to bear, and bowing to the king declared:

"Sire, your Majesty is quite right; even one hat would be too much for a fellow who has no head!"

89.—OLD WORDS TO NEW TUNES.

Plutarch tells us that Solon, by singing an elegy of a hundred verses in length, composed by himself, excited the Athenians to war with the Megarians. This may readily be believed. To be compelled to listen to a song of a hundred verses would excite almost any one to war, even at the present day. But the old Puritan psalm singers outdid the Greeks in this respect. The writer has a copy of the Covenanter's Psalm Book, dated 1595. In it, among other lugubrious tunes, is the one used to the 119th psalm, and to this tune are set the 176 verses in long array, stringing out their dreary length page after page. We may well believe that a people who could stand such doses as this, could burn their neighbors at the stake for witchcraft. Some of the versions of the Psalms as used by the modern psalm-singers are somewhat improved as to versification, but are yet lamentable failures as to rhyme and rhythm. But there is this to say in their favor, that the quantity to be used at any one sitting has been reduced somewhat from 176 verses.

If the Psalms must be sung in their original phrase or anywhere near it, let the original Hebrew tunes (if such they can be called) be used. But if these lines are to be set to modern tunes of the Gospel hymn order, a re-arrangement of idiom and rhythm must take place, or the result upon the musical listener will not be productive of a worshipful frame of mind.

90.—THE COMPOSER'S DEBT TO NATURE.

Many a composer has been indebted to some sound or tone in nature for the suggestion of musical ideas. Nature suggests and man elaborates the melody, though some writers would have us believe that the composer is simply the amanuensis of nature, in many cases. But we must remember that music is art, and that nature supplies nature, not art.

A good composer will turn to account a suggestion from any source, however humble. Mendelssohn took pleasure in acknowledging his debt to nature in these matters. While Mendelssohn was not a Beethoven, while he could not so well depict the rugged, the grand, the heroic, as did that musical Jupiter, yet Mendelssohn was the tone poet of the forest and field, the bright sun, and the blue sky.

A friend of his relates how they were walking in the country one day, and getting tired, threw themselves on the grass in the shade and were there pursuing their conversation. Suddenly Mendelssohn seized him by the arm and whispered, "Hush!" A moment later the composer told him that a large fly had just then gone buzzing by and he wished to hear its sound die away in the distance.

Mendelssohn was at that time working on his overture to "A Midsummer Night's Dream," and not long after it was completed. He then showed his friend a certain descending bass modulation with the remark, "There, that's the fly that buzzed past us at Schonhausen."

91.—SONTAG'S REVENGE.

Henrietta Sontag, one of the greatest "queens of song," had to go through at least one severe struggle before she attained the enviable position which she maintained as the greatest singer Germany had produced. It is said that at the beginning of her career she was hissed off the Vienna stage by the friends of her rival, Amelia Steininger. But in spite of this defeat, Sontag persevered until all Europe was at her feet.

Many years later, when she was at the height of her fame, she was one day riding through the streets of Berlin. Soon she came across a little girl leading a blind woman. The kind-hearted songstress was touched by the woman's helplessness, and she impulsively beckoned the child to her with, "Come here, my child, come here. Who is that you are leading by the hand?"

The answer was, "That's my mother, Amelia Steininger. She used to be a great singer, but she lost her voice, and she cried so much about it that now she can't see any more."

Sontag inquired their address and then told the child, "Tell your mother an old acquaintance will call on her this afternoon." The great singer was true to her word. She searched out their lowly abiding place and undertook the care of both mother and daughter. At her request, a skilled oculist tried to restore the woman's sight, but it was in vain.

But Sontag's kindness to her former rival did not stop here. The next week she gave a benefit concert for the poor woman, and it was said that on that occasion Sontag sang as she had never sung before. And who can doubt that with the applause of that vast audience there was mingled the applause of the angels in heaven who rejoice over the good deeds of those below.

92.—A SECOND NAPOLEON.

Boucher was a violinist who succeeded in attracting the attention of Charles IV, of Spain, and was finally appointed special violinist to his Majesty. This man bore a great resemblance to Napoleon I, and when he was traveling in Russia, the Emperor Alexander, noticing this, sent for him and showed him a French uniform consisting of a three-cornered hat, sword, and a colonel's uniform of the Chasseurs of the French Imperial guard, and a cross of the Legion of Honor. "Now," said the Czar, "this uniform once belonged to the Emperor Napoleon, and was captured during the campaign of Moscow. I have noticed your likeness to him, and desire you to put on this uniform; I will then present you to my mother, who has often desired to see Napoleon."

When Boucher had arrayed himself as the Czar had requested, he was conducted to the apartment of the Empress, and her son assured her that she saw a perfect counterpart of the great Corsican.

93.—A SINGER'S SENSE.

Santley, the English baritone, is a man of wide musical experience and of great operatic ability. But more than this, he is a man of solid nerve and good sense.

This was shown by his cool actions and language one night in 1865, when he was singing the part of "Papageno" in Mozart's "Magic Flute." In the same cast were Titiens and Di Murska.

The London theater was crowded with an enthusiastic audience. In the last act some gauze, which had been used to represent clouds, caught fire from a gas jet behind the flies. Immediately one of the stage hands ran out on a narrow strip of wood over the stage and with a knife cut away the burning material which fell blazing on the stage.

The audience, seeing the fire, would quickly have lost all presence of mind; but Santley, who was on the stage at the time, walked to the front and called out to the audience: "Don't act like a lot of fools! Its nothing."

Then he immediately took up his interrupted song and went on with the scene. This quieted the people and a panic was doubtless averted by the singer's presence of mind.

94.—HAYDN'S NOBLE ENGLISH PUPIL.

Haydn was delighted with London in most of its aspects, but we have an idea that there was one kind of pupil that he was perfectly willing to leave behind when he returned to his beloved Vienna. But probably he found them there as well as in London. They are not limited to England.

One day a nobleman called on him and, expressing his fondness for music, said he would like Haydn to give him a few lessons in composition at one guinea per lesson. Haydn promised to gratify him and asked when they should begin.

"At once, if you have no objection;" said he, drawing from his pocket one of Haydn's quartets. "For the first lesson let us examine this quartet and you tell me the reasons for some modulations and certain progressions that are contrary to all rules of composition."

Haydn could offer no objection to this. They then set to work to examine the music. Several places were found which, when asked why he did this and that, Haydn could only say he wrote it so to obtain a good effect. But "My lord" was not satisfied with such a reason and declared unless the composer gave him a better reason than that for his innovations, he should declare them good for nothing. Then Haydn suggested that the pupil rewrite the music after his own fashion; but this he declined to do, though he persisted in his question, "How can your way, which is contrary to all rule, be the best?" At last Haydn lost all patience with this noble critic, and said :—

"I see, my lord, that it is you who are so good as to give lessons to me. I do not want your lessons, for I feel that I do not merit the honor of having such a master as yourself—I bid you good morning, my lord"—and showed the upstart the door.

95.—LABLACHE AND TOM THUMB.

Perhaps the greatest basso the stage has known was Lablache. He was a very tall and powerfully built man, with a head which was said to be the "finest that ever decorated a human body." His voice was powerful beyond description, yet was subject to the most complete control; and withal Lablache could enjoy a joke.

He happened to be in Paris at the same time as Tom Thumb, he of the minute proportions. One day a Frenchman from the rural districts, having come to town for the express purpose of seeing the "General," asked of a wag the way to Tom's stopping place. This joker, instead of giving the diminutive general's address, gave that of Lablache. Hastening to the address given, the rustic rang the bell and was confronted by Lablache himself. The amazed visitor stood confounded, but managed to gasp: "A thousand pardons, Monsieur, there must be a mistake. I hoped to see Tom Thumb."

Lablache immediately saw the point and replied gravely: "Sir, there is no mistake, I am Tom Thumb!"

"But—how—I—Tom—why! I thought Tom Thumb was very small!"

"Yes, yes; before the public I am small, very small, indeed—only so tall," holding his hand two feet from the floor; "but here at home," raising himself to his full height and sending out his voice in full, deep tones, "here at home I sing and take my ease."

The Frenchman departed full of wonder and satisfaction.

96.—A COMPOSER'S CHAGRIN.

Moscheles, the virtuoso, composer, and teacher, had one fault that we must say was not confined to him alone. In teaching he used frequently to forget the purpose for which the pupil was present, and instead of using every minute for the pupil's advancement, he would take up much time in relating his experiences and reminiscences, and telling about the different composers and notable people he had met in his long and busy life. And his pupils were oftentimes not averse to this, for besides being very entertaining, it occasionally concealed the fact that the lessons were not as well prepared as they might have been.

In one of his classes were Sir Arthur Sullivan, and the violinist, Carl Feininger. As they came to recitation one morning all the class was struck with the downcast expression on the face of the usually smiling Moscheles, and as the pupils came in each one would exclaim: "Um Gotteswillen, Herr Professor, what is the matter; are you ill?" But never a word did they get in reply, only a wave of the hand toward the piano, as much as to say, "You are here to study music and not to pry into my feelings. Do not chatter to me; sit down and attend to the lesson."

The last pupil to enter was Feininger, and he being Moscheles' pet pupil, felt brave enough to insist that the dear Herr Professor tell his anxious pupils what had occurred to so cast a cloud over his genial spirits.

"Well," said Moscheles, "I will tell you." So with labored breath he began: "I got up this morning—I dressed myself—I went to eat my breakfast—there was no butter—I sent my Dienstmädchen for some butter—" and then his voice burst forth in agony, almost in sobs, "and what do you think she brought it in? That butter was wrapped in a page of—*my G minor Concerto!*"

97.—THE FRIENDS, MOZART AND HAYDN.

The jealousy and dislike that has existed in the minds of certain of the great musicians for others of their guild found no place in the feelings Mozart and Haydn entertained for each other.

Haydn was writing his symphonies before Mozart

began to cut any figure in the world. But so rapid was the growth of the younger musician that he soon caught up with and distanced the elder, and Haydn became the pupil instead of Mozart. Eight years after Mozart's death, Haydn brought out the "Creation." His life extended eighteen years beyond that of the genial Mozart.

The relations between them were always of the most pleasant character, and their words always expressed a hearty admiration of each other's abilities. This was certainly a rare state of affairs. But then, of all the musical giants, perhaps, these two were the most genial and pleasant of disposition.

Haydn wrote to a friend: "Oh, Mozart! If I could instil into the soul of every lover of music the admiration I have for his matchless works, all countries would seek to be possessed of so great a treasure. Mozart is incomparable, and I am amazed that he is unable to obtain any court position. Forgive me if I get excited when speaking of him, I am so very fond of him."

Equally strong was Mozart's fondness for Haydn. When Haydn was leaving for England in 1791, the year of Mozart's death, Mozart said, in endearing phrase, "Oh, papa, you have had no training for the wide, wide world." And Haydn's answer was, "My language is spoken everywhere."

Mozart's words on that occasion, "We shall now, no doubt, take our last farewell in this world," proved true.

His defense of Haydn's music was prompt and spirited. When Kozeluch and Mozart were one day listening to a composition of Haydn's, the former called attention to certain strange progressions, asking Mozart if he should have written them so.

"I think not," replied the composer, "and for this reason: Neither you nor I would have thought of them."

One day, Mozart was approached by a Viennese professor who used to bother him by finding fault with Haydn's music. This time he had found a great error.

Finally, when Mozart could stand it no longer, he shut him up with, "Sir, if you and I were melted down together we could not furnish materials to make one Haydn."

98.—A FRIGHTENED DESDEMONA.

Manual Garcia possessed, besides a beautiful voice, a furious temper. His daughter, Maria, destined in later years to become one of the world's most celebrated *prima donnas*, inherited somewhat of this feature of her father's character, and the result was not conducive of domestic tranquillity. When Monsieur Malibran made her an offer of marriage, Garcia was enraged, and declined to sanction the engagement. The result was that there was an uproar in the establishment. As luck would have it, that night father and daughter were to sing together in "Othello," and so, for the time being, though wrath was in their hearts, the father must appear as the swarthy Moor, and the daughter as Desdemona.

In the course of the opera it becomes necessary for Othello to stab Desdemona, and at this point Maria saw her father approach and brandish over her, not the stage dagger of cardboard covered with silver paper, but a real dagger which her father had recently bought.

Terrified at what she thought was her father's revenge for her opposition to him, she shrieked out: "Father, father, for God's sake do not kill me!"

But her alarm was needless. Garcia had in his haste been unable to lay his hand on the pasteboard dagger, which was one of the stage "properties," and was forced to substitute his own. It might be added that the affrighted Desdemona afterward married Malibran and by this name scored her remarkable triumphs.

99.—RETENTIVE MEMORIES.

Elsewhere in this volume is told the story of Mozart's prodigious feat of memory in retaining in mind the celebrated "*Miserere*" of Allegri, and that, too, when he was a boy of tender years. Reference is also made to the almost incredible memory of other composers and conductors. But it is not alone those who have attained the greatest heights of musicianship that are gifted with the power of retention in its largest degree.

For instance, there was the English musician, Battishill, whose memory was such that even the longest compositions of Händel, Corelli, or Arne were always sufficiently present to his recollection, during the time he was playing them, to render the assistance of the text unnecessary. He was one day dining with Dr. Arnold, when he played from memory several passages of the doctor's oratorio of the "Prodigal Son," which he had not heard for thirty years, and which Arnold himself had entirely forgotten.

The name of Wesley is revered among English organists and composers as being affixed to some of the most valuable compositions that country has produced. Both of the brothers, Charles and Samuel Wesley, were gifted with remarkably retentive memories. Charles Wesley could play the whole of Händel's numerous choruses from memory. Samuel Wesley has given many remarkable instances of a similarly retentive memory; one of the most remarkable may be mentioned. In his early days he composed an oratorio consisting of a score of upward of three hundred closely written manuscript pages. It was afterward performed at one of the Birmingham festivals. Returning to London the composer was robbed of his portmanteau, which contained this work, and he never again heard of its contents. Nearly twenty-five years afterward, at the solicitation of a friend, he commenced to write it out afresh, which he did with the greatest facility, stating that he saw the score in his mind's eye as accurately and distinctly as if it lay before him.

The blind are generally possessed of strong memories, for the reason, of course, of the continual and dependent use made of that faculty. But even among these strong-memoried people not all have the quick grasp of that blind English organist, Henry Smart. This excellent performer and composer of much good music has been known to get a friend to read over the notes of a chorus of Händel's, and afterward go to church and perform it correctly. When asked how he was able to recollect so much without having a single sound conveyed to his ear, he would reply: "I carry the notes in my mind, and do not think of the sounds."

100.—PATTI'S DOG.

Prima Donnas, like many less distinguished folk often have a weakness for pets. Adelina Patti possessed a tiny dog of rare Mexican breed, which was a present from one of the Mexican Presidents. The little creature led a life of great luxury, and accompanied the great songstress everywhere. During an American tour the little dog, to the inconsolable grief of its mistress, departed this life. Shortly afterwards, at the close of a performance of "*Lucia*," when the *Diva* came before the curtain to acknowledge the plaudits of the audience and to receive the floral tributes showered upon her from all parts of the house, a casket of roses was handed up to her. Immediately Patti received the gift, the outer case of flowers sprang open, and then was disclosed a silk pillow upon which reposed another tiny Mexican dog to take the place of him who had joined the majority. The excitement of the audience knew no bounds at witnessing this episode, and Patti was obliged to continue to appear before the curtain fondling her new treasure.

101.—CLEMENTI'S ECONOMY.

Muzio Clementi is known to so many in the present day as merely a composer of sonatinas and of a series of *études*, that we fail to realize his true place in musical history.

He was born in Rome in 1752. By the time he was fifteen he was well known in his native city as a player and composer. He attracted the attention of an Englishman who carried him off to England to give him a broader education. There he soon became the most prominent musician of his day. His was the first music that was composed for the pianoforte, and it was on his works that the modern school of piano playing was founded.

When he was visiting Vienna, the Emperor Joseph arranged for a musical duello between Mozart and Clementi, but they were so equally great as performers that it could not be decided who was the superior.

Later in life he bought an interest in a London firm of instrument makers and music publishers, and by his energy, business talents, and economical habits succeeded in accumulating a large fortune in spite of various business reverses.

Speaking of Clementi's economy reminds us of a story told of him by Spohr. That entertaining writer met him and John Field, his pupil, in St. Petersburg, where Clementi did a large business and where Field made a name for himself as a composer. One day Spohr called on them and found teacher and pupil at the wash-tub, washing their stockings and other linen. They did not suffer themselves to be disturbed, and "Clementi advised me," writes Spohr, "to do the same, as washing in St. Petersburg was not only very expensive, but the linen suffered much from the method used in washing it."

102.—MUSIC AT SO MUCH PER NOTE.

The statistician is never satisfied unless he has a thing represented in cold-blooded figures. Some have even gone so far as to estimate how much various artists earned for every note they sang or played. For instance, one mathematician tells us that Rossini got eighteen pence per note for each note he wrote in the opera of "Semiramide."

This is certainly "drawing one's note" for goodly figures. But it pays even better to be a singer than a composer; for we are told that every time Patti sings "Semiramide" she gets fifteen pence per note. In "*Lucia di Lammermoor*" the rate is still higher, as the notes are fewer. In this opera, when she gets her best rates, "La Diva" draws her one and ninepence per note.

But these are moderate figures, when we consider the prices at which Paganini used to draw the bow. At a certain concert in Paris, in which he played some fifteen pages of violin music and at which his proceeds were one hundred and sixty-five thousand francs, it was found by some patient figurer that the "Wizard of the Violin" received nine and threepence per measure. Divided on the basis of time, his receipts were four and sevenpence for every quarter-note or every quarter-rest, half that sum for every eighth-note or eighth-rest, and so on.

This is getting musical mathematics down to a pretty fine point. Soon we will have some fellow calculating the cost to the world of each note of Gabriel's final trumpet blast.

103.—LISZT'S PRECOCITY.

The early life of the great pianist, Franz Liszt, reads, in some respects, like the story of Mozart's youth. Liszt manifested his musical genius when very young, and appeared in his first public concert when but nine years old. Shortly after this he played for a gathering of nobility at the palace of Prince Esterhazy, in whose service the boy's father was as assistant steward; and at that time six noblemen subscribed six hundred gulden a year for six years, that this prodigy might have the means for a proper education.

Adam Liszt then wrote to Hummel, the pupil of Mozart, to secure for his son tuition of this celebrated player. But Hummel's terms were higher than Liszt could afford, so they went to Vienna and sought instruction of Czerny. Czerny was so crowded with work that he declined to receive another pupil. Therefore little Franz, without more ado, seated himself at the piano. On hearing the playing of the youthful Liszt, Czerny quickly changed his mind, and not only received him as a pupil, but refused to take any tuition money from such a genius. A few years later, when they went to Paris, the boy was given the title "the little Mozart." His playing was phenomenal, and he at once became the rage in that artistic city. To show the regard in which this young artist was held—for he was at that time but eleven years old—we quote the following from a criticism of his playing:—

"I cannot help it; since yesterday evening I am a believer in metempsychosis. I am convinced that the soul and spirit of Mozart have passed into the body of young Liszt. And never has an identity revealed itself by plainer signs. The same country, the same wonderful talent in childhood, and in the same art!

"Mozart, in taking the name of Liszt, has lost nothing of that interesting countenance which always increases the interest a child inspires in us by his precocious talent. The features of our little prodigy express spirit and cheerfulness. He comes before his audience with exceeding gracefulness; and the pleasure, the admiration, which he awakens in his hearers as soon as his fingers glide along the keys seem to him an amusement which diverts him extremely."

104.—KEEPING AT IT.

Eternal vigilance is said to be the price of liberty; and we might say that everlasting practice is the price of virtuosity. This principle has been illustrated in the lives of nearly every great artist. The following episode has been paralleled in the history of several of the famous *virtuosi*:—

Lolli, a celebrated violinist of the last century, found, when he went to Stuttgart, a very superior player named Nardini. In fact, Lolli was quite eclipsed, and he felt his secondary ability very keenly. He realized his need of practice so much that he requested a leave of a year's absence from his patron prince. But instead of putting in the time at traveling, which he had declared his intention to do, he retired to a small village, and worked at his instrument until the year had expired. Then he returned; and by the increased brilliancy and effectiveness of his playing, his rival, Nardini, was forced to seek other fields of labor.

Another violinist of note, Giardini, when asked how long it would take one to play the fiddle well, answered "Twelve hours a day for twenty years!"

So our first statement would seem to be correct; the only short cut to virtuosity is to " keep everlastingly at it."

105.—A PECULIAR GENIUS.

When we read of Thomas Britton, who lived in London in Händel's time, we might almost believe that music furnished more of a bond between all classes of society in those days than in ours. Britton was a coal dealer, or, as the English say, a coal heaver, or dealer in "small coals." In spite of this humble occupation he was a great lover of music and had the loft over his coal warehouse so arranged as to accommodate an audience. Thither many of the celebrated musicians of the day and noble lords and beautiful ladies would wend their way, attracted by the music and the company they found there. In the morning Britton would be lugging a sack of coal to some customer, and in the afternoon he would be entertaining such personages as Händel, Dr. Pepusch, Jennens (Händel's librettist), Sir Roger L'Estrange, and the Duchess This, the Countess That, and Lady T'other.

The best of music was performed at these informal gatherings. With Händel at the harpsichord, Bannister, the first great English violinist, with his fiddle, and perhaps the famous soprano, Cuzzoni, to sing one of Händel's latest airs, we may imagine that never did another coal warehouse resound to such music or entertain such a company. Not only were musicians here assembled, but also writers, philosophers, and poets came to contribute their quota to this humble *salon*.

Such a condition of affairs speaks well for the democratic spirit of that day. We doubt if a man of Britton's humble origin and occupation would be thus countenanced by the English aristocracy of to-day, however musical he might be.

Britton came to his death in a peculiar way. One of the attendants at his impromptu concerts was a ventriloquist; and this man one day, in a spirit of fun, called out that Britton would die in a few hours if he did not at once drop on his knees and say the Lord's Prayer. The voice seemed to be intangible, to come from space. Britton, greatly frightened, did as he was bid; but he suffered so from terror that he died a few days after— an ignominious death for an original genius.

106.—SHAKING ALL OVER.

It is well known that Queen Victoria was formerly an excellent pianiste, and is possessed of a remarkably correct ear. Baroness Bloomfield, in her "Reminiscences," relates how on one occasion the Queen asked her to sing, and she, with fear and trembling, sang one of Grisi's famous airs, but omitted the shake, or, as we should say in this country, the trill, at the end. The Queen's quick ear immediately detected the omission and, smilingly, her Majesty said to Lady Normanby, her sister: "Does not your sister shake, Lady Normanby?" To which that lady promptly replied: "Oh, yes, ma'am; she is shaking all over."

107.—THE "OX" MINUET.

There is no sensible reason for the titles attached to many pieces of music, some of them even classical selections. Most generally they are placed there as an attempt of some publisher to "boom" his stock and sell his goods. Then, again, some peculiar titles may have their origin in incidents about as important as the following:

Haydn one day received a visit from a butcher who stated that himself and his daughter were admirers of Haydn's music; and as the young lady was soon to be married, he made bold to ask that the composer write a minuet for her wedding. Kind "Papa Haydn" consented, and in a few days the man of meat secured his music. Not long afterward, Haydn was surprised to hear this same minuet played under his window. On looking out he saw a band of musicians forming a ring around a large ox, tastefully decorated with flowers. Soon the butcher came up and presented the ox to Haydn, saying that for such excellent music he thought he ought to make the composer a present of the best ox in his possession. Ever after, this little composition was called the "Ox" minuet.

108.—NILSSON AND THE SHAH OF PERSIA.

On the occasion of the visit of the Shah of Persia to England in 1873, many entertainments and festivities were arranged for this eastern monarch, and among them an operatic representation which should include the best acts from several favorite operas. The performance was to consist of the third act of "*La Favorita*," with Titiens as Leonora, the first act of "*La Traviata*," and after a short ballet, the first act of "*Mignon*." In each of the latter operas Nilsson was to take the title rôle.

But Titiens entered an objection to this arrangement, saying that it was not fair to give Nilsson the best two places on the programme, and suggested that she be given the central place, and that Nilsson appear in the first act and the last, which was certainly a fair arrangement. But to this Nilsson demurred.

So matters stood until two days before the presentation; then Nilsson suddenly changed her mind and expressed her willingness to accept Titien's plan, by which Nilsson was to appear first in "*Traviata*" and in the last act of "*Mignon*." This change was brought about by Nilsson's hearing that the Shah would only be present from 8.30 to 9.30, on account of other festivities the same evening. Had she continued in her objections to Titiens' plan, Nilsson would have had little chance for singing to the royal party more than a few minutes.

At 8.30 on the evening set for the opera, the Prince of Wales arrived at the theater to receive the Shah, but no Shah was to be seen. After waiting half an hour the opera began. Nilsson came on the stage and saw, in disgust, that the royal box was empty. Her disgust was no-wise lessened by the fact that she had ordered from Worth, of Paris, a most magnificent dress for her character of Violetta in "*Traviata*."

Not until 9.30 did the Shah put in an appearance, and then Nilsson was through with her first appearance and Titiens was on the stage in "*Favorita*."

Mapleson, the manager, knew of Nilsson's disappointment, and was expecting to have a scene with her on the morrow, when the Prince of Wales suggested to him that it might soothe the wrathy *prima donna* if she were to be presented to the Shah that evening.

So the *impresario* hied himself to Nilsson's dressing

room and informed her that she was to be presented to the Shah. But she objected, as she had removed her gorgeous costume used in *"Traviata"* and was arrayed in a ragged old dress, with hair disheveled, and without shoes, for her character as Mignon. But Mapleson persuaded her that it was a command, and that she must obey.

They went to the royal box; but, before her arrival could be announced to his serene Highness, Nilsson had walked into the room in her tramp-like costume, and going at once to the Shah she explained in French that she had prepared "a superb costume expressly for your Majesty," but that by his tardiness he missed seeing her in it, and now could only see her in this miserable rig, and without shoes.

Meanwhile she was gesticulating with her right hand, and at the end of her remarks pointed to her bare feet. The Shah bent forward to see through his spectacles what she was pointing to, and at the same time she raised her foot to emphasize her remarks. The result was that that member came within an inch or so of the royal Persian nose.

So struck was the Shah at the *prima donna's* originality that he remained until after midnight to see her in "*Mignon.*" Nilsson was appeased, but the Lord Mayor and other notables of London were kept waiting for him from half-past nine until half-past twelve at the Goldsmith's ball.

109.—MODULATIONS.

One prominent point of difference between the old classic and the modern schools of operatic composition is in the matter of modulation. The older writers, Mozart, Cimarosa, Spontini, *et al*, used comparatively few changes of key. The tonality was preserved, or on being departed from, was left in a formal and in a perfectly clear style.

But in the modern school, as represented by Wagner, Mascagni, and the older Verdi, abruptness of modulation is no rare thing. One of Wagner's theories was that a composer should not be confined to any given succession of keys, that he should be free to "swim in a sea of tone;" but many who have essayed this tonal sea have been drowned therein. Where Wagner could swim they could only flounder and sink.

In this modern school, changes in circumstances or plot of the opera are frequently accompanied by sudden modulations in key relationship, and often the composer does not wait for "something to happen," but changes his key at will, this being the theory of the new school.

As long ago as the time of Grétry, the French composer, the *pros* and *cons* of this subject were agitated.

A musician once asked him why he did not make use of some of those sudden transitions in key, and his reply was:—

"Some day I will give the public a taste of that sort of thing, but I must have my reasons for it."

"Oh, what are they?"

"Well, for example, suppose in the plot of the opera some amorous swain, in spite of a father's strict injunctions, should attempt to make love to a fair damsel,—if the father should steal on them unawares, and astonish our lover from behind with a hearty kick, then, I assure you, I will modulate very abruptly!"

Certainly the lover would think this good cause for a sudden change of base!

110.—AN EVENTFUL CAREER.

The life of the composer of the light and popular "*Maritana*," William Vincent Wallace, was as full of strange experiences as that of the hero of many a novel. His native country was Ireland. Shortly after he was married, on the wedding journey, in fact, his young wife became jealous of the attentions he paid to her own sister, who was with them, and the couple separated, never to meet again.

Cast down by this circumstance, Wallace then drifted to Australia, where he took up his abode among the roughs and savages of the "bush." On one of his visits to Sydney, his acquaintances discovered that the man they considered to be an ordinary immigrant, was in reality a fine musician and an excellent violinist. The news was carried to the Governor of the colony, and he insisted that Wallace give a concert. This was done with great success. The Governor was so pleased that he made him a present of a hundred sheep, the staple currency of the colony at that time.

Wallace later went to Tasmania, where he narrowly escaped being butchered to make a Tasmanian savage's holiday, and on one occasion his life was saved through the romantic intervention of a chief's daughter. After this he went on a whaling voyage, and only he and three companions escaped the wreck of the vessel. His next journey was to India, where he played before sumptuous courts of several Indian princes, and after that went to South America, where he crossed the continent by a slow but sure method, *viz.*, on the back of a mule. He then came to North America, and finally landed in London, having netted a handsome sum by his playing.

In London, in 1845, he undertook to compose an opera, and "Maritana" was the result. This was such a success that it was followed by similar works. When his eyesight began to fail, he again visited the western continents, and again he figured in some interesting experiences, more interesting, perhaps, to the reader than to Wallace. One of them was that a steamboat on which he traveled blew up, and he narrowly escaped with his life; and another was that he lost nearly all his savings by the failure of a pianoforte factory in New York. But he retrieved his fortunes through concert giving, and finally ended his eventful career in the Pyrenees mountains, in 1865.

111.—NAPOLEON OUTWITTED BY A SONGSTRESS.

The iron will of Napoleon I did not confine itself to the control of kingdoms and things political, but he desired to bring under its sway all matters with which he was brought into contact. The disrespect of this military genius for the rights of other nations brought him to the defeat of Waterloo. Though he could control the majority of men who came under his notice and within his grasp, he occasionally met a miniature Waterloo when dealing with the fair sex.

It is generally conceded that the *prima donna* without a will of her own and the willingness to make it known is a rarity. And no exception to this rule was Madame Catalani, one of the first singers in the time of the First Empire.

Historians have not given Napoleon credit for being musical; but at any rate he determined, after hearing Catalani, that she should remain in Paris, that he might enjoy her vocal abilities whenever he wished. So he ordered her to come to the Tuileries. Not daring to disobey, the *cantatrice* awaited the pleasure of him who was making the thrones of Europe to tremble.

The Emperor knew that she was intending to leave Paris, and without wasting time inquired—

"Where are you going, Madame?"

"To London, sir," said the astonished and somewhat affrighted songstress.

"But you must remain here," declared Napoleon, testily; "you shall have a hundred thousand francs a year, and two months' vacation. Consider the matter settled. *Bon jour, Madame.*"

Too much frightened to declare to the tyrant that she had engagements abroad that she must keep, Catalani retired at his curt dismissal, and hastened to her apartments. A few days afterward, a document stating the arrangement was left at her house.

Determined not to be subjected to this arrangement, which was entirely opposed to her plans and wishes, she resolved to escape this bondage, even though the fetters were golden. Hence she disguised herself in the habiliments of a nun, and hastened to the sea-coast.

There she found a vessel exchanging prisoners. Seeking out the captain she secured his silence and assistance by adding a generous sum to his purse. When the vessel left France the nun was on board.

Napoleon might not have relished this stratagem and perhaps would have made the wilful lady feel that his power was not confined to Paris. But military affairs just then took a serious turn, and for this reason the Emperor had more weighty things to occupy his mind than sending after runaway opera singers.

112.—STUBBORN COMPOSERS.

Had more of the most famous composers catered to the taste of the people of their time, they would have been in receipt of larger incomes and would have held positions that were closed to them on account of what was called their stubbornness. Undoubtedly there was a good deal of the stubborn element in some of them, and a great deal of admiration for self and the works of self. That is right. A fair amount of self-appreciation is a good thing.

Many times these men did right in refusing to grant the demands of critics or of a public that was unappreciative of their artistic strivings. A great composer is always ahead of the times in which he lives. As Lowell says, success is posthumous. They were right in refusing to descend to the level of the commonplace, and, in the majority of cases, were right in refusing to alter their standard and their written works to suit a taste that was temporary or vitiated in character.

But there was occasionally a middle ground that might have been occupied without harm to the artistic interests involved, and with great advantage to the composer's financial welfare. When they refused to see this, or seeing it, refused to act as good judgment dictated, then we can only assign stubbornness as the reason. One instance will serve to illustrate our meaning.

Schubert once had an opportunity to obtain the conductorship at a certain opera house. He was sadly in need of such an appointment, as his income, despite his many compositions, was next to nothing. But before the position was awarded, he was to compose and conduct certain music to the satisfaction of the officials. But the composition he presented contained difficulties that were evidently insurmountable, and Schubert was asked to alter it somewhat to make it suitable to the singers and the circumstances. He gruffly refused. After two rehearsals the trouble only seemed to grow worse and at the final full rehearsal an attempt to sing the obnoxious part only resulted in a grand failure.

The manager then announced that the presentation would be postponed and asked Herr Schubert in the meanwhile to make such changes as would insure the performance, especially in the part assigned to one of the soloists. At this Schubert's wrath got the upper hand of his good judgment and shutting up his score with a bang he shouted, "I alter nothing," and left the house. That ended his prospects as an opera director.

113.—CLERICAL WIT.

Good old Father Taylor, when pastor of the Seaman's Bethel, in Boston, was once preaching on "social amusements." As it happened, but unknown to the speaker, Jenny Lind, who was then singing in America, was in his congregation. He roundly denounced card-playing, dancing, the theater, etc., but in speaking of music gave it his unqualified approval. After dwelling on the power of music in the religious service, he paid tribute to the generosity of the great vocalists, especially to "that greatest and sweetest of them all, now lighted on our shores."

At this point he was interrupted by a boor seated on the pulpit stairs, who shouted out to know if any one who died at Jenny Lind's concert would go to heaven. Taylor's prompt reply was:—

"A Christian will go to heaven wherever he dies, but a fool will be a fool wherever he is—even if he is on the steps of a pulpit."

114.—A PATIENT PUPIL.

The fine arts are, perhaps, in the matter of the time involved, the most difficult of all studies to conquer. One cannot master music or painting by mere force of will; one must, as it were, grow into the chosen art, not jump into it. The reason we have so much poor art, and art that is not art at all, is because there is so much of this jumping attempted.

The proper growth is brought by continuous application, day after day, for years. This is true in all departments of the musical life. Yet it is a truth that seems the most difficult of realization to all but about one-tenth of one per cent. of the people generally.

Every teacher finds that the majority of his pupils expect to play the piano or violin well in a year; and as to singing, why, Lord bless you, they expect to give concerts in half that time. All this is not so much the fault of the individual pupil as it is a general misapprehension of the depth of art and of the difficulties that beset the student's path. To express the whole matter in a few words, the public ideal is a low one. We do not aspire to play or sing well, *i. e.*, artistically; we simply desire to sing or play; if it be in a very ordinary or slovenly manner, that does not matter.

Not all can have the talent, time, money, and health necessary to make a great artist. But all may do well what they set out to do. A simple thing well done is preferable to a complex one abominably done. Oh, that music pupils and their parents could recognize this!

Some schools realize that music is "a long road to travel," and insist that a student, upon entering, shall give evidence of his expectation of completing a course of study. For instance, we read that the conservatory at Milan, Italy, requires each pupil to declare his intention and ability to stay in the school until the seven years' course is completed. Not many half-prepared pupils are turned out of that school. That is one European standard. In America a fair damsel will unblushingly apply for a diploma before she should be allowed to leave a musical kindergarten.

In former times students were content to abide by the adage "*festinate lente.*" Years were spent in technical drill. But the years so spent produced great singers. As an extreme example of this painstaking study, we may cite the method used by Porpora with his pupil, Caffarelli.

For five years this celebrated teacher (who perhaps gave instruction to more great singers than any teacher since has done) held his willing pupil to the practice of various scales and exercises which were written down one at a time. During the sixth year Caffarelli was drilled in articulation, pronunciation, and declamation, points in which many modern singers are sadly deficient.

Then, one day, when the patient pupil thought perhaps he might soon begin to sing something beyond scales and exercises, old Porpora turned to him, and handing him his music, said, in his curt fashion:—

"Now, young man, you may go. I can teach you no more. You are the greatest singer in the world!"

And so it was. This patient toil had brought its own reward. He was without a peer in his own time. Honors and reward and riches came to him, and at the end of his career he purchased a dukedom and retired to his castle to enjoy the large fortune his unrivaled singing had brought him. Had he rebelled against his old master's long course of training, these things and the applause of all Europe would have been lost to him, and his name would probably never have appeared in the list of the world's great singers.

115.—FIELD FOOLED.

John Nepomuk Hummel was one of the most prominent European pianists of the early part of the present century. But greatness and good looks do not go hand in hand in all cases. Though he was, in his day, ranked the equal of Beethoven, and though he was fêted and flattered in all the musical centers of Europe, the fact still remained that he was a very plain and ill-favored sort of a fellow, throwing even Schubert into the shade in this respect. In 1822, Hummel went to Russia, in the suite of the grand duchess, and there his reception was of the most flattering and brilliant kind. But there was one thing that marred that cordial reception at Moscow, and that was that the greatest composer and pianist of all Russia did not call on him. This personage was no less than John Field, the Russianized Irishman, the pupil of Clementi.

Finally, Hummel concluded that if the mountain would not come to Mahomet, Mahomet would go to the mountain, and he started out to find Field. When he arrived at Field's rooms he found him giving a lesson and was compelled to await his pleasure. Hummel, with his stout, thick-set body and plain features, and poorly dressed, looked like some German farmer; Field, on the other hand, was elegant in bearing and courtly in manner.

At the close of the lesson, Field turned to his visitor with a gruff " Well, sir, what can I do for you ? "

" I have heard so much of your playing that, as I was in Moscow on business, I thought I would come in and make your acquaintance, and hear some of it myself. I am very fond of music and understand it a little."

Field smiled at this request, coming as it seemed, from some village tradesman who dabbled in music; but he sat down to the piano and played some of his own elegant compositions in his best style. The stranger warmly applauded and thanked him. Then Field, thinking to have some fun, asked the supposed rustic to take his turn at the piano; but Hummel declared he never played without his notes, that he only played a little on the organ now and then, and so on.

But Field insisted, and as his clumsy visitor sat down to the piano, Field leaned back to enjoy the fun. And he did enjoy it, but in a different way from what he expected. Hummel took one of the themes that Field had just finished playing, and developed it into a brilliant *fantasia* in which were displayed all the intricacies of technic and beauties of expression.

Field was thunderstruck. He sprang to his feet and, catching his visitor by the shoulders, he gave him a shake and then embraced him in the hearty European fashion, crying, "You can't fool me! You are Hummel. No other man in the world can improvise like that!"

With that introduction it is needless to say that the two pianists became fast friends.

116.—SAVING A FIDDLE.

One of Ole Bull's favorite violins was a Joseph Guarnerius, called the "King Joseph," for the greatest violins of the old makers are known and named as individuals. It is not to be wondered that he was willing to brave a good deal to preserve this violin, for, irrespective of its worth as a producer of beautiful tones, there was some eight hundred pounds invested in it.

On one of the great violinist's concert trips in this country, he was a passenger on an Ohio river steamboat. In the fashion of those days the boiler burst, tearing away the forepart of the boat and setting the cabins on fire. Ole Bull found himself choking, deafened, blinded, in the midst of shrieking women and howling children, and surrounded by smoke, flame, and shattered timbers. Did he turn his attention to saving the mothers and little ones? The action of the man was characteristic.

Oblivious to all else, he rushed to his cabin, seized his precious Guarnerius, and putting it between his teeth leaped over the guards into the muddy water and swam to shore. There he tenderly examined his precious fiddle to see that it was not harmed. Ole Bull was nothing to Ole Bull at that moment. His beloved instrument occupied his mind to the exclusion of all else. The only "King Joseph Guarnerius" might have been lost!

117.—ABSENT MINDED.

Concentration of attention to the study in hand is, above all things else, a necessity for him who would produce valuable results. The ability to withdraw the mind from other affairs and to focus one's attention on the subject in hand is most valuable to a composer. Not, however that we would commend that degree of abstraction from every-day affairs that was Beethoven's habit when in the midst of a bit of congenial mental work.

In the history of absent-minded and forgetful men (that remains to be written) Beethoven must certainly have a prominent place.

It is related of him that about the time he was engaged in the "Pastoral" symphony he went into a restaurant and ordered dinner, but as there was some delay in serving the meal, his mind reverted to his composing; and when the waiter came and offered dinner, he waived him away, saying, "Thank you, I have dined," and laying down the price of the meal took his departure.

A friend once presented Beethoven with a noble steed,—and he did what you or I would do under the circumstances,—took a ride around town. After riding it a few times, he proceeded to forget its very existence, and made his journeys on foot or in coach. But he had a servant who was not so neglectful of his opportunity. This man took the horse under his care and used it as his own, after finding that Beethoven no longer inquired for it. He put it up at a stable and carefully paid the bills, lest his master should be reminded of its existence. Then, to reimburse himself for his trouble and expense, he frequently hired the horse out as he had opportunity and pocketed the proceeds.

118.—THE PRIMA DONNA OF THE EIGHTEENTH CENTURY.

As the world grows older, *prima donnas* seem to grow more sensible. It is very seldom, now-a-days, that we hear of any great piece of nonsense or extravagance on the part of these talented and captivating beings. But in the last century it was otherwise; and the records of the times are full of the scandals, intrigues, eccentricities and excesses of footlight favorites. But the difference may be in the moral and social atmospheres of the times rather than in the individuals themselves.

There were few more capricious than the great soprano, Gabriella. Of her it is related that when the Viceroy gave a grand dinner at Palermo, herself being one of the principal invited guests, she insolently remained in bed, reading, and when a messenger was sent, saying the company was awaiting her coming, she sent word that she had entirely forgotten the engagement.

That evening when she was to appear before the company in opera, she sang all her airs *sotto voce*. The Viceroy sent a messenger to the stage promising to punish her if she did not sing out with her accustomed power and brilliancy. On this she obstinately sent a reply to the effect that "while he might make her cry, he could not make her sing." This exhausted the patience of royalty and she was sent to prison, where she was confined twelve days.

But even here her caprice showed itself and made her the conqueror after all. She gave costly entertainments to her fellow-prisoners, who were of all classes, from debtors to bandits; she paid their debts, feasted them, and sang to them in her most charming manner; and she was finally released amid the acclamations of the people she had befriended.

119.—THE "HARMONIOUS BLACKSMITH."

If all the stories of musicians and their work were to be sifted for that which is the plain truth, unembellished by fancy, we fear that the number that stood the test would not make a very cumbrous volume. It is not a hard matter to concoct a pretty fair story, and it is much easier to embellish one—not, however, that the writer knows from experience. One of the stories of this suspected class is that so frequently told of Händel's air and variations called "The Harmonious Blacksmith."

The story runs thus: One day when this composer was out taking a ramble, a sudden storm came up and drove him for shelter into a convenient blacksmith's shop. While there he watched the men at work and was attracted by the melodious tones of the hammers as they struck the anvil. He kept the scene in mind and later wrote this piece, giving in it a musical imitation of the occasion.

If the reader will play this piece and then listen to the din made by some muscular son of Vulcan, we believe he will, with the writer, be unable to hear the anvil strokes in Händel's air; or when surrounded by the noise of the shop we defy him to see the parallel between the clank of the hammers and Händel's smooth and pleasant melody.

120.—THE UPS AND DOWNS OF A SINGER'S LIFE.

In another sketch we have given Italio Campanini's experience as a soldier. After the war was over and the victorious army of Garibaldi was disbanded, this young Italian—for he was only fourteen when he went into the army—returned to his native town, and for two years worked in his father's blacksmith shop. But one night his voice attracted the attention of a *connoisseur*, and it was arranged that he should study singing with this gentleman in the evening, after his twelve hours at the forge were over. But let him tell the story in his own words:—

"I was with some companions one evening in a wine shop, when a band of strolling musicians came in. They played the '*Miserere*' from Verdi's '*Il Trovatore.*' I and my companions sang the chorus. A little, weazened old man sat in one corner over a bottle of red wine. He listened to the chorus carelessly at first, and then with increasing attention. When the song was ended he rushed over to the table where we sat.

"'Which of you sang the tenor part?' he cried, excitedly.

"'It was Campanini—Italio Campanini,' some one said.

"'You?' the old man asked.

"'Yes, Signor, it was I.'

"'Where did you learn to sing?' the old man continued.

"'I have never learned,' I replied.

"The old man was Maestro Dall' Argini, a composer of local celebrity. He asked me to come to his house the next day. A number of well-known musicians were there. I sang for them—by ear, for I did not know a note—selections from '*Il Trovatore*' and '*La Somnambula.*' The end of it all was that Dall' Argini offered to become my master, and the learned musicians decided that I must become an opera singer.

"To secure my father's consent was another thing. He was a man of the people, proud of his independence, proud of his honest character, proud of his trade. 'A singer in opera,' he said. 'It is a beggar's trade. So you want to be a poor underling in a miserable chorus, a vagabond without a fixed home? Not with my consent.'

"At last I began to sing small parts in the local theaters. The first part for which I was cast was the notary in '*La Somnambula*.' I had a severe attack of stage fright. In fact, I could hardly utter a note. The audience jeered and shouted. From the crowded galleries came the cry: 'He sings like a hunchback with his shoulders in his throat!'

"'You may laugh now,' I shouted, 'but it will be my turn to laugh next, and he who laughs last laughs best.'

"But it was a long time before I laughed in Parma. Naturally enough, this little altercation ended my engagement. At that time there chanced to be in Parma a Russian manager looking for artists to complete an operatic company. I signed a contract with him for a five years' tour of the Russian provinces. My compensation was to be four lire—about three shillings—a day.

"The engagement was profitable, but a small revolution broke out, the theater was closed, and the manager disappeared. I was left without money, my luggage was seized, and I was turned out into the street without a penny or a change of clothes. The kindness of a stray acquaintance—I do not think I ever knew his name—procured me a garret in a wretched part of the town. The second day I sold my coat to a Jew peddler, and I dined on that coat for two days. I was standing in my shirt sleeves in the street when I chanced to see a notary whom I knew passing on the other side. I rushed over and put my case to him. Through his efforts a concert was arranged for my benefit.

"What had I gained in my wanderings?

"Neither fame nor fortune. I had worked harder

than ever blacksmith toiled in the smithy, and I had been at times on the point of starvation. Truly it looked as though my old father was right and it was a beggarly trade.

"But one thing I had learned, and the knowledge was worth all the hardships of those Russian days. I had learned to know my own powers and my own deficiencies. I recognized the need of cultivation. I went to Milan and placed myself under Chevalier Francesco Lamperti, the famous master. I might almost say that I worked day and night.

"I studied with Chevalier Lamperti for a year. At the end of that time I secured an engagement to sing the first tenor rôles at La Scala.

"I made my début in 'Faust.' It was my first success, and I may be pardoned for dwelling a moment on that night—a night that comes only once in a singer's lifetime, when, after years of difficult labor and long discouragement, success comes royally, suddenly, bringing in its train fame and fortune.

"Before the first act was over the audience was cheering as only an Italian audience can cheer. To the manager it meant fortune; to me—it is hardly necessary to say what those cries of 'Bravo, Campanini!' meant to the unknown tenor.

"It is easy to write of one's failures, but I do not think that any one finds it easy to write of his successes. And then the story lacks picturesqueness. There are fifty ways of starving, but, after all, there is only way of dining."

121.—SOME LIBERAL MUSICIANS.

The great musicians have been noted for their open-handedness and generosity, and some carried it to the extreme of the spendthrift. Prominent among those who devoted large sums to charity were Liszt, the wonderful pianist, and the "Swedish Nightingale," Jenny Lind.

It is told of Mozart that, not finding any money in his pocket to give to an importunate beggar, he hastily sketched a song on some blank paper, and told the mendicant to present it at a certain publisher's and he would receive a good sum. The beggar did so, and received the money. But if this is true, why was Mozart himself so often in need of money? Why did he not present his own songs and draw the cash for himself?

Rossini, although having a reputation for stinginess, was liberal toward his old parents. After the first three performances of each new opera he produced he would send them two-thirds the amount he received for composing it.

122.—HOW PAGANINI SECURED HIS FAVORITE FIDDLE.

When Paganini had only reached his seventeenth year, he had already tasted the enjoyments of flattery and applause. Having thrown off the restraints of his father's control, he plunged into all kinds of dissipation, especially into gambling, a vice that was universal in Europe at that time. Many a night did this youthful gambler lose all the proceeds of more than one concert in the gambling room; and he was at one time even obliged to raise money on his violin as security to pay his gambling debts.

On one occasion, when the youthful violinist was announced for a concert at Leghorn, he had pawned his violin, and had to make some arrangement to borrow one for use at the concert. Hearing that a certain French merchant of the place possessed a very fine "Guarnerius," he applied to him for the loan of it. This gentleman generously granted his request and placed this valuable instrument in his hands.

After the concert, when Paganini returned the borrowed violin, its owner, who himself was no mean violinist, and who had heard Paganini's performance, exclaimed:—

"I will never profane the strings which your fingers have touched. The instrument is yours!"

Paganini's delight may be imagined, for there was hardly to be found in the world an instrument superior to this one. He used it throughout his wonderful career and at his death left it to his native city of Genoa, where it rests in its glass case, having been played by but one since his death, by his pupil, Sivori, who died in 1894.

123.—LISZT ON MENDELSSOHN.

The following bit of conversation, reported to come from Franz Liszt, we are inclined to take *cum grano salis* as to the intensity of some of the expressions used. If other writers are to be believed, the gentle Felix was hardly of so jealous a disposition as this sketch would have us believe. But, be that as it may, we infer from it somewhat of the personal characteristics of Liszt as well as of Mendelssohn.

Said Liszt: "Mendelssohn, on one occasion, drew a picture on a blackboard of the devil playing his G minor concerto with five hammers on each hand instead of fingers. The truth of the matter is, that I once played his concerto in G minor from the manuscript, and as I found several of the passages rather simple and not broad enough, if I may use the term, I changed them to suit my own ideas. This, of course, annoyed Mendelssohn, who, unlike Schumann or Chopin, would never take a hint or advice from any one. Moreover, Mendelssohn, who, although a refined pianist, was *not* a virtuoso, and never could play my compositions with any kind of effect, his technical skill being inadequate to the execution of intricate passages. So the only course open to him, he thought, was to vilify me as a musician. And, of course, whatever Mendelssohn did, Leipzig did also. However, I was, once, more than fully revenged on him.

"I well remember meeting him at dinner at the Comtesse de P——'s, in Paris. He had been unusually witty and vivacious at dinner, and after dessert the Comtesse asked him if he would not favor us with one of his last Lieder, or, in fact, anything he chose to select. He most graciously condescended to sit down at the piano, and, to my astonishment, instead of treating us to one of his own compositions, he commenced my Rhapsodie, No. 4, which he played so abominably badly, as regards both the execution and the sentiment, that most of the guests, who had heard it played by myself on previous occasions, burst out laughing. Mendelssohn, however, got quite angry at their mirth, and improvising a finale after the thirtieth bar or so, dashed into his Capriccio in F sharp minor, No. 5, which he played through with elegance and a certain amount of respect. At the conclusion we all applauded him, and then, when he begged me to play something *new and striking*, as he somewhat viciously referred to my compositions, I determined I would have some revenge and fun at his expense. So I seated myself at the piano, and announced that I would perform the Capriccio, Op. 5, Mendelssohn, arranged for *concert performance* by myself.

"In a second the guests had comprehended that I intended being revenged on Mendelssohn for butchering my poor Rhapsodie, although I suppose many thought it a rather hazardous attempt to play a difficult composition in a new garb or arrangement on the spur of the moment, especially with the composer sitting within two yards of the keyboard. However, I did what I had announced to do, and at the conclusion, Mendelssohn, instead of bursting out with indignation and rage at my impudence and liberty, took my right hand in his, and turned it over, backward and forward, and bent the fingers this way and that, finally remarking laughingly, 'as I had beaten him on the keyboard, he thought his only way for vindication was to challenge me to box, but that now, since he had examined my hand, he would have to abandon that decision!' So everything passed over smoothly, and what might have been a very unpleasant meeting turned out a most enjoyable *contretemps.*"

124.—MARA'S REVENGE.

Madame Mara was blessed with a rascally husband who persisted in too frequently looking on the wine when it was red. Notwithstanding the brutality and drunkenness her liege lord engaged in, she supported him and kept him in money for many a day. At one time this gentleman was for some offense separated from his wife by order of the King of Prussia, and made to play the big drum in a regimental band instead of the violoncello in the court orchestra.

In spite of her husband's loose habits, Madame Mara determined to be revenged on the king for this treatment, and after a while her opportunity came. His Majesty was entertaining the Czarowitz of Russia, and had arranged a grand concert as a part of the pleasures to be offered to his distinguished guest. Mara was ordered to take part. But instead she took to her bed, and sent word to the theater that she was too ill to sing.

On the evening of the concert, shortly before time for the performance to begin, a military escort was sent to her house, and the officer in charge insisted that she get up and go with him to the opera. Mara declared that she would not.

"Don't you see I am in bed and cannot leave it?" exclaimed she.

"If that be the case, I must take you and the bed too," answered the officer.

So Mara was forced to go weeping to her dressing-room, and finally to accompany the guard to the theater. Then she thought of the old saying, "You can lead a horse to water, but you can't make him drink," and though she were made to go to the opera she determined to sing in such a manner as would make the king repent of his order.

For a good part of the evening she kept to her resolve. But suddenly the audience were astonished to notice a complete change in her style of singing and acting. She had changed from her poorest to her best mood, and she seemed to excel herself in the brilliancy of her singing and the intensity of her acting. And Mara at her best was wonderful.

The secret of this sudden change was that Mara had bethought herself that if she went on in her first careless style, the heir to the Russian throne would carry away with him a very poor opinion of her abilities, and as this would be very undesirable she suddenly changed her policy, making the king the victor after all.

125.—CHOPIN'S TECHNIC.

The coming of Chopin into the field of piano composition marked a new era in the treatment of that instrument, both in the technic of composition and in the technic of interpretation. While nearly every great composer felt called on to essay the various forms of composition and for a variety of instruments, Chopin devoted himself exclusively to the piano, using the orchestra only as incidental to his piano works.

The technic of the schools that had preceded him was inadequate to the performance of his compositions. so much so that even as great a player as Moscheles confessed himself unequal to the task of properly playing Chopin's music.

In this connection, it is related that Chopin went to Kalkbrenner, a celebrated pianist and teacher of Paris, hoping to get some valuable technical instruction from a man of such celebrity. Kalkbrenner criticised his playing severely and advised Chopin to attend his classes in the Conservatoire to learn the proper fingering. Chopin answered this advice by placing one of his own

"Études" on the piano and asking Kalkbrenner to play it. But the arrogant old fellow was utterly unable to do it, for he found his old style of technic inadequate to the demands made upon it by the music of the younger composer.

126.—SPOHR AS A HORN PLAYER.

Ludwig Spohr, besides being a violinist and composer of note, was a man of much resource, and had a goodly fund of humor. He relates many interesting experiences in his "Autobiography," from which we get the following story. He tells us that in 1808, when Napoleon entertained various sovereigns of Europe at Erfurt, there was announced to be given before these potentates some of the great French tragedies, by actors brought from Paris for the occasion, prominent among whom was the great Talma. Spohr and some of his pupils took a pedestrian trip from Gotha to Erfurt, more in the hopes of seeing this celebrated French tragedian than the assembled sovereigns.

On their arrival they found, much to their chagrin, that the common people were not to be admitted to the theater, as every seat was reserved for the royal personages and their suites. This was a dilemma. But Spohr was equal to it. He had come there to see Talma, and see him he did. He sought out four musicians of the theater orchestra and bribed them to allow himself and his pupils to take their places in the theater. But even then he was met by another obstacle. Three of these musicians were violin or 'cello players. So far as they were concerned all was well, for Spohr's pupils could play those instruments. But the fourth was a horn player; and here came the trouble, for none of the four visitors could play that instrument.

There was nothing for it but Spohr must learn to play the horn; so he set about it, practiced all day, and by evening was ready to play his part. At the theatre they were placed with their backs toward their royal audience, and forbidden to look around to satisfy their curiosity concerning the rulers of the earth. But Spohr was also equal to this emergency, for he had provided himself with a small mirror, and by this means was able to see at least the reflections of the sovereigns of Europe. But he finally became so absorbed in the magnificent acting of the tragic artists that he handed over the mirror to his pupils and gave his entire attention to the stage.

The severe practice that he had been through in learning to play the horn at such short notice, resulted in a pair of swollen and painful lips. On his return to Gotha, when his young wife expressed surprise and alarm at his negro-like appearance, he coolly told her that his lips had come to that condition by the frequent kissing of the pretty Erfurt women. But when the truth came out the joke was on him.

127.—SECURING MUSIC UNDER DIFFICULTIES.

Of the two hundred and forty-seven men of the name of Bach who were known as musicians, there were over fifty who were distinguished as composers and performers. In that part of Germany where the most of these quiet, home-loving people lived, they had been for generations so prominent in local musical affairs that the town musicians were known as "the Bachs," even after there had ceased to be any of the name among them.

But of all the Bachs, John Sebastian was "the" Bach. He is generally known as simply "Sebastian," for the name "Johann" is found so constantly in the family that to use it alone would fail to distinguish the particular "Johann" that was meant. Out of the twenty-three most prominent Bachs, the first name of sixteen was "Johann" and six of them was labeled as "Johann Christoph." But there was only one "John Sebastian," and it is an incident in his early youth that we here relate.

At the age of ten years, little John Sebastian lost both his parents and was taken from Eisenach to Ohrdruff, where he made his home with his elder brother, one of the "John Christophs." The little fellow had begun his musical study with his father, and now continued under the tuition of his distinguished elder brother. Even at this age, his great genius began to manifest itself, for he would come to his lessons with his music learned by heart. Soon he began to aspire to higher and more difficult music than his teacher would allow him. It seems that John Christoph had laid away on the upper shelf of a certain cupboard a manuscript volume of pieces by Buxtehude, Frohberger, Pachelbel and other noted composers of that day, and this book the little Sebastian modestly requested be given him for study. His brother curtly refused and locked up the cupboard. But the young seeker after knowledge was not to be so easily defeated.

Determined to gain possession of the coveted treasure, he one night managed to get his hands through the openings of the latticed cupboard door, and, rolling up the manuscript, drew it out. Then for six months he would utilize the moonlight nights copying the music, and each night would again place it back in its proper place. But at the end of that time his nocturnal occupation was discovered and the brother was cruel enough to confiscate the result of his hard labor, and, it is said, burned it before the boy's eyes.

128.—IN BÜLOW'S CLASS-ROOM.

Von Bülow, the eccentric pianist and conductor, was even more severe with his pupils than Liszt. Tears were not infrequent things in Liszt's class-room, and yet his gallantry and winning personality did much to dull the sharpness of his cutting criticism.

Not so with Bülow. His classes were large, and he called out whom he chose to play what they had prepared. The rest sat trembling in expectation of their turn. An awkward English girl once went to the piano and, because of her great fright, managed to play her piece with so large an assortment of blunders that the irate Doctor cried out: "*Ach, Gott!* you play the easy passages with a difficulty that is simply enormous!" This saying might well be kept as a stock quotation with every teacher, so frequently is it applicable.

129.—VIOTTI'S TIN FIDDLE.

Had the world not had a Viotti it might not have produced a Paganini. Viotti fixed the principles of violin playing, especially with regard to the bowing. His playing was characterized by "a great nobility, breadth, and beauty of tone, united with a fire and agility unknown before his time." On his work was based Paganini's brilliant and dazzling technic.

While Viotti was noted for his independence of bearing, he was also a kind-hearted man and a pleasant and companionable gentleman. It is related of him that, strolling on the Champs Elysées one night with a friend, they came across a blind old man making music on some instrument that seemed by its tone to be a cross between a fiddle and a clarinet. Having their curiosity excited by the strange sound, they found the old fellow using a fiddle made of tin. On inquiring of him as to his instrument, they learned that he was miserably poor and did not have money enough to buy an ordinary violin, so his nephew, a tinker by trade, had made him this one of tin.

Viotti offered to buy this queer violin, but the old man declined to part with it until he was promised enough to buy a new one. Then Viotti took up this queer instrument and played on it in his inimitable way; his friend passed the hat and secured a good sum for its former owner. When the old man heard such wonderful music come from the tin fiddle he declared that he did not know it was so good, but since it was capable of such grand music he ought to have had double the amount he had received for it.

Viotti good-naturedly let him have his way and paid him twice the price agreed upon. After the master's death in London, when his instruments and effects were disposed of, this tin fiddle was sold for but a few shillings to an amateur lover of curiosities.

130.—LISZT'S PLAYING AND HIS GENEROSITY.

Franz Liszt was the Paganini of the pianoforte. We can hardly realize at this day the excitement he created by his wonderful playing. Europe had seen many great players, among them Hummel, Herz, and Thalberg; but no one of them aroused the public to such a pitch of ecstatic enthusiasm as did Liszt. They conquered by their mere brilliancy of effects; he by his greatness of intellect and his poetry of conception, united with a technical skill that was beyond the limits of their comprehension.

He had a certain majesty of bearing, a commanding sway; he carried his audience by his strong personal magnetism. He would come on the concert stage with the step of a conqueror. Tearing his gloves from his hands, he would seat himself at the piano, run his fingers through his hair, and then attack the instrument with the mien of a commanding general. Whether it was because of his magnificent playing, or whether the surrounding excitement reacted on their sensitive natures, the feminine part of his audience would go wild with excitement. Ladies of high rank would throw their jewels at his feet, and perhaps faint in their ecstacy. After the concert there would be a wild rush for the stage to see Liszt, and even to touch the hem of his garment, and to contend for the pieces of broken piano strings that Liszt had shattered in his playing.

As Jenny Lind was noted among singers for her

generosity, so was Liszt among pianists. A prominent instance of this was when thousands of his countrymen were rendered homeless by an inundation of the Danube. Though Liszt was in Italy, he hastened to Vienna the next morning after hearing the news, and there he began giving concerts for the benefit of the stricken people; and it was not for two months that he ceased, by means of his art, to pour a flood of gold into Hungary.

It is said that his direct contributions to charity, if added to the amounts which he raised by his concerts, would make a sum-total of millions. With his wonderful art, his extensive learning, his magnetic temperament, his kindness of heart, his broad sympathies, and his great beneficence, it is little to be wondered that he was worshiped by all who knew him.

131.—FROM HUMBLE ORIGIN TO WEALTH AND FAME.

The goddess of song seems to have chosen her most talented devotees from the humbler walks of life. Among the *prime donne* we find some of the greatest to have been children of strolling actors, cooks, shopkeepers, and the like. And among singers of the other sex we find porters, school teachers, valets, and coachmen. Very few of the greater singers have sprung from the higher walks of life. We give the circumstances of the discovery of two renowned sopranos, and the list of similar discoveries might be indefinitely extended had we the space and our readers the patience.

Some time during the middle of the last century, Cardinal Gabrielli, who was attached to the Papal Court, was walking in his garden, when his ears were delighted with a stream of joyous melody which, though evidently coming from an untutored throat, still showed remarkable power and sweetness. On investigation, he found the songstress to be the little daughter of his favorite cook. She had been taken to the theater by her father, and there her ready memory had retained some of the favorite melodies of the operas she had heard.

The cook had not the means to give the girl the education she deserved, and so that was provided by the liberal Cardinal, whose name she afterward took. La Gabrielli became one of the greatest singers of her day, and delighted nearly all of the crowned heads of Europe by her powers and beauty.

She had a large income and traveled with a royal retinue. But when she retired from the stage it had become greatly reduced by her generosity as well as by her luxurious habits.

The discovery of the vocal powers of Angelica Catalani was made in a different way. At the end of the last century there arose a queer kind of complaint in a certain town in Italy, concerning the singing at one of the churches. It was declared that one of the young novices sang with such power and brilliancy that the people gathered at the church for miles around, and the service became more of a concert than a religious service. This came to the ears of the Bishop and he ordered the scandal to be stopped, which was very easily done by not allowing the young girl whose voice made such a commotion to sing, except in the chorus. Angelica's father had destined her for the cloister and could hardly be persuaded to give up his cherished design of making her spend her life in the dark walls of a convent. But, allured by the promise that the girl had a gold mine in her throat, he finally allowed her to be taken from the convent and to be placed in the hands of the best masters for her vocal education.

Thus, snatched from the convent at the age of twelve years, Catalani began her career, which was one of the most brilliant known to art. No more beautiful person has graced the operatic stage, and no more cultivated or flexible voice is recorded in operatic annals. But her very abilities hurt her career as an artist, for she sacrificed true art in her anxiety to display her wonderful powers of vocalization. Her career, like that of Gabrielli, was crowned with riches and fame.

132.—GALLANT HAYDN.

When in London, Haydn once visited the studio of that celebrated portrait painter, Sir Joshua Reynolds. He there saw a picture of Mrs. Billington, one of the best known singers of her day. Reynolds had represented her listening to the song of the angels. On being asked for his opinion of the painting, Haydn remarked: "Yes, it is a beautiful picture; it is just like her; but there is one strange mistake."

"A mistake! How is that?" exclaimed Reynolds, who could hardly believe his ears.

"Why," said the gallant composer, "you have made Mrs. Billington listening to the angels, when you ought to have painted the angels as listening to her!"

133.—ROSSINI AND THE ITALIAN SCHOOL.

It is the fashion nowadays, by the admirers of the modern school of opera, to deride the works of Rossini and the Italian school. They point out his lack of dramatic truth, his sacrifice of the sense to the music. Still there has perhaps never lived a man who could excel him as a writer of *bel canto*.

The faults of Rossini's music were faults not of the man, but of the time. Rossini was, in his way, a reformer. Prior to his time the composer had been at the mercy of the singer, but with Rossini a new era dawned. He wrote not only the framework of his music, leaving the soloist to ornament at pleasure, but the whole aria, note for note, and insisted that it should be sung as written.

Then he had faith in himself and his music. He knew he was ahead of the public, and he did not drop back to keep pace with them. When, at the first appearance of

"The Barber of Seville," the audience expressed its disapproval of certain innovations, Rossini shrugged his shoulders, went home and went to sleep. When "*La Donna del Lago*" was pronounced an utter failure, Rossini openly and loudly proclaimed it a complete success. When "*La Gazza Ladra*" did not meet the approval of the critics, and he was accused of violating the rules of musical grammar, he retorted:—

"So much the worse for the grammar. Reform your grammar; it must be defective."

He might have said "so much the worse for the critics," for the public soon recognized the beauty of the works in question, and Rossini, next to Verdi, ranks as the typical Italian composer.

134.—LIVES OF LABOR.

Verily, the old classic composers seemed to take literally the command "be not weary in well doing." Händel, whom Beethoven declared to be "the monarch of the musical kingdom," left nearly four hundred compositions, most of them of considerable length, including his forty-three operas, nineteen oratorios, and one hundred and fifty cantatas.

Haydn wrote much more than Händel, his compositions being about eight hundred in number. But many of these were of no great length. The principal ones were one hundred and eighteen symphonies, eighty-three string quartets, twenty-four operas and fourteen masses. Haydn's life was more quiet and his disposition more tranquil than was Händel's. While the latter composer had to fight his way in the musical world, Haydn was enjoying the patronage and support of Prince Esterhazy, in whose musical establishment he reigned supreme.

Another writer who put forth an astonishing number of compositions was Johann Chrysostom Wolfgang Theophilus Amandeus Mozart. That Mozart died young was not owing to the weight of so long a name, probable as that might appear. Händel had seventy-one and Haydn seventy-seven years in which to turn out these long arrays of compositions, while Mozart was cut off with thirty-five short years. But in those years his labor was unceasing; and as a result his catalogue shows between six hundred and seven hundred works, large and small. In the larger forms were forty-nine symphonies, twenty-three operas, twenty-eight masses and litanies, thirty-one string quartets, and fifty-five concertos; to say nothing of thirty-three sonatas for piano, forty-five for violin, and ninety sonatas and pieces for the organ.

The catalogue of Beethoven's works shows as many or more compositions than that of Haydn. If we reckon all the smaller numbers as individuals, we find over eight hundred and twenty-five works, of which some two hundred and fifty were vocal; but many of these were combined in sets, and frequently several would appear in the same *opus*. Of this number but one was an opera and only nine were symphonies; yet those are the "great nine" symphonies of the world.

135.—A GREAT QUARTET.

The stories told of the *prime donne* are so many and so wonderful, that it is with relief we turn to the career of some of the opposite sex.

The great quartet of singers,—Rubini, Tamburini, Mario, and Lablache,—who were on the stage the first half of this century, have hardly been excelled in musical history. Every one of these men was an artist of the highest ability, and the records of their feats of vocalism might well fill a volume.

Though not a great actor, the first of this quartet, Rubini, captured his audiences by pure feats of vocalism. His command of his voice was beyond description. On one occasion, however, he overstepped the bounds of nature. He was singing a passage where he had to attack and hold with great power a high B flat, and he took the note with such force that the sudden contraction of the lungs resulted in a broken clavicle. In spite of this he finished his part in the opera. So great was his popularity that he for a time held a position in the opera at St. Petersburg at £20,000 a year.

It is told of Tamburini that when singing in Palermo during the carnival season of 1822, the *prima donna* being scared from the house by the antics of the revelers, this great baritone donned her costume and took her part in the opera with the superb falsetto tones he had cultivated. Even in the duets he would sing his own notes in his strong baritone voice and then change to the falsetto for the lady's part. It need not be added that the carnival revelers were delighted with their success in procuring amusement.

Mario, of all the tenors one of the greatest, was an exception to the rule that great singers spring from the humble walks of life. He was an Italian count; but forsook the dignity of his inheritance for that career which nature had mapped out for him. His singing was noted for possessing that which Rubini lacked, *i. e.*, a strong sense of the dramatic. He was not so successful in the flights of ornamentation to which Rubini was addicted, but this was more than compensated by his rendition of the arias of modern writers that required more artistic intelligence and poetry. He was a highly educated Italian gentleman, in this respect being the opposite of many who have perhaps been endowed with as fine powers of vocalization as himself.

The last of the quartet, Lablache, was in his way the most wonderful singer the world has possessed. His was a remarkably strong bass of over two octaves in compass. He was a very tall and strongly built man; indeed, so great was his strength that he took pleasure in carrying off singers from the stage under his arm, when the plot allowed of it. It was said of him, " he was gifted with personal beauty to a rare degree; a grander head was never more grandly set on human shoulders." His voice was the most powerful of any of which we have record; and his stage presence and artistic education made him the foremost bass singer of musical history. In this he was unique; there were none to rival him or dispute his claim to greatness. As a youth he sang at the funeral of Haydn and later at that of Beethoven. He was, when in England, the singing master of Queen Victoria.

136.—REC'D IN FULL OF A/C.

The Irish composer, Field, married from a somewhat peculiar reason, if we may believe his version of it. While yet this originator of the style of music called the "nocturne" was single, he numbered among his pupils one attractive young lady from whom he found it exceedingly difficult to collect the amount of her tuition bill.

Finally, Field concluded to proceed to law in the matter, that is, to use one form of law—for he proposed to the slow-paying damsel and was accepted. He made no secret of the fact that she was his pupil and he married her to get rid of giving her lessons for which she never paid, and for which he felt sure she never would.

This may be a good plan. Who can say but it is applied more than the world knows. But what if the teacher is already the happy possessor of one, or if he has several debtors among the fair sex?

137.—WAGNER'S WORKING COSTUME.

Of the score of greatest composers, perhaps none was more eccentric than that founder of the modern German operatic school, Richard Wagner. The caller who was unaware of one of his peculiarities might suffer a mild shock; for on entering the room where his visitor was seated Wagner would throw the door wide open before him, as if it were fit that his approach should be heralded like that of a king, and he would stand for a moment on the threshold, a curious mediæval figure in a frame.

The mystified visitor, rising from his seat, would behold a man richly clad in a costume of velvet and satin, like those of the early Tudor period, and wearing a bonnet such as are seen in portraits of Henry VI, and his three successors. Buffon used to put on lace ruffles and cuffs when he wrote, and Wagner had his composing costume—that of a Meistersinger—or rather several costumes, for he would vary his attire not only according to his own moods, but according to the faces of people who came to see him.

Alexander Dumas, calling upon him made some good-humored remark about his own ignorance of music—which he had once defined as 'the most expensive of noises'; but his pleasantries were listened to with such a smileless stolidity that he went home in a huff, and wrote his contemptuous protest against 'Wagnerian din —inspired by the riot of cats scampering in the dark about an ironmonger's shop.'

On the day before this protest was printed Wagner returned Dumas' visit, and was kept waiting for half an hour in an anteroom.

Then the author of the "Three Guardsmen" marched in, superbly attired in a plumed helmet, a cork life belt and a flowered dressing gown. "Excuse me for appearing in my working dress," he said majestically. "Half my ideas are lodged in this helmet and the other half in a pair of jack-boots which I put on to compose love-scenes."

Snubs of this sort—of which Wagner encountered many—rankled deep in his mind and made him say that the French were Vandals, whereas, in truth, their quarrel was not so much with his music as with him personally and with his uncivil followers.

138.—CHERUBINI AS A REVOLUTIONARY FIDDLER.

We have read of the Englishman who, knowing the temper of the French people and French weather, instructed his valet, when they were in Paris, to bring him each morning information on two points; first, what kind of weather there was, and second, what form of government. This is not so much overdrawn as one might at first think, for in the last hundred years France has seen at least ten changes in its form of government. The first of these changes was accompanied by such an outpouring of blood as the world has never before or since seen in a civilized country. But, as is frequently the case, the horrible was accompanied by the ludicrous. The following incident was more enjoyable to the beholder or to the reader than to the main actor, not less a musical personage than Cherubini.

Once, during the exciting days of 1792, Cherubini ventured to take a ramble on the streets, and as a result was soon in the hands of a mob. They knew him to be a musician, and insisted that the talent with which he had delighted the king and court should now be displayed for their gratification. Cherubini refused to satisfy them, whereupon murmurs of "Royalist, Royalist," were heard, and that meant a speedy exit from this world for Cherubini.

Another kidnapped musician, seeing the danger the great composer was in, thrust a violin into his hands and persuaded him that his only safety was in playing for them. The whole day these musicians had to play for the revolutionary and blood-thirsty mob, and at last were mounted on some casks in a public square, and made to play till the riotous feasters had devoured an impromptu banquet and had dispersed at a late hour.

139.—CONSCIENTIOUS ACTING AND SINGING.

The public does not realize the nervous and mental strain the great actors and singers undergo when on the stage, portraying the characters they represent for the pleasure and entertainment of their auditors. Of course, in many cases, the action becomes mechanical and the emotion a cut-and-dried counterfeit. But on this score it may be said that it is the highest art to present emotions from an intellectual standpoint, without being subject to the uncertain whim of the moment.

It is the highest art to conceal art.

Per contra, another school declares an actor should always feel the full extent of the emotion he portrays.

Be that as it may, the proper presentation of the composer's ideas and emotions is a serious study with the conscientious actor. He may study for weeks and months without being able to embody in action his own or the composer's ideas to his satisfaction.

A good example of this is given us in the words of one of the most dramatic singers of Beethoven's time, Madam Schröder-Devrient. This talented woman was the first to fill the *rôle* of " Leonora " in Beethoven's only opera, *Fidelio*. She describes her efforts to adequately present the composer's intentions in the following words:

"When I was studying the character of 'Leonora,' at Vienna, I could not attain that which appeared to me to be the desired and natural expression at the moment when Leonora, throwing herself before her husband, holds out a pistol at the governor with the words, 'kill first his wife.' I studied and studied in vain, though I did all I could to place myself mentally in the situation of Leonora. I had pictured to myself the situation, but I felt that it was incomplete, without knowing why or wherefore.

"Well, the evening arrived. The audience knows not

with what feelings an *artiste* who enters seriously into a part, dresses for the representation. The nearer the moment approached, the greater was my alarm. When it did arrive, and as I ought to have sung the ominous words and pointed the pistol at the governor, I fell into such utter tremor at the thought of not being perfect in my character, that my whole form trembled, and I thought I should have fallen.

"Now only fancy how I felt when the whole house broke forth into enthusiastic shouts of applause, and what I thought when, after the curtain fell, I was told that this moment was the most effective and powerful of my whole representation.

"That which I could not attain with every effort of mind and imagination, was produced at this decisive moment by my unaffected terror and anxiety. This result, and the effect it had upon the public, taught me how to seize and comprehend the incident; so that which at the first representation I had hit upon unconsciously, I adopted in full consciousness ever afterward in this part."

140.—THE PECULIARITIES OF GENIUS.

Men of genius live a double existence. Their better and greater selves are within. They show their true being in their works. The man of genius is wrapped up in his contemplation, in his study, in his evolution of some thought, or some art work. The external life is a necessity, of course, but is more of an unpleasant incident than an enjoyable reality. Let those whose whole life is external and superficial give their time and effort to the mere matter of living pleasantly. The man of genius has something deeper and better to do. But as the everyday life is to be lived, let it come as it may, and within it he will do as the caprice of the moment moves him, without regard to the conventionalities of the world.

This doctrine seems to express the plan of life of many of those who have given to the world its most imperishable art and ideas; and to none does it apply better than to Beethoven.

His was a rugged, impetuous, and in some respects, careless nature; wrapped up in his inner life, he paid little attention to externals, and was careless of the opinions of others. As his deafness increased, he became more peculiar and less observant of the rights of others. He could hardly hear his piano, and yet would thump and bang it in vain attempts. As he composed he would pace his room, shouting out his melodies in an unmusical voice.

Then, to cap the climax, he would dash a pitcher of water over his hands to cool his feverish pulse. The results were that the landlord would complain of damaged ceiling and flooded rooms, and the other tenants would declare that they would not stay in the house with such a noisy fellow. So off he would go to some other place, and would frequently be paying rent on several places at once.

Then, tired of moving about he would undertake to keep up his own establishment, or would take possession of apartments in the home of some patron that he had perhaps deserted in a moment of anger. One of his admirers kept certain rooms always ready, saying to his servants, "Let them be ready, Beethoven is sure to come back again," and after some more experiences with inexorable landladies, back he would come without notice or warning. Had it been a man of lesser genius, these whims and eccentricities would have been given no quarter. But the peculiarities of genius are forgiven.

141.—HÄNDEL'S YOUTH.

Händel's father determined that his boy should devote himself to the law; but the future composer evinced a propensity for music that nothing could restrain. He was strictly forbidden to touch a musical instrument; but this mandate was overcome by using an old clavichord which was stored in the garret, to which the boy would steal while the rest slept. When he was six years of age his father set off on a journey to the court of a prince in whose service a relative was. The little Händel was determined not to be left behind, and followed the carriage on foot, begging to be taken in. His father finally relented and took him to the court, where he attracted the notice of the prince by his organ playing. The prince was interested in the boy's future, and persuaded the father to allow him to make a serious study of music.

From the age of nine to twelve Händel composed a church service every week for voices and instruments. He made rapid progress in the study of composition, and, by the time he was fifteen, had written three operas, each of which was performed many nights in the city of Hamburg. From this on, a steady stream of composition flowed from his fertile mind, culminating in those master-works, the series of oratorios, which were the product of his latter days.

142.—A VIOLIN FOR EIGHTEEN PENCE.

The ability to recognize the good points of others in musical matters, or to have the grace to acknowledge the superiority of more talented or better educated people is not, to say the least, common among professional musicians.

But this is true: The greater the real merit of a man, the quicker he is ready to recognize that quality in others; while, by a continual depreciation of the work and ability of others, one only shows his smallness of soul, and frequently creates in the minds of his hearers exactly the opposite impression to that which he desires. In proportion as we have merit we will recognize merit in others. Greatness has an affinity and admiration for greatness that will not be silent.

Homage to one that excels us but proves our own right to appreciation. We at once think more of an artist or teacher who speaks enthusiastically and appreciatively of the work of some brother musician. But how often we are told what Mr. A. or Miss B. can *not* do, and what failures they are; and how seldom do we hear what they *can* do, and how little are their abilities and their successes mentioned?

There is a lesson for us in the words and actions of two of London's great musicians on the occasion of Paganini's first appearance in England.

When this greatest of fiddlers had ceased his playing, Mori, himself a fine violinist, got up from his seat and solemnly inquired of those in his neighborhood, "Who'll buy my fiddle? Who'll buy a fiddle and bow for eighteen pence?" Even Mori's "Strad" went a begging at that price under the spell of the violin-wizard's playing.

Another great musician was present, John Cramer. His tribute to Paganini's playing was the simple words, "Thank heaven, I am not a violinist!"

Cannot the rank and file of the musical profession learn something in this matter of giving credit where credit is due, from the attitude of those who head the army? Or do we even recognize that our armies have commanding generals?

143.—MENDELSSOHN AT WORK.

Bach used to call composers who could do nothing at writing music without hearing it first on an instrument by a peculiar name. He dubbed them "harpsichord knights." Mendelssohn belonged to a different order of knighthood. A friend once called on him, and finding him engaged in writing music excused himself and offered to call again. But Mendelssohn would not hear of it. He had the gentleman come into his studio, and there carried on an animated conversation with him, all the while going on with his work. But let the caller speak of his visit:—

"I remained, and we talked on all kinds of subjects, he continuing to write the whole time. But he was not copying, for there was no paper but that on which he was writing. The work whereon he was busy was the grand overture in C major. It was a score for full band. He began with the uppermost stave, slowly drew a bar line, leaving a good amount of room and then extended the line to the bottom of the page. He next filled in the second, then the third stave, and so on, with pauses and partly with notes. On coming to the violins, it was evident why he had left so much space for the measure. There was a figure requiring considerable room. The longer melody in this part was not treated differently from the other instruments; but like the other parts had its bar given it, and had to wait at the end of one measure till its turn came in the next.

During all this there was no looking forward or backward, no comparing, no humming over, or anything of the sort. The pen kept going steadily on, slowly and carefully, it is true, but without pausing, and we never ceased talking. The "copying out" therefore, as he called it, meant that the whole composition had been so worked out in his mind that he beheld it there as if it were actually lying before him."

144.—A DOUBLE DOSE OF BRAHMS.

Von Bülow was a remarkable orchestral conductor; remarkably proficient and remarkably self-willed. There was one city in which he generally received hearty, or at least loud applause, whatever he chose to have his orchestra play. It came about in this way: On one of his concert programmes he had a long and abstruse Brahms symphony. Now Brahms is not a writer to be easily understood or generally enjoyed, and in this case, what applause there was, came from gratitude that the end of the lengthy work had been reached, rather than from appreciation of the work itself. Not satisfied with this half-hearted applause, Bülow turned to the audience and said:—

"What, do you not like it? I will teach you to!" and ordered a repetition of the whole work. Succeeding audiences applauded Brahms' symphonies out of sheer self-defense, if for no other reason.

145.—UNFAILING SIGHT READING AN IMPOSSIBILITY.

Very frequently we hear of people who "can read anything at sight." Such people are more rare than the frequency of this claim would lead us to suppose. In fact, if one real, good, live example of the man who can read anything at sight were to be produced he would find that he had no competitors in the field. This may seem a strong statement. There are so many who can read almost anything that may be put before them that, when reading of their prowess in this line, we are apt to think they have accomplished that which we may almost say no man has yet done. We hear of the great feats of Liszt, Mendelssohn, Mozart, and others. But by all accounts Bach was their superior in reading and execution, and here is Bach's experience.

Bach was certainly a giant in composition and performance. His memory was prodigious, his playing unapproachable. He himself began to think he was invincible and frequently expressed to a friend his belief that he could play anything at sight. The friend had great faith in Bach's abilities, but could not quite swallow that. So one day he laid a trap for him. Selecting a certain piece of music that was much more difficult in reality than it was in appearance, he laid it with others on his organ desk. Then he invited Bach to breakfast, and while he was arranging the meal, Bach, as was his custom, sat down to look over the music that happened to be on the desk. In a few moments he struck this particular piece; he tried it, tried it again, stopped, and tried again. Finally, he called out to his friend, who was laughing at him in the next room, "No, no, one cannot play everything at sight, it is not possible."

146.—A SHARP REJOINDER.

Many of the great musicians have been the recipients of the bounty of royalty. While some of the great composers have been allowed to live in obscurity and to suffer in penury, others have, for a time at least, enjoyed the good graces of kings, queens, and princes. To the bounty of Prince Esterhazy we are beholden for much of the work of Haydn; and from that day to the period when Wagner was surrounded by royal patronage, we find the appreciation of the genius of the great composers continually increasing.

While in some cases, that of Haydn, for example, servility to royalty is the result, in others the musician has retained his native independence of spirit. Of the latter, Mozart was one. This is instanced in a reply he made to Austrian Emperor, Joseph II, when that royal personage criticized his opera, "*Il Seraglio*," on the first appearance.

"My dear Mozart," said he, "this is too fine for our ears; there are too many notes."

"I beg your majesty's pardon," Mozart sharply replied, "there are just sufficient notes," a rejoinder which did not add to the esteem in which Mozart was held by the court.

147.—TWO KINDS OF BILLS.

Musicians occasionally have streaks of good luck, but these bits of good fortune are so rare as to deserve especial mention at the hands of the historian. That incident of Paganini's gift to Berlioz has been told and retold with a gusto that would prove its unique position. Some musicians (but very few) are born rich; some achieve riches, and some—still less in number than those who are born to wealth—have riches thrust upon them.

We wonder how many of the fraternity would use the riches thrust upon them as did the composer Balfe, when, once upon a time, fortune smiled on him.

Balfe was about to set out from Paris for Italy. His carriage had arrived; he stepped into it; and just as he was about to give the word to start, a gentleman hastily drove up, and, asking for the composer, handed him a small packet, with the request that he accept it, but that it be not opened till he was well on his journey. Balfe, though greatly surprised at the request, murmured his acceptance, and hardly had the stranger left till his curiosity prevailed, and he tore open the packet.

Out dropped a letter and with it a thousand-franc note. The missive declared that the writer had been charmed by Balfe's talent, and that, wishing to serve the young composer, he risked sending the enclosed bank note, hoping it might be of use. As Balfe's exchequer was about depleted at this time, he considered himself to have certainly met a streak of good luck.

While he was thus congratulating himself up came another stranger and handed him a second communication,—this time asking that it be given immediate attention. Balfe complied and opened the letter, feeling that he would not now be surprised at a shower of bills. And, true to his guess, out dropped a bill—for over six hundred francs, and with it a request that the account be immediately paid. The bill was of a different kind from that brought by the first messenger. With a sigh he handed over his thousand-franc note and pocketed his change.

Our composer then hastily set out on his journey, fearing other notes and bills,—not of the first kind, however. He had the satisfaction of knowing that, had he restrained his curiosity a few minutes longer, he might have honestly said he could not pay the account presented, and later found himself possessed of a thousand francs.

148.—VON BÜLOW AS A POLITICAL SPEAKER.

Von Bülow was an inveterate speech maker. At his recitals and orchestral concerts he frequently took opportunity to express his sentiments on various affairs, and he did not always confine himself to things musical, but occasionally ventured into a political harangue, but not always with credit or safety to himself.

On one occasion he could not forbear to slur the Emperor and to express his disgust at the dismissal that royal personage had given to Prince Bismarck, whom Bülow heartily admired. Two years before Bülow's death he made his final appearance as leader of the Philharmonic concerts in Berlin. The programme closed with Beethoven's " Heroic " symphony. The eccentric leader could not resist this opportunity for making a speech.

After reproaching the Germans for lacking the necessary spirit to move in the matter of erecting a monument to Beethoven and making it necessary for Liszt, a Hungarian, to do so, he then said that all knew of the dedication of the Heroic symphony to Napoleon, and then after that general had disappointed Beethoven, how he changed his dedication to an Austrian prince.

" We musicians," he continued, " know well what hero would receive the dedication if the composer were living to-day—namely the man that has done the greatest things for us Germans, that Beethoven of politics, Prince Bismarck ! "

Then, after eulogizing Bismarck, he took his handkerchief from his pocket and, dusting his shoes with it, left the stage. This peculiar action was a slur at the Emperor, who had recently dismissed Bismarck from the chancellorship and had publicly declared that any one who did not like his policy could shake the dust of Germany from his shoes and take his departure.

Even the Emperor of Germany had no terrors for Bülow.

149.—LIND'S FIRST ENGAGEMENT.

There never was on the stage a sweeter or more lovable disposition than that of Jenny Lind. Like the rest of mankind, Miss Lind had her troubles, and serious ones, but they never affected her serenity of temper or her kindness of heart.

The circumstances of her wedding to Otto Goldschmidt, whom she met on her American tour in 1851, are well known. Lind was under the management of P. T. Barnum, and for a time Goldschmidt was the pianist of the company.

But her narrow escape from a marriage with a less enjoyable personage is not so well known. Not long before her trip to this country she became acquainted with a certain Claudius Harris, an officer in the English army, and the result of this acquaintance was their engagement. Now Harris was a very religious fellow and quite bigoted. He kept urging her to leave the stage; and in fact his family thought she could not do better than spend the rest of her life in atoning for her theatrical career. Finally, she was persuaded, and gave a series of six farewell operatic presentations. No one thought at that time that this would be her permanent farewell to the opera, but it proved to be such.

When it came to making the arrangements for her wedding, Harris wished a promise inserted in the wedding contract to the effect that she was never to go on the operatic stage again, and he objected to her having full control of her earnings, saying that it was unscriptural.

So the engagement was nearly broken off. Harris

terrified her by threats of torment here and hereafter if she broke her word. She became reconciled to the engagement. After their reconciliation, she sat at the piano singing to him, but, turning around she found him asleep! Finally Harris became more and more repugnant to her and the engagement was broken. Not long after she found a worthier man in Mr. Goldschmidt, and married him in 1852, after a year's acquaintance.

150.—BEETHOVEN'S FIRST TRIUMPH.

The story of Beethoven's first triumph as a composer is told in a very interesting way by Meyerbeer. When Beethoven was scarcely sixteen years of age he was invited one evening by his good friends, the Von Breunings, of Bonn, to spend the evening with them in the company of a number of well known musicians. Among them were Capelmeister Ries, the brothers Romberg, Count Waldstein, several members of the orchestra and others.

After there had been some music performed by various persons, Count Waldstein announced that he had received a trio in manuscript, and that he wished very much to hear it; but he desired not to mention the name of the composer until the work had first been performed. He then called on the two Rombergs and young Beethoven to try the composition *prima vista*. They complied. The work was found to be original in form and full of vigor and life.

Many expressions of admiration were given as to the trio, and much comment was excited as to who its composer might be. One declared it was too passionate to be from Haydn's pen, and another added that it was too gloomy to be by Mozart. Ries declared that at any rate it was by a man who thoroughly understood his work.

Finally Count Waldstein announced that the trio was composed by young Beethoven. The musicians looked as if something had fallen from the clouds. Then succeeded the most hearty congratulations, and the young composer went to his humble home that night with a fresh inspiration for his life work, brought by this first triumph as a composer.

151.—HÄNDEL'S DUEL.

Not many of the great composers have gone down in history as having taken part as one of the principals in a duel. Among them, perhaps this honor must be awarded solely to Händel. The cause of this affair was to be found in one of the curious customs of his day.

In the early part of the last century it was the custom for the director of an opera to play the accompaniments on a harpsichord which had its place on the stage. Distinguished personages who were present often claimed a seat on the stage and felt free to interpose a running fire of audible conversation and comment. This is now relegated to that part of the audience who have little musical understanding and less of good manners.

In the early part of Händel's career he was associated with a composer named Matheson, a man of talent, but of no great depth, but from whose writings we may catch some enjoyable glimpse of the customs of his time. On the occasion in question, in Matheson's opera of "Cleopatra," the composer was acting the part of Antony, and Händel was seated at the harpsichord. When Antony died, early in the opera, Matheson came into the orchestra and desired to take Handel's seat as director. There was some excuse for this wish as Matheson had been the regular director of the opera.

But Händel, with that irritability which characterized him later in life, crustily refused to give up his place, whereupon a violent quarrel ensued, and as they were leaving the theater Matheson gave him a hearty slap in the face. Händel drew his sword, Matheson defended himself, and a duel was fought then and there. Luckily, perhaps, for our musical literature, Matheson's sword was broken against a metal button on his opponent's coat, and the honor of each was vindicated! Soon after, the two composers were at peace and hearty good friends again. This was a good example of a discord, prepared and resolved.

152.—PAGANINI'S GENEROUS DEED.

In the later years of Paganini's life his avarice grew apace with his fame. He was the wizard of the violin world. People fought for admission to his concerts, and raved over his playing. All the while a golden stream was flowing into his coffers; but with it his passion for wealth, instead of being satisfied by his large income, grew stronger, and at the end was, next to his love for music, his ruling passion.

While his skill made him a millionaire, yet he lived as though stricken with poverty. In order to save some of his precious gold he would limit the amount of his food to an insufficiency.

When sick he would refuse to have a doctor called in. He would quarrel with the druggist, and if the medicine seemed to him expensive he would take only one-half or one-third as much as ordered.

When Paganini reached the summit of his fame he lost all the generosity that his miserly nature ever contained. He even refused to play at the charity concerts given in Paris and Marseilles; by this lack of humanity, so opposite to the generosity of great musicians generally, he aroused the contempt of the people to such a degree as to be hooted on the streets.

The friends of the great violinist, knowing that he was publicly charged with great avarice, thought to allay these stories by having him get the credit for doing a notable deed of generosity. At that time the composer, Berlioz, who gave rich promise for the future, and who even then had composed some effective works, was suffering from a sad lack of funds.

So these friends arranged that Paganini was to present Berlioz in his hour of need with twenty thousand francs, and it was to be ostentatiously heralded as a fine piece of generosity. Knowing, however, that the violinist would not consent to part with even twenty francs to be thought generous, they raised the twenty thousand among themselves, and only besought Paganini to allow the use of his name, to which he obligingly consented.

Berlioz thinking the gift came from a brother musician who wished by it to recognize his merit and his struggles, accepted it and blessed the hand that bestowed it; and even the music histories and biographies of to-day praise this act of brotherly kindness and generosity on the part of that great artist, Paganini.

153.—A GENTLE CRITIC.

Mendelssohn was of gentle disposition, and was a kindly critic. This was evinced on one occasion when he heard what he considered too harsh criticisms on Donizetti's music. His ideas of music were entirely in opposition to those of this Italian composer of light operas. The friends and acquaintances who surrounded him one evening at a representation of one of Donizetti's operas knew this and sought to enter further into the good graces of this idol of the musical world at that time by flinging at the Italian's work harsh and contemptuous criticisms.

Finally Mendelssohn could endure it no longer, and tired of their attempts to curry favor with him at the expense of another composer, cried out:—

"I like it; and do you know, I should like to have composed such music myself!"

154.—ART BEFORE BUSINESS.

Beethoven was accustomed to spend the summer months in the country; and there, in the open air, in the woods and fields, his genius seemed to have the freest fancy. He once took lodgings in the village of Modling, that he might enjoy the beautiful scenery of that neighborhood. A four-horse luggage wagon was to transport his furniture and music, and it was piled high with the composer's *lares et penates*.

Beethoven walked on before. But no sooner were they outside of the city than the beauties of nature awoke his creative spirit, and he became oblivious of the reason of the journey. Musical ideas crowded thick upon him; he jotted them down, selected and arranged them, and all the while the wagon and its contents were forgotten. Finally, he bethought himself of his goods and hastened to his journey's end.

When he arrived there, tired and dusty, he found his belongings scattered around the market place. The driver of the caravan had arrived at his journey's end, and, after awaiting his employer for two hours, had dumped down his freight in the market place and returned home. It is needless to say that Beethoven had paid the man in advance for his services, or he would not have left in such a hurry. Of course, Beethoven was angry at this state of affairs, but he soon saw the ludicrous side of the matter, and securing help, was able to get his goods under cover by midnight.

155.—THE "DEAR SAXON."

An interesting story is told of one of Händel's experiences when he was in Italy. The Italians so enjoyed his wonderful powers of playing that they gave him the title of "the dear Saxon." He entered in a friendly rivalry with Scarlatti, in Venice, and after many trials of skill the general verdict was that the Italian excelled on the harpsichord, but the German carried away the palm on the organ.

Some time afterward, Händel was invited to a masked ball, and in the course of the evening he sat down at the harpsichord, and astonished all those present by his masterly improvisations. Presently Scarlatti came in, also *en masque*. Walking quickly to the instrument he listened a moment, and then called out, "It is either the devil or the Saxon!"

Händel achieved this enviable reputation when only twenty-one years of age.

156.—BÜLOW BITS.

The biographer of von Bülow will find no trouble in securing anecdotes characteristic of this whimsical player and conductor, for the peculiar things he did were legion. His criticisms, while often severe, were certainly to the point and were stated without hesitation or reserve. Especially cutting were his remarks about singers. He had a great antipathy to the majority of tenor singers. One especially did he dislike, and speaking of his singing, said, "Do you call that singing? I call it a disease."

While conducting a rehearsal of "Lohengrin" at Hanover he became enraged at the singer's rendition of a certain passage and, throwing his baton at him cried, "You don't sing like a "Knight of the Swan," but like a knight of the swine!"

A caller once noticed as the principal picture in his apartments that of the leader of the ballet. On his friend's expressing surprise, Bülow said, "Yes, she is the only woman of the artists on the stage who does not distress me by bad singing."

When this eccentric pianist met any one to whom for any reason he took a dislike, he would turn and hasten away in an opposite direction. Once in Copenhagen an accomplished player of the 'cello who was the unfortunate possessor of a very large nose was presented to him. Bülow gazed at him an instant, then, without returning the player's salutation, exclaimed, "That nose is impossible!" and fled away.

In America we sometimes hear the phrase "put a head on him," but the German idiom for the same phraseological gem is to "give one a nose." When Bulow was leading the Meiningen orchestra, on one occasion the duke wished a certain piece played. The conductor through some whim declined. The duke insisted. The next day Bülow appeared at rehearsal with an enormous false nose on his face. At the close of the first piece, he said to the orchestra, "Gentlemen, you will wish to know where I got this nose? I will tell you. His Highness gave it to me yesterday."

These are some of the whimsicalities of greatness; greatness viewed from its comical side. Viewed as an interpreter of the great masters from Beethoven to Wagner, on piano or orchestra Bülow was one of the very elect. A man of prodigious memory, of wide learning, of an all-conquering technic, he was a universal genius who concentrated his abilities upon music, yet to whom music was but one department of learning. At this writing there is no one that may take up his fallen mantle.

157.—AN INTERRUPTED CONCERT.

Paganini had a cowardly horror of England, due to some peculiar experiences he had while there. He had a great deal of pride and egotism, and continually suspected other violinists—jealous of his fame and ability—of wishing to assassinate him.

When he was besought to go to France, he would have declined from this fear of assassination, had he not been told that he would accumulate great riches from the trip; but finally his avarice overcame his cowardice.

One of the circumstances that made him dislike England was an experience he had in London. One night, in the midst of a brilliant concert, a respectable citizen arose from his seat, and facing the audience, interrupted the proceedings with the following impromptu speech:

"Gentlemen, do you not blush at spending a guinea to come and hear a miserable player, a mountebank, who knows only how to get sounds out of a wooden box, mounted with catgut? Could you not make better use of your money? Would you not do better to give it to the poor? Look at that big charlatan, who is just like the devil; he laughs at your simplicity and puts your money into his pockets. You are a set of fools!"

Hardly had he finished this tirade, when Paganini, greatly frightened and thinking he was followed by assassins, had fled from the concert hall and was on his way to Manchester.

158.—COÖPERATIVE COMPOSITION.

In 1837 a certain charitably disposed Princess hit on a novel way to gather in money for the homeless Italian patriots then in Paris. Her plan was to bring into the musical market a composition which should be the combined work of six of the greatest pianists then before the world.

The theme that was chosen was a duet from Bellini's "I Puritani," and the composers who took part in this composite composition were Liszt, Thalberg, Pixis, Herz, Czerny, and Chopin—a brilliant array. From the number of composers this work was called the "Hexameron." Each one wrote a variation on the given theme and Liszt furnished the introduction and finale.

This was not the first time that Liszt had taken part in such composition. In 1823 Diabelli, the Vienna music publisher, issued a series of fifty variations on a waltz theme, by fifty prominent composers of the time. Among them were Czerny, Hummel, Kalkbrenner,

Kreutzer, and Schubert. The twenty-fourth variation was by Franz Liszt, then eleven years old; and despite his youth, his variation is on a par with those of the older and more celebrated composers. This is the only one of Liszt's earlier compositions that has been preserved.

159.—AN ABSENT-MINDED CONDUCTOR.

We have elsewhere spoken of the growth and culmination of Robert Schumann's sad malady. The more serious phases of this affliction were preceded by an occasional absence of mind that sometimes produced ludicrous results.

A characteristic instance of his forgetfulness occurred when he was once conducting a rehearsal of Bach's "Passion Music." The choir had begun the great opening chorus and were singing bravely along, when it was noticed that his beat grew less and less decided, and finally stopped altogether. He then laid down his baton, rapidly turned over fifty or sixty pages of the score before him, and became absorbed in reading a movement in the second part of the work. The chorus kept on singing and Schumann kept on reading, utterly oblivious to what was going on around him.

After a while he became conscious of the singing, and finding that what he heard did not agree in the least with the music he was reading, he stopped the singers and cried out to them: "Good heavens! ladies and gentlemen, what on earth are you singing there?"

160.—COSTLY ADMIRATION.

There has never been a vocalist who secured more favor on these shores than Jenny Lind, the "Swedish Nightingale," as she was called. The people went wild over her singing; in fact, to rave over the young lady was at that time the proper thing to do, as it has been later to go into ecstacies over a certain fluffy-haired pianist.

In Baltimore, Lind was the recipient of a popular serenade. Upon her appearance on the balcony of the hotel to acknowledge the compliment thus tendered her, there was a loud and enthusiastic shout from the crowd beneath. In the midst of this uproar she dropped a valuable shawl. It was eagerly seized by the crowd, and in a moment was torn into small pieces and carried away as mementoes of the songstress.

Such proceedings may be highly complimentary to the artist; but, save as a matter of advertising, are not particularly profitable.

161.—WINE AND MUSIC.

There seems to be a close relation existing somehow between wine and music. Those countries that produce the most wine seem to be likewise the most successful in turning out good music and plenty of it. The world would hardly know it if all the music written outside of Germany, Italy, and France were to be lost. There has some good music come from England and Russia, but its absence would not be greatly felt. England's great musician, Händel, was thoroughly German in birth, temperament, education, and style of composition. Italy, France, and Germany are the great wine-producing countries, and might be called likewise the great musician-producing lands.

Then, I wonder if a liking for the juice of the grape has anything to do with fecundity of musical ideas. Of all the great composers, and likewise those who come very near the limits of greatness, hardly one can be mentioned who was averse to "the cup that cheers." A teetotaller among composers is a *rara avis*.

On the other hand, it might be said that it would have been better for several musicians of great fame if they had heeded the injunction to "touch not." Lulli, Mozart, and especially Schubert, all spent too much time over their cups for their own good, and they have not been without followers in this respect among musicians of lesser fame. Doubtless the great composers could have lived without their wine and beer, but doubtless they never did.

162.—SCHUBERT'S "ERL-KING."

Perhaps none of the great composers deserve our pity more than Franz Schubert. Poor as the legendary church mouse, obliged to eke out a scanty living in the uncongenial and poorly paid occupation of teaching school, he was unknown by musicians and not understood by publishers. The following incident is a sample of the reception given his music by some of the gentry who grow rich off of the products of other people's brains.

In 1817, Messrs. Breitkopf & Härtel, of Leipsic, received from Vienna a manuscript setting of Goethe's "Erl-king," by Franz Schubert.

"Vienna?" exclaimed the publishers,—"Franz Schubert? There is something wrong here. Franz Schubert lives in Dresden; he occupies the high position of Royal church composer, he is a highly respectable man, aged forty-nine; what has he to do with Vienna or Erl-kings?"

They send the manuscript on to the Franz Schubert of Dresden, and ask for an explanation. He replied: "About ten days ago I received your letter, in which you forward to me a manuscript, 'The Erl-king,' that professes to be by me. With the utmost astonishment I inform you that this cantata was never composed by me. I will use every endeavor to discover who has so discourteously sent you this bit of patchwork (machwerk), and expose the scoundrel who has so misused my name."

It is not known whether Breitkopf & Härtel declined

Schubert's "Erl-king," but the ballad composed in 1816 was not printed till February, 1821, when it appeared in the first part of his "Lieder."

Schubert sold some of his songs to publishers for as little as tenpence apiece. When the publishers refused to issue them, some of his friends rallied to his assistance, and from their own pockets paid the expense of publication.

163.—ROYAL HONORS TO A SINGER.

The careers of many of the noted *prima donnas* read like romances rather than history. Fiction has nothing more sensational or brilliant to present than the adulation, the almost worship, accorded to some of these women by an admiring public. So many of the great singers met this flattering reception at the hands of the public that it is hard to choose one as an example. But we will here speak of two incidents of Madame Malibran's career.

On the last visit of this celebrated singer to Venice, the ovation she received was such as might have been awarded to some conquering general returning from his victories. As her gondola entered the Grand Canal, she was greeted by the blare of trumpets, the noise of bands, and the shouts of multitudes. This homage continued during all her stay in this city. When she appeared in public the admiring crowds were so great that she had to be protected from the crush by armed police; and when she went out in a gondola the other vessels of a similar sort that followed her were so numerous as to obstruct the passage of the canals. On her departure from this enthusiastic people she was presented with a magnificent diadem, studded with diamonds and rubies.

In Milan her reception was hardly less flattering. One night she was deluged with bouquets, the leaves of which were made of gold and silver, and her enthusiastic hearers recalled her twenty times. It is little wonder that she fainted at the end of the performance.

164.—THE DEAF BEETHOVEN.

The deaf Beethoven and the blind Händel are pitiful pictures. For many years Beethoven could hear no note of music, yet in this time he put forth some of his mightiest works.

At the first performance of his immortal Ninth Symphony, Beethoven himself conducted. But he could not hear a single tone from the orchestra and chorus. When, at the close of the work, the audience loudly applauded, Beethoven was entirely oblivious of it until the lady who sang the alto solo part had turned him around facing the people, so he could see the clapping of hands. It was a touching sight, and the people were deeply affected by the condition of this grand old man, who had to see, instead of hear, the applause for his music.

165.—THE HISTORY OF A VIOLIN.

Ole Bull's favorite violin was one of old Gaspar di Salo's creations.

Its history was so varied as to deserve mention. For a hundred and fifty years or so it had reposed in the museum at Innspruck, where it had been placed by a cardinal as being a fine example of the work of its maker. In 1809 the French soldiers sacked that place, and this valuable instrument was carried off by a soldier and subsequently sold to Herr Rhehazek, a Viennese official, who was a collector of violins, and who had put nearly all his wealth into his fine collection of instruments. When Ole Bull visited Vienna, in 1839, he saw this fiddle and determined to possess it. But no, Rhehazek would not part with it, and all Bull could get out of him was that if the violin were to be sold he should have the first opportunity to purchase it at four thousand ducats. The violinist agreed, although he knew it was a big price.

Two years later he was one day dining with Liszt and Mendelssohn in Leipzig, when a letter was handed him bearing an official seal. It was from Vienna, and announced the death of the old violin collector. Rhehazek had told his son that Ole Bull was to have the first opportunity to buy the di Salo violin, and the son faithfully wrote him that he could now purchase it. Liszt declared that Ole must be crazy to pay so much for a violin he had never heard; and Mendelssohn said it was a piece of extravagance that only a fiddler could be capable of. But Ole Bull persisted in buying the violin, and with it won some of his greatest triumphs.

166.—"VORTS" *VS.* MUSIC.

In this century it is considered necessary to have a congenial theme and inspiring words before a composer can do his best in giving the text a musical setting. But this was not the case in the first half of the last century. Counterpoint, *i. e.*, musical mathematics, held the boards then. The words were secondary in the composer's eyes; and the main thing was whether the music was good as music, and not whether it illustrated the sentiment of the language.

Even the great Händel seemed at times to care little for the words set to his compositions. Perhaps there is a great deal to be said for this view of the matter, for who goes to hear an opera on account of its beautiful words? How many operas have been borne into public favor by the beauty of the music when the words were mere trash? Even in church music, in how many cases are the words understood by the congregation? If the singers don't give the people the opportunity to understand the words, why scan the composition of the poetry very critically?

With Händel it was natural that the music should hold first place in his affection. His ideas about the value of the poetry to which he set his music may be illustrated by the following incident:—

There was a certain Dr. Morrell who arranged many of Händel's librettos for him. This personage one day ventured to give Händel some advice as to what kind of music should be set to certain words. This at once aroused the choleric Händel.

"Vat," he exclaimed, "Vat! you deach me music? My music ish goot music. Damn your vorts! Here,"—sitting down to his instrument and playing through a melody,—"here are mine ideas; you go and make vorts to dem."

Yet in some of his greater compositions, his oratorios, Händel carefully chose his words from the Scriptures, and in many cases the musical settings are highly beautiful and in perfect accord with the sentiment of the Word.

167.—FRENCH WIT.

Grétry, the French opera composer, was a man of considerable wit and enjoyed a good joke. He was able to take a hand in a bit of fun when occasion offered. At one time, when going on a trip through Switzerland, he met with a German baron who proposed that they should travel together.

As soon as they had begun their journey, Grétry began a conversation with his lordship, saying, "Ah, sir, how enchanted I am with—,"

"Sir," interrupted the baron, "I never talk in a carriage."

"Very well," said Grétry, and subsided into quiet.

The baron had evidently considered that he had a garrulous traveling companion, and that it was best to shut him up in the beginning of the journey.

That night when they halted at an inn and had

divested themselves of their dusty traveling robes and were comfortably settled before a roaring blaze, the baron turned to Grétry, saying :—

"Now, my dear sir, how glad I am that ——."

"Sir," said Grétry sharply, "I never talk in an inn."

The nobleman saw the joke, and the two then entered into friendly conversation.

The next day they were ascending Mount Cenis. Grétry espied a small cross stuck in the ground and inquired of the guides what it meant. He was answered sharply with one word, "Silence!"

"How now," thought our Frenchman, "are these some more German barons?"

But he kept quiet until the end of their climb, when the guides told him that any conversation or noise might, by the vibration of the air, loosen some of the masses of snow and cause an avalanche.

168.—TOO LITERAL.

An English singer, Anna Storace, when visiting Vienna, sang before the court on a certain gala occasion, and was the recipient of many compliments. The Emperor, passing her in the *fête*, politely asked her if she was enjoying herself, and also if there was anything he could do for her. Not understanding that court language must not always be taken too literally, she calmly replied, "Yes, your Majesty, I am quite thirsty; will you get me a glass of water?"

The effect of this request on the bystanders may be imagined. The Emperor, however, had the good sense not to be offended, and, ordering an attendant to wait on the lady, smilingly passed on.

169.—IMAGINATION A FACTOR IN HEARING MUSIC.

One cannot but regard with pity the semi-insane actions of the people who rave over the playing of some popular artist, and lose their good sense, dignity, and self-possession in their mad worship of the idol of the hour.

The latest craze of this style has been over that excellent pianist, Paderewski, when people—that is to say, women—have thrown themselves at him, wept over him, kissed him, and made fools of themselves generally.

Certainly, emotional playing affects emotional people. But if we subtract from such scenes the maundering sentimentality, the shallow brain, and the feeling that it is "the proper thing" to rave over the unfortunate object of their sentimental vaporings, popular artists might then venture before the public without a body-guard to ward off the emotional female.

Those who best appreciate good playing, and who really have the deepest emotional nature, do not manifest their sentiments on the surface for the benefit of a curious crowd.

In this sentimental excitement the imagination is a powerful factor. This was proved by Liszt on one occasion. Excitable ladies were affected by Liszt's playing just as, in later days, they have been by that of Paderewski.

In this instance Liszt found himself surrounded by a bevy of beautiful dames and damsels, a circumstance which, by the way, was not opposed to his tastes, for Liszt was a lover of the beautiful, to which feminine beauty was no exception. Of course, the universal desire was that he should play for them, that he should produce for them "the ecstacies, the artistic raptures, which his magnificent talent never failed to evoke." Overcome by their persuasions, Liszt seated himself at the piano and played. By his wonderful skill some of the ladies were soon overcome with delight; some even fainted!

In telling a friend of the matter afterward, Liszt said: " Believe me, I played many wrong notes intentionally; indeed, so palpable were some of my errors, that had I been playing at any elementary music school I should certainly have been expelled as an impostor!"

So much for the power of imagination. Had some other than Liszt played the same music perfectly, the ladies would have thought it not worth their while to faint.

170.—MUSICAL AND NON-MUSICAL ACCENT.

The matters called "time" and "accent" in music are stumbling-blocks for many a pupil and for many people who profess to understand the tone-art. If music students have trouble in understanding these subjects, it is small wonder that so stupid a body as the average court jury should need a detailed explanation of these somewhat common technical terms; and it would need a musician who not only understood his subject, but one who was able to express his ideas in clear, terse language, and to employ apt illustration, to elucidate the matter.

Such a musician was found, when, in 1833, there came up for trial before an English court a case of violation of copyright, and Cooke, the composer, was called as an expert witness. In the course of the examination the following dialogue took place:—

"Now, sir," said the lawyer, "you say that these two melodies are identical but different; what am I to understand by that, sir?"

"What I said," replied Cooke, "was that the notes in the two arrangements are the same, but with a different accent, one being in common, the other in triple, time; consequently the position of the accented notes is different in the two copies."

"What is musical accent?" glibly inquired the counsel.

"My terms for teaching music are a guinea a lesson," said Cooke, much to the enjoyment of the spectators.

"I don't want to know your terms for teaching; I want you to explain to his Lordship the Judge and to the jury what is 'musical accent.'" Here Sir James Scarlett, the questioner, grew warm and inquired,—

"Can you see it?"

"No."

"Can you feel it?"

"Well," drawled Cooke, "a musician can."

Again the lawyer put the question and the court required it to be answered.

"Will you explain to his lordship and the jury, who are supposed to know nothing about music, the meaning of what you call accent?"

"Musical accent," replied the witness, "is emphasis laid on a certain note, just in the same manner as you would lay stress on any word when speaking, in order to make yourself better understood. Let me give you an illustration, Sir James. If I were to say, 'You are a *jackass*,' the accent rests on jackass; but if instead I said, '*You* are a jackass,' it rests on you, Sir James; and I have no doubt the gentlemen of the jury will corroborate me."

171.—VON WEBER TO A BAWLING CHOIR.

Appropriateness of expression is a thing foreign to many choir singers and choristers. Many cultivate the *fortissimo* habit until all hopes for a *pianissimo* or even a *piano* passage vanish. Outside of the excellent effect of an occasional change from a strong, lusty tone to a subdued and quieter passage, there is another matter to be considered, that of suiting the sound to the sense,— the volume of tone to the sentiment expressed by the words.

A chorus was once heartily rebuked by von Weber in a manner that no doubt left a permanent impression. He was conducting a rehearsal of his " Jubel Cantata " in London. In the course of this work occurs a beautiful prayer for chorus. The singers attacked it with a loud and lusty tone, in a " hammer and tongs " style, as a German would say, when suddenly Weber called a halt, saying:—

"Stop! do not sing like that. Would you bawl in that manner in the presence of God?"—words that might appropriately be framed in almost every choir loft.

Not only in chorus and choir, but especially in church and Sunday school do we find people singing prayerful words in a manner which cannot be better described than in Weber's language—"bawling in the presence of God."

172.—AN INTERRUPTED OPERA.

Mozart once created quite a sensation in a theater he was visiting. It was at Marseilles. He had gone to the opera *incognito* to hear one of his own works performed. All went well till, in a certain passage, through some error in the copyist, the orchestra played "D" where Mozart had written "D sharp." This change of one note made a decided difference in the harmony, and turned the superior harmonic effect intended into a very ordinary sounding affair.

No sooner was this done than Mozart sprang to his feet, crying out: "Play D sharp, will you; play D sharp, you wretches!" It may be imagined that such actions produced quite a sensation. The orchestra and singers stopped their performance and the audience began to hiss him down and cry, "Put him out!" and he was about to be summarily ejected from the theater, when he announced who he was.

When it was known that it was Mozart, the tumult subsided, and cries of "Mozart! Mozart!" rang through the house. The very ones that were about to expel him now conducted him to the orchestra, and he was compelled to direct the opera, which was taken up anew. This time the missing D sharp was played in its proper place and produced the intended effect. At the close of the opera a perfect ovation was tendered the composer, and the people were not content until they had escorted him in triumph to his hotel.

173.—BEETHOVEN PUNISHED.

What would we have done for Beethoven anecdotes without Ries? Here is one that this pupil of the master tells in his enjoyable style:—

"One evening I was to play a sonata of Beethoven's which one does not often hear. As he was present, and as I had not studied this sonata with him, I declared myself willing to play the others, but not this. The company turned to Beethoven, who at length said: 'Now, you will not play so badly that I cannot listen.' In the end I was obliged to play. Beethoven turned, as usual, toward me. When I made a mistake in the left hand, he tapped me on the head with his finger, which the Princess L——, who leaned on the piano opposite, laughingly observed. After I had finished Beethoven said:—

"'Well done! You do not need to learn sonatas with me first. The finger tap only proved my attention to you.'

"Later he played, and chose the D minor sonata, Opus 31. The Princess, who expected that even Beethoven would make some mistakes, stood behind his chair while I turned the music. Soon he blundered noticeably. The Princess gave him a few not very soft strokes on the head, with the remark:—

"'If a pupil receives a finger stroke for a false note, then the master must be punished with a full hand for greater mistakes.'

"Every one laughed, Beethoven first. He then began

again and played wonderfully, especially the adagio, which was inimitable."

174.—VIOLIN COLLECTORS.

It has long been a source of satisfaction to *virtuosi* and wealthy amateurs to make collections of old and rare violins. While this keeps these valuable instruments out of use for a time, it certainly acts as a preservative, and future generations get the benefit of what we are deprived.

Paganini had in his collection, among other Cremonas, a "Strad," a small Guarnerius, an Amati, a "Strad" bass, and the large Guarnerius, which was given to him and which he loved so much that he gave it to Genoa to keep sacred from the profaning touch of any succeeding artist. I believe this wish has been followed in every case, with one exception, that of his pupil, Sivori.

A good example of the wealthy amateur was Gillott, the millionaire Birmingham (Eng.) pen manufacturer. He had a penchant (excuse the pun) for collecting violins and letting them be unused and uncared for. He was not a player himself, and it is a question whether he realized the possibilities of any one of his valuable collection. At his death there was found in one room of his factory over £40,000 worth of fiddles and in other rooms many 'cellos and basses. At one time he had about five hundred instruments collected together, making probably the largest number of valuable Italian instruments ever owned at one time by a single person.

175.—POT-BOILERS.

Most composers are driven to the writing of "pot-boilers," *i. e.*, music that does not contain their best effort, but which is written to please the public and bring in a needed supply of the "filthy lucre." Händel did much of this kind of work and sent out many inferior compo-

sitions, but was not proud enough of them to sign his name to them. Once, when attending a kind of promenade concert with some friends, Händel said to one of them, "Come, sit down, let us listen to this piece. I want your opinion of it." In a few minutes his friend said:—
"It is not worth listening to; it is very poor stuff."
"You are right, sir, it is very poor stuff. I thought so myself when I had finished it."

The friend hastened to apologize, but Händel cut him short, saying that the music really was poor, as his time for writing it was limited, and assured him that his opinion was as correct as it was honest.

176.—GOUNOD'S FAUST.

Gounod will always be best known as the author of "Faust." But with all the beauty and popularity of that work it was not well received at first. In fact, had it been we might suspect its value. Chappell & Co., the London publishers, bought the right of English performance from Gounod for £60. It lay on their shelves for some time, until one day Colonel Mapleson, husband of the great *prima donna*, Titiens, and *impresario* of Her Majesty's Opera House, being at his wits' end for something new and attractive to produce, turned for assistance to his friend, Tom Chappell, head of the firm of Chappell & Co. This gentleman handed the Colonel the manuscript of "Faust," remarking that its merits, if it had any, remained to be discovered. Colonel Mapleson carefully removed the cobwebs and dust from the work, mute witnesses of British musical perspicacity. In a few weeks the public were wild with delight, and Gounod's name as a composer of the highest order was widely proclaimed.

177.—MADAME PATTI.

Adelina Patti has every claim to the distinction of a "Queen of Song." She was born, of musical parents, at Madrid, on February 10th, 1843. She made her first appearance in 1850, as a child of seven years of age, at Tripler's Hall, New York, when she sang and acted. From her seventh to her tenth year she travelled as a prodigy through South America, where she was at once received with that extraordinary enthusiasm which has always attended her progress everywhere. Her first appearance in London was at Covent Garden, in the opera of "*La Sonnambula*," on May 14th, 1861, when she at once took everybody by surprise, and she immediately shot into the front rank of popularity. She had arranged to sing for Mapleson at the rate of £40 per week, singing four nights a week. The same *impresario* subsequently paid the Diva no less a sum than £1,000 for each performance during his American opera tours. Some ingenious American mathematician made a calculation as to how much Patti received for singing each separate note in Rossini's "*Semiramide*," with the result that he discovered she put into her pocket $7\frac{7}{10}$ cents *more per note* than Rossini received for writing the entire opera.

Wonderful accounts are recorded of Patti's American journeys. The railway car in which she travelled from city to city was a marvel of workmanship, and cost £12,000. The drawing-room was decorated in white and gold, and on the ceiling was displayed several figures painted by Parisian artists of eminence. The wood-work was of sandal wood, the curtains of heavy silk damask, and the walls and ceilings were covered with gilded tapestry. The lamps were of rolled gold, and the furniture throughout was upholstered in silk damask of the most beautiful texture. The bath, having hot and cold water, was of solid silver! The key of the outer door of the car was of 18 carat gold, and a Steinway grand pianoforte, costing £400, had a case of sandal wood.

Adelina Patti's home is amongst the Welsh hills. Her castle, near the town of Neath, is named Craig-y-nos, which is the Welsh for "night rock," or "rock of the night." Here the great singer lives in a style befitting her exalted position in the realm of song. The magnificent conservatory, a sort of winter garden, illuminated with myriads of electric fairy lights, has been described as "a hall of enchantment."

Patti is very fond of billiards. In the billiard-room is a huge orchestrion, made in Switzerland, which plays many tunes, from *"La Fille de Madame Angot"* to the "Pilgrim's March" from Wagner's *"Tannhauser."* A theatre, complete in every department, is also a feature of this palatial dwelling-place. There is room in it for a band of twenty performers, and the necessary scenery for mounting six or more of the *Diva's* operas is on the spot. All that Patti has to do when she wishes to sing in any particular opera for the delectation of her friends, is to send for her head scene-shifter and give her orders as she would to her cook or coachman. Patti's diamonds are quite in keeping with the glories of Craig-y-nos, and are almost as wonderful as her notes. At one of her appearances in New York she is said to have worn no less than £60,000 worth of precious stones.

Patti's pets include some remarkable parrots. One, named "Cookie," exactly copies his mistress's *fioriture*. Another is gifted with some linguistic capabilities, which he can use with excellent effect when occasion requires. If a guest knocks at the door, Charlie will cry, "Entr-r-rez." When he is asked "How are you?" he will reply, "Pas mal; et vous?" which of course is in very polite French. But when a guest ventured to sprinkle some water on his poll, Charlie replied (in vigorous English) "You *pig!*"

178.—AN EVEN DISTRIBUTION OF HONORS.

Dr. Arne was once placed in a somewhat similar situation to that of Solomon when the two women each claimed the child. His disposition of the case was as fair as that of the king, only the distribution was more even, as even as Solomon threatened to make the division of the child in question.

Dr. Arne was a very prominent English composer who lived in the first half of the last century. He had been called upon to decide on the merits of two singers. Their merits, by the way, were based largely on their own appreciation of their powers, rather than on that of other people. After hearing them, Dr. Arne cried out to one of them,—

"You are the worst singer I ever heard in my life!"

"Then," exclaimed the other, "I win."

"No," answered the just judge, "you can't sing *at all!*"

179.—RAPID COMPOSITION.

There are many instances of rapid work on the part of the great composers; and their facility and quickness of composition causes great wonder and admiration. But our admiration is often misdirected. When we hear of some of the speedy writing of great works by Mozart or Mendelssohn we are apt to think that this speed was of the composing powers as well as of pen, but, in fact, such was seldom the case. These great musicians generally did their composition mentally without reference to pen or piano, and simply deferred the unpleasant manual labor of committing their music to paper until it became absolutely necessary. Then they got credit for incredible rapidity of composition. But it is no light matter to quickly and correctly pen a long and complicated composition. One has only to copy a piece of music or to try to put into notes some piece of music previously memorized, to realize this. And then, when the instrumentation of a composition for twenty-five different kinds of orchestral instruments is considered, the arranging of the bars and the writing of the numerous signs of expression, the manual labor becomes no insignificant task. It is no infrequent thing to find over two hundred notes in a single measure of a full orchestral score.

While many shorter things, such as overtures, might be fully arranged in mind before touching pen to paper, that cannot be said of the larger works. In these, composition and writing probably went, to some extent, hand in hand.

That enormous work of Händel's, the oratorio, "Israel in Egypt," he wrote in the space of twenty-seven days; while that greatest of oratorios, the "Messiah," he composed in the remarkably short time of twenty-three days! The opera, "Rinaldo," Händel wrote in just two weeks.

Mendelssohn wrote his overture to "Ruy Blas" in two days. He was waited upon by a committee two days before the concert at which "Ruy Blas" was first given, and in the course of their remarks they said that owing to the lateness of the day they could not expect him to write an overture. This rather nettled Mendelssohn, and although he had another concert and rehearsals to attend in the intervening two days, he was ready with the "Ruy Blas" overture when the time arrived.

But few wrote music more rapidly than Mozart. The overture to "*Don Giovanni*" he wrote in one night, working with but slight intermission until seven next morning. He had it all arranged in mind, but had put off the writing until the last moment. That night the orchestra played it at sight. He composed the G major symphony in ten days; but a greater feat than this was the writing of the whole of the "Marriage of Figaro" in the month of April, 1786. The *finale* of the second act of this opera he wrote in one day, and that while he was so ill as to fall fainting from his chair ere it was finished.

But for rapid composition the palm must perhaps be awarded to the Italian composer, Coccia; for of him it is recorded, that he composed the opera of "Donna Caritea" in *six days*. This opera was first performed in Turin in 1818. But such rapidity cannot be conducive of valuable works unless it be by much greater composers than was Coccia.

180.—FRIENDS.

The music of Rossini and Meyerbeer would lead us to expect that they might have some personal affinity. Nor would we be mistaken, for they were intimate friends. The friendship would seem to have been real, for it was of such a character as took a real enjoyment in the work and successes, each of the other.

Once, when listening to a performance of "Roberto," the two were seated in a box at the opera house in Paris.

Rossini was so delighted at a certain piece that he jumped up, and, turning to the composer, said:—

"If you can write anything better than that I will undertake to dance on my head!" "Well then," replied Meyerbeer, "you had better begin practicing, for I have just finished the fourth act of *'Les Huguenots.'*"

181.—HAYDN'S RECEPTION BY PRINCE ESTERHAZY.

Haydn spent some time in the service of Count Motzin, a wealthy noble. At an entertainment given by the latter there was present Prince Esterhazy, whose wealth and station exceeded that of his entertainer. During the evening there was played a symphony by Haydn which so delighted the Prince that he determined to take its composer into his service. So he sent word to Haydn to come to his palace. At the appointed time Haydn appeared before this august personage. The Prince glanced carelessly at the slight figure that stood before him and said:—

"Is this, then, the composer of the music I heard last night?—a Moor, I should judge, by his complexion." The composer blushed in embarrassment. "And you write such music? You do not look it. Haydn—Haydn—I recollect the name; and I believe I was told that you were not well paid for your labors?"

"I have not been fortunate, your Highness, I ——"

"Well, you shall have no reason to complain in my service. My secretary shall fix your appointments; and name whatever else you desire. Understand me, for all of your profession find me liberal. Now then, Sir Moor, you may go; and let it be your first care to provide yourself with a new coat, a wig and buckles, and heels to your shoes. I will have you respectable in appearance as well as in talents; so let me have no more shabby professors. And do your best, my little dusky, to recruit in flesh—'twill add to the stature; and to relieve your olive with a shade of the ruddy. Such spindle masters would be a walking discredit to our larder, which is truly a spendthrift one."

So saying he laughingly dismissed the humble musician. But to-day who knows aught of that proud prince as compared with the fame of that same Joseph Haydn.

182.—PROVING IDENTITY.

Here is a story that has been told of more than one *prima donna*, but at present is related of Sigrid Arnoldson. If it is true, this lady has proved the statement that a great intellectual gift proves an easy passport to anything.

When she was in Rome, she went one day to the *poste restante* to call for a registered letter. She was asked for her passport to establish her identity, but she had left it at her hotel. Her reiterated assurance that she was indeed Sigrid Arnoldson failed to satisfy the officials, until at last the happy thought occurred to her to sing to them. "Assai, assai!" they exclaimed when the song was finished; "here is your letter, for no one but Sigrid Arnoldson can sing like that."

183.—A GREAT THIEF.

By all of the composers whom we call great, with one notable exception, other men's ideas have been held sacred. Genius is sufficient unto itself. No more would Mendelssohn have thought of stealing musical ideas from Beethoven than Beethoven would of appropriating them from Mozart, or Mozart from Bach. True, after a man once gives his ideas to the world they become the world's property. But they are the world's to use, not to claim as its own productions.

The great exception to this code of musical morality was one who was himself so great as to have no need of using other people's brains; yet perhaps he thought that very ability would excuse wholesale stealings on his part.

This monumental thief of musical ideas was—Händel.

Händel's originality was fertile, and his treatment of musical themes was superb; yet, rather than go to the trouble of composition, he would frequently appropriate right and left, taking a theme here, a melody there, a chorus yonder, until the question has almost become, "What really is Händel's?" To many, Händel is a musical god, a sun around which revolves the lesser orbs—all other composers. Händel's abilities have been recognized by all of his craft, and especially in England is his music most popular, and deservedly so. But still, in the light of modern research, one must continually question how much of it was originally his own. We do not speak at random in this matter. Reference to our illustrations of Händel's wholesale borrowing will prove the above statement.

Two of the best choruses in "Israel in Egypt" ("He

spoke the word," and the "Hailstone") were taken almost note for note from works of Stradella. In the second part of this oratorio are portions from a *magnificat* by Erba, composed about 1690. A certain *Te Deum* by Uria furnished him with material for no less than nine numbers of the "Dettingen *Te Deum*," and six of the oratorio, "Saul," and his opera, "Theodora," also betrays to some degree the same source.

For his "Time and Truth," parts of an unpublished work by Graun were made to serve; and the chorus, "Hear Jacob's God," from "Samson," is the "*Plorate Filiæ*," from Carissimi's "Jephtha." Even the favorite "Harmonious Blacksmith" has been traced to Corelli.

Dr. Crotch once made a list of twenty-nine composers from Josquin des Pres to Hummel, who furnished the "Dear Saxon" with material which he incorporated into works "by Händel."

We might say of Händel's works as a musician once said of a certain composer's oratorio, "Well, if another flood should occur, it would be well to preserve his music as affording specimens of the works of all previous composers."

There is one thing about Händel's appropriations, however, that must not be overlooked. It was the man's very genius that enabled him to be such a thief. A lesser genius would have been found out at once, and have been hissed off the stage. But Händel's abilities transformed everything he touched, to a greater or less degree, and imparted to it a certain Händelian flavor that one can hardly mistake. His castles were frequently builded upon other men's foundations; but because of the character and treatment of the superstructure we forgive this borrowed basis. The world is richer for his work; yet there will arise the question, why, when he could have depended entirely on his own genius, he did not do so. As among the old Roman gods some lied and some stole, so among our musical gods Händel must be remembered as the thief *par excellence*.

We may join with Mr. Prout when he says, "The more I study Händel the less I feel sure what is Händel's and what is not. No one in all the whole range of composers has robbed in such a wholesale and unprincipled manner as this dear old boy has done; but with all his faults I love him still."

184.—VON BÜLOW'S MEMORY.

A young composer called on von Bülow one day to get his opinion of a pianoforte concerto. Von Bülow declared he was too busy at that moment, but promised to look at it at his leisure. That same evening, at a party, von Bülow was asked to play, and to the amazement of the youthful aspirant for fame, who happened to be present, he sat down and played the entire concerto from memory. When he was director of the famous Meiningen orchestra, not content with conducting without a score, he endeavored, though without success, to induce the members of his band to learn their music by heart. The orchestra lacked both Bülow's prodigious memory and his matchless enthusiasm.

185.—THEIR FAVORITE SURROUNDINGS FOR COMPOSITION.

The great composers have each had their own ways of writing out their masterpieces, and some of them chose peculiar surroundings to witness the birth of their musical ideas. Some of these surroundings, while they may seem an odd choice to us, were very commonly chosen by literary and musical men of past days. The tavern and the wine room are not now regarded as productive of great ideas. But, be that as it may, much of our greatest music has come to light of day by that route.

Beethoven was often seen to jot down in his tavern and coffee room visits some musical idea that occurred to him; but not so much of his music first saw the light of day there as was the case with Mozart or Schubert, for Beethoven did much of his composition while walking in the country lanes or fields. There is a large gnarled oak tree shown near Vienna in which he frequently sat composing, and utterly oblivious to his surroundings. Many another musician has climbed up to that seat, but to whom has come the inspiration of a Third or Ninth Symphony?

Mozart loved company, wine, and good fellowship, and we read of operatic managers driven to despair by the fact that he would linger in the wine-room or at the billiard table when they were in sad need of perhaps an overture that he had promised, but had put off writing until "to-morrow." But the overture was sure to be forthcoming just at the last moment, for was it not all completed in his head and had it not been for many days or weeks? It was the manual labor of writing out that he shirked. Who that has copied music can blame him?

Schubert lingered much at the tavern. Well, perhaps it was more cheerful than his home. No clatter of plates and glasses or chatter of busy tongues could stay the flow of his beautiful melodies. The fountain must flow even though the world thought naught of the stream. Many of his songs went to the publisher for tenpence apiece, while their author lacked the necessities of life.

Haydn would shut himself up in his sixth story garret and pen the symphonies which paved the way for Mozart and Beethoven. So absorbed in his work would Haydn become that the absence of food or fuel was unknown; the joy of composition was enough to produce oblivion to all minor matters such as food. But a scolding wife may have had somewhat to do with his voluntary isolation. While hunger and music are not incompatible, we find no instances where the muse has been awakened to loftier flights by a scolding wife.

Rossini was another "jolly good fellow" who could compose divinely, not only when at the tavern but after he had been turned out of it. After a night of revelry his compunctions of conscience would cause him to sit down to work at the dawn of day and note his inspirations which were arranged into permanent shape later in the day, perchance while entertaining visitors and friends. Withal, Rossini is noted as being one of the laziest of musicians. It is related that a friend once found him composing in bed, doing his writing there that he might keep warm. A piece of music had fallen off the bed, and, rather than get up after it, Rossini turned over and wrote out another duet to take its place.

Mendelssohn was a well-balanced man, and a man of few idiosyncracies or unpleasant peculiarities. Scholarly and refined, he was in every sense a gentleman. He, like Mozart and others, composed mentally, did all the drudgery of composition in his head, even to the details of orchestration, and left nothing to experiment on paper or at piano. A friend relates that when once calling on Mendelssohn he was told by that composer to sit down and talk to him, and while a lively conversation was carried on, Mendelssohn was all the while writing music as fast as pen could fly, and each measure for each instrument was completed as he went.

Wagner was a genius, and in some ways a queer genius. When he wished to compose he desired absolute quiet and freedom from disturbance, and at these times not even his wife or his favorite servant dared interrupt him. But his queerest fancy was that he could compose better if he were dressed in the costume of the age that the opera which he happened to be working on represented, or the character whose music he was then writing. He wished to place his surroundings in harmony with his mental attitude, and who can say that this peculiarity did not aid him in the wonderful historic accuracy for which his operas are noted.

186.—A KIND ACT.

Paganini was not, as a general thing, noted for deeds of charity. In fact, he became quite a miser in his later days. For this reason the following incident is all the more peculiar.

He happened, in the course of a walk on the streets of Vienna, to come across a miserable little fellow sawing away on an old fiddle. On inquiry the great violinist learned that the boy was trying to maintain an invalid mother and several little brothers and sisters by his street playing. Paganini, touched by the boy's destitute circumstances, took the old fiddle and began to play in his marvelous manner; and after a crowd had collected he himself passed around the hat and collected a goodly sum from the bystanders, adding to it all the money he had in his own pockets.

187.—PUBLIC CRITICISM.

Critics who give vent to their ideas in public places should be sure of their neighbors before using a loud utterance.

Mendelssohn's "Midsummer Night's Dream" overture was first given in Paris. There had been reserved for the composer a seat in one of the prominent boxes, and in the same box were some well-known musical amateurs who were, as it happened, ignorant that the composer of the music to which they were listening was in their company.

After the music had progressed for some time one of the gentlemen got up to take his leave, saying, "Yes, it is good, very good, but we shall not relish the rest;" and they left the box, ignorant of Mendelssohn's presence. Perhaps their idea in leaving was that they were satisfied and pleased and had had the worth of their money, and did not care to undergo an attack of musical indigestion by a continuation of the feast! Perhaps such was the case, but we doubt if Mendelssohn took that view of it.

188.—FUN ON THE STAGE.

Actors and singers have their fun on the stage as well as off. On looking over stage annals we find how this one would take a few whiffs from his cigar when the stage business kept him behind a bit of scenery for a minute; how that one would have a pot of her favorite porter handed up through a trap if occasion offered; how this or that irrelevant remark, made under the breath, came near upsetting the whole course of mimic events. As a piece of stage fun calculated to disturb the gravity of those in the immediate vicinity, the following was a fair sample:—

In the opera of "The Corsair," during a duet which took place on the Corsair's vessel, the audience could see that the people on the stage were suffering in the attempt to restrain their mirth. The cause, invisible to the house, was that some joker, during the rocking motion of the ship, had stuck his head up through a trap and, offering a couple of basins, had solicitously inquired, "Any gentleman require the services of the steward?"

Some actors and singers identify themselves with the character essayed, and their emotions are stirred to their profoundest depths by the joys and sorrows, the good and evil, the love and hate that make up the sum of such characters. Others, on the contrary, consider it a vitiation of art to permit their feelings to dominate them in any degree. They must always be above and superior to the character and the emotion if they are to dominate that emotion and are to be free from the caprice of the moment.

So far do some singers carry the latter idea that their simulation of a part becomes, as we might say, automatic; and while their auditors think them torn and swayed by some passionate emotion, they may be enjoying some bit of by-play on the stage, entirely opposite to the assumed emotion.

For instance, it is related that Mme. Devrient, when, as "Leonora," she offered Haizinger, the "Florestan" of the evening, the crust of bread that the libretto prescribes for the latter, and he was somewhat slow in taking it, impatiently whispered to him:—

"Why in the deuce don't you take it? Do you want it buttered?"

189.—THE THIRTY-THREE VARIATIONS.

Beethoven was an enemy to all quackery and shallow pretensions, and disliked the meaningless style of composition that was so prevalent in his day.

Diabelli, the music publisher, importuned him to write a series of variations, which was a very popular style at that time; but Beethoven declined to write that kind of thing, till, one day, he threw a manuscript in at the publisher's door, with the exclamation:—

"Here are three and thirty for one; but now, for God's sake, leave me in peace!"

Diabelli had asked Beethoven to be one of the fifty composers to contribute to the book of fifty variations; but instead of joining the fifty and writing one, he himself wrote thirty-three variations on the Diabelli theme. This series of variations is one of the best known of his smaller works.

190.—A DESERVED CHASTISEMENT.

Franz Liszt used to take great pleasure in relating various happenings of his youthful days, and none gave him more merriment than the recital of a trick he tried to play on Czerny, with whom be began to study when but nine years of age. Czerny was very kind and Liszt always spoke reverently of him, but he could not forget this prank of his childhood. Probably the consequences of it fixed it definitely in his memory.

It seems that Czerny had kept the youthful Liszt at work considerably longer on a certain Clementi sonata than the latter found agreeable; and so the boy, knowing that complaints to his father would be useless, as good Adam Liszt had great respect for Czerny's teaching abilities, resolved to try a little strategy. So he took the offending sonata and in a certain place marked an unreasonable fingering over some of the notes. Then taking it to his father he innocently said:—

"I think it's about time for me to stop my lessons with Czerny; just see this ridiculous fingering he has marked for me!"

Liszt, senior, was surprised at such work on Czerny's part, but thought he had best see the teacher before taking any action in the matter, and perhaps having had some experience with the youthful Franz before. So he took the book to Czerny and asked for an explanation. Czerny gave him one; and though the two old fellows may have had a hearty laugh at the youngster's ready invention, that did not deter Liszt, *père*, from administering a lively thrashing to a certain young man when he reached home.

191.—IL TROVATORE.

If the following story of Verdi is true, it speaks better for his discernment as to the popular musical taste than it does for his care for the artistic standard of his works. But it probably should be taken *cum grano salis*. At any rate, the Verdi of to-day is not the Verdi of "*Il Trovatore.*"

It is related that when Verdi was putting the finishing touches to his "*Il Trovatore*" he was one day visited by a friend, an able and conscientious musical critic. Verdi played him several portions of the work and asked him

his opinion of them. First came the "Anvil Chorus."
"What do you think of that?" asked the composer.

"Trash!" laconically answered the critic.

Verdi chuckled to himself and said, "Now look at this, and this, and this," at the same time showing other numbers.

"Rubbish!" came the answer.

Verdi showed his delight at these answers to such a degree that his friend demanded to know what he meant by such conduct, when the master replied:—

"My dear friend, I have been composing a popular opera. In it I resolved to please everybody save the great critics and classicists like you. Had I pleased them I should have pleased no one else. What you say assures me of success. In three months '*Il Trovatore*' will be sung, and roared, and whistled, and barrel-organed all over Italy.

And such proved to be the case.

192.—MUSIC *VS.* COMMERCE.

We seldom hear of professional musicians leaving the field of music for that of commerce; or, in this country, of combining commercial business with the profession of music. There can be no serious objection urged to such a combination, however. When one is used to seeing the sign, "John Smith, Teacher of Music and Mender of Kettles," it loses its oddity, and surely no one can object if John teaches his music properly and does not punch another hole in his kettles for each one he mends.

The commercial and the professional instincts are not necessarily opposed to each other, but frequently where one is well developed the other lies dormant. The reason is that it takes years of apprenticeship to develop either, and that which is first developed generally remains the ruling passion.

Mozart had a pupil who, in spite of the greatness of

the teacher, could only be brought to a fair standing as a vocalist and a third or fourth-rate position as a composer. Now, as a general thing a man most admires in himself those abilities which he is least successful in handling. And so it was that Michael Kelly thought more of his abilities as a composer than as a singer.

But after some years of professional life, Kelly found that his income was not satisfactory, and went into the wine business. As a wine importer he prospered. His friends joked him about the change of occupation, and Sheridan, the wit, declared his sign should read: "Michael Kelly, Composer of Wine and Importer of Music."

193.—A NARROW ESCAPE.

The favorite compositions of the public are frequently not the favorite ones of their composers. And very frequent is it that works to which the composer has given the most time, labor and thought find less favor in the eyes of the public than others which are not so satisfactory to the writers.

An example of this is seen in Beethoven's well-known song, "Adelaide." Just as he finished writing this song a friend of his, a Herr Barth, called on him and found him with the manuscript, still wet from the pen, in his hands.

"Here," said Beethoven, holding out the score to his visitor, "look at that; I have just written it and don't like it. There is hardly enough fire in the stove to burn it, but I will try," and he was about to commit it to the flames, when Barth got his permission to try the song. Barth sang it, and liking it very much, persuaded Beethoven not to destroy it. "Adelaide" is now perhaps the most well-known of all Beethoven's songs.

194.—A PYROTECHNIC VIOLONCELLO.

In the " good old times," each player in the orchestra used to have his candlestick fastened to his music desk. We read of one of the old masters who, at a certain place in one composition, had the violinists stop playing and rap the tin shades of their candlesticks with their violin bows, then go on playing as if nothing had happened. And we may remember how old " Papa " Haydn, when his patron prince had a fit of retrenchment and was about to discharge his orchestra, had each one of the players, one at a time, in the progress of the " Farewell " symphony, to rise, blow out his candle, and take his departure, until only the leader was left. This ruse secured the continuation of the orchestra's existence.

It was told by an English clergyman, who was quite a good player on the violoncello, that when his candle began to get dim he would, if a few bars of rest offered opportunity, hastily snuff his candle with his fingers; and, not to spoil the carpet, he would quickly thrust the burnt wick into the sound holes of his 'cello and continue his performance. This was all right, if he wished to make an ash-box of his instrument. But once a wag, observing his peculiar trick, determined to have some fun at his expense, and, just before the playing began, managed to interview the parson's 'cello.

Shortly after the music was well under way, our friend spotted a favorable rest and took occasion to snuff his candle, and deposited the results in his favorite place, when bang! went the 'cello into uncountable pieces, and the good parson sprawled on the floor. Down went 'cello, parson, and all. A 'cello ne'er made so much noise before. Doubtless he treated his next instrument to a better fate than that of an ash-bin.

195.—MISDIRECTED AND REPRESSED TALENT.

Perhaps more talent than the world has ever known, more genius than it has ever recognized, has been repressed and coffined by the obstinacy, stupidity, or prejudice of parents. Many a child, born to astonish the world in some line of art, has been pushed into some uncongenial occupation and its talents lost to humanity.

But in some cases chance, a strong will, or Providence has overruled the plans of the parents, and genius has run its course. There are enough of these cases in music alone to warrant our previous statement that in many instances where the parents' will has prevailed the world has been the loser.

We have only to mention that Händel's parents had arranged that he was to be a lawyer; that Tartini was to be moulded into a priest; that Schubert was compelled to teach school for many a day at a mere pittance; that Schumann could hardly escape from the court room, following his parents' will, to his congenial music; that Weber was kept for some time from his chosen profession; that Zelter was apprenticed to a stone-mason; that Berlioz' parents were determined to make a poor doctor where a great musician was the result; that Bülow became a doctor of law ere he realized that music was his life work,—we have only to realize all these instances and to partially grasp what these men have been to the world to believe that but a part of the talent and genius that the race is endowed with comes to the surface. We can never know the number of cases in which it is repressed, stifled, murdered beyond resurrection in this life.

196.—THE DISCOVERY OF A TENOR.

The tenor is always the *rara avis*. He is hard to find, he is harder to train, and if we may except the *prima donna*, he is hardest to control. No wonder, then, that operatic managers have to start out on tenor-hunting expeditions and are supremely happy if they capture a good specimen of the bird.

In 1820, Count Palffy, the manager of the Vienna Opera, was at his wits' end for a good tenor. So he set out with Salieri, the composer and conductor, to scour the country round, seeking for the voice the latter wished for his last new opera. After chasing down several rumors of wonderful voices, tired and disgusted, they sought the comfort of a village inn. It was a holy day, and the peasants were passing in procession from one shrine to another, singing as they went, the most of them making more noise than music—if the truth be told.

Suddenly Salieri jumped up, rushed out into the crowd and caught one awkward country youth by the arm, commanding him to "Sing, Sing!" The fellow did so, and his tones were full, free, and of wonderful musical quality. But alas! his appearance! Bullet-headed, short, thin, ugly-featured, and — bow-legged! But Salieri cared nothing for his appearance. He declared his legs had nothing to do with his singing, and leading him back to the inn the composer threw open the piano and begged the tenor to begin. He chose an Italian aria, and as the last sounds of a high C died away his listeners warmly encored him, for the long sought-for man was found.

"What is your name?"
"Anton Haizinger."
"And your occupation?"
"Under school teacher."
"Your salary is yearly?"

"One hundred gulden and free lodgings."

"Ye gods! and you have thousands lying in your throat! I engage you immediately for the Royal Opera."

The look of joy which had filled the eyes of the amazed singer died away as, after a moment's hesitation, he replied: "It is impossible; I can't leave here." "Why not, you young fool?" cried Salieri. "I cannot; if I go away from Willersdorf I—I must leave Lise—and—" answered the blushing lover. "Ha, ha!" laughed the count. "Well, my man, I will give you lessons free and a hundred gulden a month the first year and after that double the amount, so you had better let Lise wait a couple of years." "It—no," murmured the amorous swain, "she would marry the miller's son, and I can't go—I won't go," and with a hasty bow he made his departure.

Palffy felt himself outraged, but the wily Italian only laughed and said: "Have him removed to Vienna; the fatal charmer will be faithless, we will accidentally meet him, and he will then gladly accept your offer."

Now, the office of school teacher in Austria is held by governmental appointment. Palffy knew how to pull the wires and some months later found the unsuspecting tenor in Vienna. 'Twas not long ere his beloved Lise verified his darkest forebodings, and found a handsomer man; yielding to the entreaties of Salieri, who had chanced (?) across him, Haizinger sought solace for his wounded heart in the divine art. A year passed and scarlet posters announced the début of this wonderful tenor. He was to appear as "Tamino" in the "Magic Flute," and far and near had been spread the predictions of his wonderful success.

A great crowd had gathered to hear the new tenor. Haizinger was so affected by stage fright that he had to be flung onto the stage by the manager when the time came for his appearance. He was awkward, and even his wonderful voice seemed to have failed him. But later in the evening his self-assurance returned and his singing was rapturously applauded. From that time on his success was assured; and for thirty years he held sway as one of the foremost tenors of all Europe.

197.—A LONG ENCORE NUMBER.

Many audiences contain a certain proportion of people who are unappreciative of the fitness of things, and who proceed to show their enjoyment of singing and playing at the wrong time and in a very obnoxious manner.

The effect of many a fine solo in oratorio or dramatic passage in opera has been utterly spoiled by some of these enthusiastic people whose zeal exceeds their good judgment. The end of a scene or act is the proper place for one to give vent to his enthusiasm.

Ordinary people can frequently get a repetition of some favorite number or occasionally a whole scene; but few can encore the whole opera and have it all over again.

When Cimarosa's "Secret Marriage" was first performed, it was before the Emperor of Austria and his Court. This august personage was delighted with the performance and at the conclusion invited all the singers to a royal feast. Compliments were numerous and the wine flowed liberally. Finally the Emperor desired to hear the opera repeated, and so they one and all went back to the opera house and the whole opera was given again. Imagine this done with one of Wagner's music dramas!

198.—"ENGLYSHE MEETRE."

Dr. Christopher Tye, a prominent musician of the time of "good Queen Bess" once undertook to set to music the Acts of the Apostles. This was no slight task; but the good old doctor plodded through fourteen chapters and then gave it up. His reasons for undertaking such an endless and thankless task is told on the title page as follows:—

"The Actes of the Apoftles, tranflated into Englyfhe meetre, and dedicated to the kynge's moft excellente majeftye, by Criftfer Tye, doctor in musyke, and one of the gentylmen of hys grace's mofte honourable chapell, wyth notes to eche chapter, to fynge, and alfo to playe upon the flute, very neceffary for ftudentes after their ftudye, to fyte theyr wyttes and alfoe for all Chriftians that cannot fynge, to reade the good and godlye ftoryes of the lives of Chrift and his apoftles."

One verse will suffice to show the improvements that were made on the usual reading in order to get the Scripture into "Englyfhe meetre." It reminds one of the arrangements of the Psalms in the books of certain Psalm-singing sects. The verse quoted is the first of the fourteenth chapter.

> "It chanced in Iconium,
>   As they oft tymes dyd ufe,
> Together they into dyd come
>   The fynagogue of Jues;
> Where they dyd preache and only feke
>   God's grace then to atcheve,
> That they so spake to Jue and Greke
>   That manye dyd beleve."

Composers now-a-days think they must have words that furnish some inspiration. What would they do if confined to such a *libretto* as the above sample?

But those were the days of counterpoint, of the mathematical in music; and the composer wrote his vocal fugue without reference to the sentiment of the words. Though Händel wrote much that was expressive of feeling, we defy one to find much sentiment in some of his works. Take the "Amen," "All We Like Sheep," and "For Unto Us," choruses in the "Messiah," for example. They are simply fugues, set to words, to be sure, but essentially instrumental in character. No one would think of writing that style of vocal music now-a-days.

The day of writing instrumental music for voices is past. Our time demands true sentiment in words and a corresponding sentiment in the music.

199.—"THE DEVIL ON TWO STICKS."

The following story of Haydn rests on a rather insecure foundation for truthfulness; but we give it for what it is worth.

There was, in Vienna, an actor named Kurtz. This man, wanting the music arranged for a certain farce or light opera, called on Haydn to see if he could do the work satisfactorily. Haydn declined the commission. But Kurtz insisted that he should try. Said he, "Sit down at the piano and play an accompaniment to my actions." Then Kurtz imitated the motions of a swimmer, throwing himself on a chair for support; suddenly he called out, "I am sinking! save me! I shall be drowned!" Meanwhile Haydn played music fitting to the situation and delighted the comic actor with the result. At last Haydn consented to write out the music he had played and set it to the opera. This was the origin of "The Devil on Two Sticks."

200.—IMPOSITIONS ON MUSICIANS.

There are many drafts made on musicians' time and good nature that thoughtfulness on the part of their friends and acquaintances might obviate.

People do not realize the time and effort it takes to prepare for a public performance. This does not matter so much if the musician be an amateur with plenty of leisure; but if he be a professional, busy with teaching or playing, and with hardly leisure to keep posted on his own specialty, let alone keeping abreast with the advance of the world along other lines, it would seem to require considerable " cheek " to add to the musician's work and subtract from his pleasure by such thoughtless requests.

Of course it is not in all cases that such an invitation brings a subtraction of pleasure, for it is a real pleasure to sing and play to an appreciative audience, be it large or small. But the trouble is, that in many cases he is desired to sing or play something light and trifling in order to amuse a non-musical audience.

If he has any conscience and refuses to give trash,—if he chooses some music that is really good, music that he is not ashamed to see on the programme, his hearers are not interested. But if, on the other hand, he descends to the level of the musical education of the average person, he loses in artistic self-respect.

In the larger cities musicians generally receive a stated sum for their services in such affairs, as funerals, weddings, private gatherings, and musicales. One way of getting entertainment out of some well-known musician is to invite him to dine, thinking he can hardly decline to play or sing when enjoying his entertainer's hospitality. But even this scheme is not always successful, as the following shows:—

When Fischer, the celebrated oboe player, who was remarkable for the oddity of his manner, played concertos at the grand concerts given at the rotunda in Dublin, a noble lord, who had been enraptured with the rare talent he displayed, came up to him, and having complimented him, gave him a pressing invitation to sup with him the following evening, adding, "You will bring your oboe with you."

Fischer, who was a little nettled at that sort of invitation, hastily replied, "My lord, my oboe never sups."

A similar story is told of a celebrated violinist who was invited to dine at a certain mansion, and after dinner was asked to play. Upon saying that he did not have his violin with him, his hostess expressed surprise that he had not brought it. But he excused himself by saying that his violin had no necessity for dining.

201.—THE HALLELUJAH CHORUS.

The uninitiated who attend a performance of Händel's "Messiah" are frequently surprised when, at the first notes of the "Hallelujah Chorus," the whole audience rises to its feet. Some think this custom arose from the desire to pay homage to the words. But if that be the case, they might well stand during the whole oratorio. Others imagine that it was because of the intense enjoyment in the music some audience had a hundred and fifty years ago, which brought them to their feet.

But this is said to be the truth of the matter: At one of the early performances of this grand oratorio, the king of England, George I, was present. During the singing of this chorus, His Majesty, either greatly enjoying the music, or perhaps simply desiring to change his position, stood up; at once the courtiers and people followed suit, thus originating a custom which is quite pleasant in view of the physical relief afforded by the change of posture in a two-hour performance.

202.—BEETHOVEN *A LA* CUPID.

Beethoven was a man of stern and rugged disposition, a man whose exterior was rough and whose actions were frequently peculiar; but at the same time he had a very gentle and kindly side to his nature. Those who did not happen to see his character displayed in that light thought him hard-hearted and boorish, but that was because they saw him at his worst.

Beethoven had his own love affairs, and, as the following incident shows, was not averse to helping other people in theirs.

In 1811, Beethoven was staying at Toplitz, and took his meals at a certain inn where, as it happened, an actor named Lowe, was accustomed to dine, and, at the same time, engage in the enjoyable occupation of making love to the landlord's daughter. The actor and his fair damsel had arranged that Lowe should come for his dinners after the other guests had gone, and only Beethoven remained. They calculated that he would not be an offensive third party, because of his deafness.

But, as the stories generally go, the irate parents stepped in and ordered the actor to discontinue his visits. This he was compelled to do, and for a time the lovers were disconsolate. But who ever knew of an actor so easily discouraged? Lowe was seized by a bright idea. He met Beethoven on one of his daily walks, having purposely taken the road frequented by the master. Beethoven recognized him and at once asked why he had deserted the inn. This gave Lowe a chance to tell his tale of woe and to timidly ask Beethoven to take charge of a letter to the maiden. "Why not?" pleasantly observed the gruff composer, "you mean what is right."

He placed the note in his pocket and started off without taking any more notice of the actor. Lowe started after him saying:—

"I beg your pardon, Herr van Beethoven, that is not all."

"Well, what then?" said the master.

"You must also bring back the answer."

"Well, then, meet me here at this time to-morrow," and again Beethoven started on his way.

As may be imagined Lowe was promptly at the place next day and received from his lady-love the reply at Beethoven's hands. And in this way the greatest of composers continued to serve the lovers as long as he stayed in that place.

203.—WAGNER AND THE BEGGARS.

Wagner had a favorite walk near his Bayreuth home, which ran through some two miles of beautiful scenery, and over this route he could wander undisturbed, for the little Franconian peasant boys and girls who saw him from afar would not molest him, having heard from their parents that the affairs of Germany would somehow get out of joint if they disturbed the great man in his meditation.

One day a small maiden was so hardy as to loiter in his path and beg for a *Silbergroschen.* With a smile of surprise Wagner lifted the child, kissed her, and presented her with a golden tenthaler piece, for, though keen to make money, he was free in expenditure when he had any whim to gratify. The news of his liberality brought out a troop of Franconian beggars of all sizes; but the composer's mood had changed, and he plied the backs of his tormentors with the famous ebony and gold staff given him by the Männergesangverein of Vienna. The Burgomaster of Bayreuth was much agitated over this affair, and had serious thoughts of providing the composer with an escort of policemen, so that his path might be kept clear every day.

For some time Wagner did not put in an appearance at Angermann's Brauerei, where he had been accustomed to spend an hour or two every afternoon; and it was rumored that he intended to leave the city. But he had only secluded himself for one of his periodical paroxysms of composition, during which he was unapproachable; but after he had again returned to the outer world he came back to his usual haunts, and magnanimously forgave the beggars he had beaten.

204.—VOX POPULI.

The day has passed when a singer could be forced on the public by royal favor, irrespective of the singer's worth or the public's willingness. But in the last century such things were still possible.

In a certain city in France a royal favorite, named Laulaire, was being forced before the public through favor in high places. She was received the first evening with hisses, whistles, and cat-calls. These being prohibited by the governor, the next night the whole audience seemed to be afflicted with an epidemic of catarrh, and the coughing and sneezing during that performance was something wonderful. But the governor had a remedy for catarrh; it was heroic but successful. When some of the audience were removed to prison the rest had a very quick recovery. The next night a young man brought a small dog to the theater with him, on whose tail he would accidentally step, and then the people cried, "Take the animal away!" but with their glances directed toward the singer and not to the diminutive canine. This resulted in more arrests.

The following night the climax came. One of the auditors was so incensed that he threw his boot at the singer. Instructions were then given to the soldiers at the doorways to arrest whoever came out with but one boot on. As it happened, the very first man to appear was minus a shoe. He was at once arrested. But strange to say, the next man also had a shoe missing, and the next, and the next. Every man in the house was in the same plight, and the soldiers were thoroughly disgusted. The next day the singer gave up the contest and left the place.

205.—WHAT'S IN A NAME.

In answer to this question we must reply, everything, to some people. To illustrate this we can do no better than to quote some of Liszt's experiences. When he was a boy he used occasionally to enjoy a prank at the expense of his audiences. He writes:

"When I was very young, I often amused myself with playing school-boy tricks, of which my auditors never failed to become the dupes. I would play the same piece, at one time as of Beethoven, at another as of Czerny, and, lastly, as my own. The occasion on which I passed myself off for the author, I received both protection and encouragement: 'It really was not bad for my age.'

The day I played it under the name of Czerny I was not listened to; but when I played it as being the composition of Beethoven, I made certain of the 'bravos' of the whole assembly."

This proves what is frequently true,—that people enjoy the composer's name more than they do his music. Liszt also gives another experience which proves that to many people the name matters more than the music. It was at a time when he had been bringing out many of Beethoven's works. Says he: "Beethoven's glory is consecrated. The most ignorant among the ignorant shelter themselves behind his colossal name; and even envy herself, in her impotence, avails herself of it, as with a club, to crush all contemporary writers who appear to elevate themselves above their fellows. This winter I devoted several musical performances almost exclusively to the bringing forward duets, trios, and quintets of Beethoven. I was sure of being wearisome, but I was also sure that no one dare say so. There were really brilliant displays of enthusiasm; one might have easily been deceived, and thought that the crowd were subjugated by the power of genius; but at one of the last performances an inversion in the order of the programme completely put an end to the error. Without any explanation, a trio of Pixis was played in the place of one by Beethoven.

"The 'bravos' were more numerous, more brilliant than ever, and when the trio of Beethoven took the place assigned to that of Pixis, it was found to be cold, mediocre, and even tiresome, so much so, indeed, that many made their escape, thinking it was a piece of impertinence in Monsieur Pixis to presume to be listened to by an audience that had assembled to admire the masterpieces of the great man.

"I am far from inferring by what I have just related that they were wrong in applauding Pixis' trio, but he himself could not but have received with a smile of pity the applause of a public capable of confounding two compositions and two styles so totally different; for, most assuredly, the persons who could fall into such a mistake are wholly unfit to appreciate the real beauties in his works."

206.—A COSTLY FIDDLE.

Jacob Stainer, of Absam, in the Tyrol, lives in the records of violin construction as the greatest of German makers, if not the only one worthy of more than passing mention. He worked in the latter part of the seventeenth century, and his violins came to be highly valued even in his own day. There is a record that at Dresden he sold a violin to a certain count in the suite of King Charles VI for a goodly sum of gold; and besides this the count undertook to supply him as long as he lived with a hundred florins every month, a good dinner each day, a new suit of clothes every year, as well as two casks of beer, his lodging, fire, and lights. As Stainer lived some sixteen years after this, the violin must have cost the count a goodly sum, all told.

207.—BACH'S GREAT WORKS. HOW ENJOYED BY SOME.

Bach is one of the most famous names in the history of musical art. There are records of 247 Bachs, who, in one way or another, distinguished themselves both by composition for, and performance on, the organ. John Sebastian Bach's last and in some respects greatest work, "The Art of Fugue," was left unfinished by the failure of his eyes. His friends urged him in his old age to write a treatise on fugue and fugue making. He started to do so, but, after writing a few pages, threw away the work in disgust, exclaiming, "I cannot teach by precept, only by example," and then recommenced the work on a different plan. He took one simple subject, and on it wrote sixteen fugues and four canons, in every style of composition. This work on "Fugue," the "Passion Music," and the "Well-Tempered Clavichord" are considered the most splendid results of his genius.

But while this grand music of the old "cantor" of Leipzig is, to some, an exposition of the highest form of art, to others it is nothing but a dreary succession of sounds which falls on ears unattuned to its grandeur. But there is still another class, though we hope it be small, that sees for Bach's music a purpose which, though it may savor of utility, does not of dignity.

The use to which a proportion of modern concert-goers puts Bach's music has its precedent in the custom of a certain count who lived in Bach's day. This noble was particularly fond of Bach's music, and at the same time was occasionally troubled with insomnia.

At these times he would have one of his musicians play a particular set of variations "of a soothing and rather cheerful character," as we are told, variations that were written for him by Bach, and which so pleased him that he presented Bach with quite a sum of money.

We are not accustomed to thinking of Bach's music as soporific in character, and yet if one glances over an average audience during a programme containing a goodly amount of Bach, we may see that with some people it has that tendency.

208.—PECULIAR ENGLISH.

Not every singer, even though he be able to excite the plaudits of thousands by his song language, can succeed in making a hit by spoken language. The well-known singer, Brignoli, seemed to be successful in both lines, as witness the following. It became necessary, one evening, for some one to apologize for the non-appearance of the *prima donna*, as she was suffering from a sore throat. The manager sent Brignoli before the curtain to make the necessary excuses. So the tenor went forward and said:—

"Ladies and gentlemen, I regret to zay zat Madame N—— ees a leetle hoarse zees evening."

Peals of laughter greeted this announcement; the tenor looked puzzled, and, thinking the people had misunderstood him, he roared out:—

"I zay zat Madame N—— ees a leetle hoarse zees evening!"

This was greeted by another explosion of mirth; then, to cap this lucid explanation, some one in the gallery roared out, "Then if she is a little horse why not trot her out?" That explained to the puzzled tenor the cause of the laughter and he was then able to join in the fun.

Another instance of a musician's English failing him at a crucial moment was when, some years ago, Paderewski played in Boston with the Nikisch orchestra. One of the orchestral soloists became very much excited at the private rehearsal, and stood up and made a little speech to the orchestra, fairly glowing with patriotic pride: "You see, Paderewski—my countryman—a Pole—he is like Cæsar—'He came, he saw, he *enquired!*'"

209.—ORIGINAL TAPESTRY.

"I was not rich enough to buy good pictures, so I made myself some tapestry such as I am sure every one cannot have." The tapestry in question was truly such as few could have and still fewer could manufacture; for it was Haydn that spoke and the hangings referred to consisted of over forty compositions in canon form, mounted and hung in his bedroom in the way customary for paintings and engravings. Had it been some composers we might think it a monumental exhibition of vanity or pride in their own abilities, but Haydn's nature was hardly of that kind.

210.—THE MANUAL LABOR OF COMPOSITION.

It is hard for us to realize the amount of laborious writing and copying there is for a composer to do before he has his manuscript ready for the printer. The manual labor necessary is enough to deter one from composition, even were he gifted with the composing ability. A good way for the student to appreciate this is to try copying, in a clear, exact hand, a few pages of complicated music, or, better still, transposing a few pieces from one key into another.

Beethoven, although averse to details, and though not as profuse with his signs of expression and nuance as some composers, has given us, in his manuscripts, an example of care and exactness, as well as of deep thought and continued study.

In his overture in C, Op. 115 (the manuscript of which, by the way, he sold to a London publisher for £15), besides the labor of writing the mere notes, it was no inconsiderable task to properly indicate the dynamic effects intended. For instance, the sign *sf.* occurs in this score more than fifteen hundred times, and besides this there are hundreds of other signs such as *p.*, *piu.*, *pp.*, *f.*, *ff.*, *fff.*, *sfp.*, *sfpp.*, *cres.*, *dim.*, etc.

It means something besides God-given genius to be a great composer,—something more than the ability to improvise music. It means days and years of slavish toil.

211.—A BURIAL PLACE DENIED.

The incidents connected with Paganini's death and burial were as peculiar as was the life of that very peculiar man.

The great violinist died at Nice, Italy, in 1840. When a priest came to administer the last sacrament, Paganini, not believing that death was so near, postponed this final consolation of the church. The priest departed, and in a few hours the violinist died without the presence of a clergyman. This priest reported that Paganini had refused the sacrament; so, when application was made for a burial permit, it was denied by the church. The Governor of the province, and even the King, petitioned the Bishop to allow the body to be interred in sacred soil, but the decree was not altered.

A law suit was entered upon by the heirs, and a waiting room was provided for the corpse, where it could pass the time till sentence was pronounced.

While this law suit was being carried on in a bitter way to secure a good Catholic burial according to the rites of his church, and while Paganini was quietly and patiently awaiting the decision as to where should be his last resting place, a Jew proposed to one of Paganini's friends to purchase the remains, offering 30,000 francs for the embalmed mummy, for the purpose of exhibiting it in England and elsewhere!

The body reposed in a pest house for three years, awaiting interment. Finally a funeral was conceded by the Pope, and in a small boat the remains of the greatest of violinists were carried to Genoa, his birthplace, and in 1845 were interred near Parma, in a splendid tomb erected by his son.

Paganini left to his son a fortune amounting to £80,000. In his will he left a fixed sum for masses which were to be said for the repose of his soul. It is certainly to be hoped that his soul found rest sooner than it was permitted by the church for his body to rest.

His native city of Genoa has preserved Paganini's violin, a valuable Guarnerius, and since his death no hand has touched it save one, that of his pupil Sivori, for whom it was removed from its glass case.

212.—VON BÜLOW'S PECULIARITIES.

Von Bülow was more Gallic than Teutonic in his bright sayings and caustic wit. He was a curious fellow and fascinating despite his peculiarities. With his passage from the stage the musical art of our day lost one of its most representative men.

He was so bothered by admiring ladies who requested his signature that he had his secretary write them, and was greatly bored if this useful personage was absent and he had to pen his name himself. But he recompensed himself by writing as abominably as possible.

At one concert where he played only Beethoven sonatas, he seemed to be very happy over the fact that the audience applauded him most in that sonata, which, as he said, "I played like a pig."

He took a peculiar course toward a conductor who came to his assistance at the last moment, in a certain concert, the musician who should have conducted being intoxicated and unable to appear. At the end of the concert von Bülow went to the one who had volunteered so kindly, and was very effusive to him before the audience, and even embraced him. He was extravagant in testifying his satisfaction, and there was much applause at the scene. Von Bülow, after the concert, said, "Did you see my little scene with the conductor?" When asked why he was so desperately demonstrative, and why he made such a scene, he replied: "Ah! you ask that? I expected you would." But why not? It did me no harm, and it may do him good. Besides, I was so grateful that the conducting was no worse, that I could not restrain myself." After having been recalled three or four times at one concert by deafening cheers, he was prevailed upon, almost by force, to sit down again before the piano and play another piece. Satan knows what deviltry possessed him, but in mad defiance of the public he began the "Marseillaise" and went through it with intense energy and feeling, unheeding the auditors, who, after the first moment of incredulous surprise, rose to their feet and attempted to drown the hated strains of the French revolutionary hymn in groans and hisses.

213.—NOT AT FIRST SIGHT.

There are different ways of singing at sight. So Händel found out one time, on a visit to Ireland. He was detained at a certain point for several days, and wishing to prove some copied parts of the "Messiah," he arranged to have several choristers of the town where he was, meet him and study the music with him. But one fellow failed so completely that Händel turned on him in wrath and cried:—

"You schountrel! Did you nod dell me dat you could sing at sight?"

"Yis, sorr, Oi did. And Oi can; but not at *first* soight!"

Very many readers at first sight seem to be blessed with the gift only of "second sight."

214.—RESTORING AN ORGAN.

Many of the pipe organs used in our churches are poor affairs. The church committee that is vested with purchasing power seems generally to be chosen, like jurymen, on account of entire absence of knowledge of the subject in hand,—in this case of music in general and organs in particular. The result is that they are at the mercy of the organ builder in matters of construction, though he is at their mercy in the matter of money; for in many cases the main consideration is to expend as little as possible and get in return not the best action, stop combinations, and material,—but the greatest possible quantity of external display.

Consequently we find organs having the tone quality poor, the key action hard and stiff, the stops requiring the muscle of a Sandow for manipulation, the swell slamming like a window blind, the tremulant rattling like a wheezy horse, and the balance of pedal and manual registers such as to make the word "balance" a misnomer, to say nothing of the pipes being generally out of tune.

True, these various ills may not often coexist in the same organ; but frequently we find several of them dwelling in—discord together.

The cause of this state of affairs is anxiety, when purchasing, to get quantity rather than quality, and afterward allowing the instrument to go for months and years without proper attention. An organ should be regulated, adjusted, and tuned at least once a year, by a competent man, and not by the "tramp" tuners that leave an instrument in worse condition than they found it.

It is poor economy to try and rebuild or restore an organ. After it reaches a certain age it is best to replace the instrument with a new one, having used in it as many of the old pipes as the builder sees fit. Improvements are constantly being made in mechanism, and the latest and best action should be secured rather than patch up an old one.

Snetzler, an English organ builder, but originally from Germany, once reported to a committee concerning the restoration of an old organ in these words :—

"Gentlemen, your organ be vort von hundert pound just now. Ven you spend von hundert pounds on him to fix him up he will den be vort fifty!"

215.—AN EXCITING MUSICAL DUEL.

Madame Malibran was a woman of delicate and responsive nervous organization, but with a fiery spirit and an indomitable will. On the occasion of her second marriage, after the ceremony had taken place and the guests assembled at her home, she asked the great pianist Thalberg to play. He did so, but only on condition that she should sing. Though tired and nervous from the fatigues of the day, she sang, but in a manner that was hardly like her normal self.

When she had finished she turned to him, saying, "Now it's your turn, Mr. Thalberg." Then a musical duel took place which we will let an eye-witness describe:—

"He had not been married that morning, and the presence of such a listener putting him on his mettle without unduly exciting him, he drew from his instrument all that wealth and suppleness of tone which made it the most harmonious of singers. As he went on, Malibran's face gradually changed, her lack lustre eyes became bright, the mouth gradually expanded, the nostrils began to quiver. When his last note had died away she said: 'Admirable! Now it's my turn.' And forthwith she intones a second piece. But this time there was no appearance of either fatigue or listlessness, and Thalberg, absolutely bewildered, sat watching the transformation without being able to believe in it. It was no longer the same woman, it was no longer the same voice, and all he could do was to say in a low voice, 'Oh, madame, madame!' She had barely finished when he said animatedly, 'Now it's my turn.'

"Only those who heard Thalberg on that evening may perhaps flatter themselves that they have known the 'whole man.' Part of Malibran's genius had communicated itself to his masterly but severe style; he had caught the feverish passion of her soul. Currents of electric fluid ran from his fingers over the keyboard. But he could not finish his piece. At the last bars Malibran burst into violent sobs, she hid her face in her hands, she shivered from head to foot, and we had to carry her into the next room. She did not remain there very long; in a few moments she reappeared, with proud uplifted head and flashing eyes, and, rushing to the piano, she exclaimed: 'Now it's my turn.' She resumed that strange duel, and sang, one after another, four pieces, increasing in grandeur as she went, unconscious of everything around her in her growing excitement, until she noticed Thalberg's face bathed in tears as her's had been."

216.—AN INTERRUPTED STRAIN.

Musicians are sometimes affected in composing by events of the most trivial kind. It was a casual and unimportant matter of this character that accounts for a certain peculiarity in one of Schumann's compositions. In his "Humoreske" the reader may remember that the short section headed "Einfach und Zart" is interrupted by a short theme of entirely different character from the context. A member of the Schumann family gives the following as a reason for this peculiar break in the continuity of the piece:—

"When the master was engaged upon the section referred to, a strolling carol seller came down the road, followed by a crowd of children, and calling attention to his wares by blowing a pipe upon which he could play three notes. With the flow of his sentimental melody arrested by the itinerant and obstreperous music, Schumann at once proceeded to make the pipe theme the motive of an intermezzo, accompanied by a throng of semiquavers to stand for the children. The episode dies away (the man's pipe becomes faint in the distance), and the composer then resumes his interrupted strain."

217.—A MUSICAL TRAGEDY.

The attributed history of the Italian musician, Stradella, might supply a good plot for as bloodthirsty an opera as any one of modern Italian school of opera composers might wish. Indeed it has been so used by two composers, Flotow and Niedermeyer, and it is a coincidence that both operas on this subject were brought out in the same year, 1837. There is no doubt that

Stradella was a musician of much ability, as is attested by some 150 compositions of his that still exist. He died in the latter part of the seventeenth century (about 1681), but there is no reliable historical record as to the manner of his death or that it was brought about by the chain of events related in the story. But to the tale; we give it for what it is worth:—

Alessandro Stradella was, during his life, one of the foremost musicians in Italy. One historian calls him Stradel, and so it is possible that he was originally from north of the Alps, and his name plain Alexander Stradel. At any rate he was celebrated as a violinist, a singer, and a composer. Among his pupils in Venice was Ortensia, a beautiful young lady, whom a certain nobleman had enticed from her parents. Teacher and pupil soon fell in love with each other and fled from Venice. The noble, thus deprived of his fair mistress, swore vengeance and dispatched two assassins who were at any cost to overtake and remove the offenders in true Italian style. After searching in various places, these ruffians learned that Stradella and the fair one were living in Rome, and there they quickly hastened.

Learning that on a certain night Stradella would go from his house to a church where an oratorio of his composition was to be given, and in which he was to sing the principal part, they determined to surprise him and Ortensia on their way home, and put into effect their master's wishes. They traced the composer into the church and kept close eye on him throughout the service. But one element they had not calculated on—that was the effect of Stradella's music. It so overpowered them and softened their hearts that they gave up their purpose, and instead related to him their mission.

That night the lovers fled to Turin, and the hired assassins went to Venice and reported that the couple had escaped to Turin and that they were afraid to follow them there. Still mad for vengeance the nobleman secured the services of two other bandits more desperate than the others, and, disguising them as merchants, sent them off to Turin.

Meanwhile Stradella had secured the good will and assistance of a certain duchess who placed Ortensia in a convent and kept the musician in her own service as chapel master. He kept within the palace walls for some time, till one night, thinking that vengeance no longer pursued him he ventured to take a walk on the ramparts of the city. But the assassins were on the watch and quickly attacking him, left him with what they supposed fatal wounds.

As good fortune would have it, Stradella recovered from the attack and signalized his recovery by marrying his charmer. But such good fortune was too good to last. The Venetian noble was continually on his track, having sworn never to give up his pursuit of revenge. A short time after his wedding, Stradella visited Genoa to superintend the performance of one of his operas, and it was there that vengeance overtook him and his wife. The assassins easily discovered their stopping place, and, gaining entrance to their bedchamber, stabbed them both, this time fatally.

218.—BEETHOVEN'S GRATITUDE.

In spite of his occasional petulance of temper, Beethoven had a warm heart for those in distress; and, moreover, he seldom forgot any one who had rendered him a good service, although he did at times impute selfish motives to his friends when they advised him for what they considered his own good. When his mother lay ill at his old home in Bonn, he hurried to her from Vienna, but arrived in time only to witness her death. After the funeral he found himself reduced to the verge of starvation. Had it not been for the violinist, Ries, who advanced him some funds, he would have suffered the pangs of hunger.

Many years afterward, the son of this violinist came to Beethoven for musical instruction and presented a note of introduction from his father. The great composer gave him a warm reception, a thing many aspirants for his instruction did not receive; and besides having his request that Beethoven should oversee his musical education granted, he was given this message to his old father in Bonn:—

"Tell your father I have not forgotten the death of my mother."

219.—CHOLERIC HÄNDEL.

The possession of genius seems to give a man the right to set at defiance the conventionalities of life. Beethoven was somewhat rough and unmannerly, and acted in a way, when in polite society, that, were it not for his genius, would have entitled him to the appellation, "a boor."

Händel was also in a position where he could snap his fingers at some of the senseless doings of the society of his day as well as at the wilfulness of his singers.

Together with all musicians who ever took part in any concert or musical entertainment, Händel greatly desired that the performance be not interrupted by the late or noisy entrance of careless patrons. Even when conducting performances at the residences of royalty, if the young Prince and Princess of Wales were late in their coming he would give them a good scolding. And if, after the rehearsal had begun, the maids of honor or other attendants made any disturbance it so irritated the master that he would not confine himself to rebukes, but would swear at the offenders and call them names; and then the good princess would calm them with, "Hush, hush, Händel is in a passion."

220.—MUSIC *VS.* CONVERSATION.

Music is one of the most powerful known incentives to conversation. To appreciate this statement one has only to use his powers of observation at the next social gathering he may happen to attend. Things may have been as dead as a door nail before, but let some one begin to play or sing and at once numerous individuals more sociable than polite feel urged to start conversation with their neighbors. Such an occasion seems quite a test of true politeness, and yet were one to intimate on such an occasion that any law of good breeding had been infringed much offense would be taken.

Were the musicians to follow the plan taken by Corelli, the great violinist, a better state of things might gradually come about.

On one occasion he was performing at the house of Cardinal Ottoboni for a select gathering. Observing the cardinal taking part in what seemed to be an interesting conversation with a guest while he was playing, Corelli laid down his instrument in the middle of his performance, politely remarking, "I fear my music interrupts your Grace's conversation!"

221.—THE WORLD'S REWARD TO GENIUS.

Wealth and great musical genius do not seem to go hand in hand. Some few of the greater composers have achieved wealth. Some were born to riches, and a few have had riches thrust upon them.

There are some plants that flourish on the bleak mountain side, amid storm and wind. Musical genius seems of such a nature. Adverse circumstances have surrounded nearly all who have been in the highest degree possessed of this gift. It would seem that such adversity were necessary to the development of genius.

Beethoven was the son of an impecunious singer of

irregular habits; Mozart had a continual struggle with poverty; Schubert was frequently on the verge of starvation; Bach was known to go barefooted for want of shoes; Rossini was set to earning his own living when but seven years old; Haydn, the son of a poor wheelwright, acted as a servant and valet in order to obtain instruction; Weber, Spohr, Glück, Wagner—but why go on? All went through the "storm and stress" period and all came out conquerors; not in a financial, but in an intellectual sense.

This would seem to prove that poverty is an impetus to great works. Affluence and ease have produced little in this field of labor. They seem to enervate the mind and to stifle genius. Doubtless, there have been many talented men among the wealthy classes of different countries, perhaps some with the genius of Haydn or Weber; but the motive power was lacking. They were born under the same condition that Rossini secured for himself—a condition that was fatal to even his energy.

Rossini achieved wealth and fame in the first half of his life. Nearly everything he produced was greeted with the acclamations of the musical world. Wealth poured in upon him. Then, when "William Tell" did not receive the customary amount of applause, Rossini retired from active composition, and for the last forty years of his life he did nothing but enjoy the fruits of his early talents and industry. This was the only instance, as far as we know, where a really great composer has allowed the productivity of the best years of his life to be blighted by the influence of wealth.

But Rossini was an exception. Poverty followed some of the great geniuses, even in their latest day. Others accumulated only a tithe of what would have been the reward of equal genius in other walks of life.

Mozart left to his family but sixty gulden in money and personal property to the amount of four hundred gulden.

The inventory of Schubert's effects, which consisted

entirely of wearing apparel and a little music, showed sixty-three gulden. Yet Schubert left as a legacy to the world six hundred songs, ten symphonies and numerous other compositions, from which the publishers reaped a golden harvest.

Beethoven fared better. After his death his furniture and music were sold; and when the expenses of his last sickness had been paid the residue amounted to nine thousand gulden, *i.e.*, something over eight hundred pounds. Well did the trustee of his estate remark, "He was only a master; he knew but his art, leaving to others the gain."

Truly, success is posthumous.

222.—AN OBESE BASSO.

The great basso, Lablache, besides being a very tall man was remarkably large and heavy. In fact, he was so large that, when living in London, he had a cab of extraordinary size built for his use, as the ordinary "growler" persisted in breaking down under his weight; and it was considerable more trouble to get out from a wrecked vehicle than it was to get into it. It is told that when he was one time singing in Havana, as he was riding along the street in a cab, the bottom of the carriage was crushed through by his heavy weight, letting his feet down on the ground. The cabman knew nothing of the accident but continued to drive on, serenely unconscious of his employer's plight. So there was nothing for the elephantine basso to do but to run along, keeping up with the cabby's pace, all the while calling to the driver to stop. Those who saw Lablache's plight had a hearty laugh at the spectacle of those fat legs sticking out from under the cab.

At another time he was cast in an opera for the part of a prisoner who had wasted away by years of incarceration in the dungeon. When this mountain of flesh came walking down the stage singing, "I am starving," the whole house broke into a roar of laughter, and the obese basso had to make an ignominious exit, followed by the shouts of the audience.

What a pair Lablache and Mme. Alboni would have made.

223.—PRESERVING IDENTITY.

The dislike that Mendelssohn had to being mistaken for Meyerbeer has had parallels among musicians of lesser note.

The public hardly has a fair chance to see the features of the conductor as he sits with his back to the audience. Sir Julius Benedict and Arditi, both most excellent opera conductors were much averse to being taken for each other. The fact that Sir Julius was bald-headed did not help matters any, for Arditi also suffered from a depletion of hirsute appendage.

On one occasion Benedict was seen to go into the *prima donna's* dressing room just before the evening's performance, and, taking up a hairbrush carefully arrange his scanty locks so that they would cover as much space as possible. When asked his reason for the re-arrangement he answered, "Oh, I don't want to be taken for Arditi while I am directing."

Shortly afterward in came Arditi and with a couple of brushes began to so arrange his hair as to cover as little as possible of the baldness. When questioned as to his reason for making himself look as bald as possible, he said, "Why, I don't want to be mistaken for Benedict."

224.—A GREAT GERMAN SONGSTRESS.

Henrietta Sontag had to combat a great prejudice from her very first appearance on the stage. This was the idea held by the musical world of that day that a German could not sing. Old Frederick the Great was not alone in this prejudice. Sontag made her *début* in

1820, when but fifteen years of age; and so short of stature was she at that time, that they had her wear shoes with heels four inches high. As time went on, she became one of a group of great sopranos, of which the others were Fodor, Pasta, Malibran, and Catalani.

In Berlin Sontag met Count Rossi, and, as an ardent attraction sprang up between them, they became engaged, but the engagement was kept a secret for some time, owing to the probable opposition of the Count's relations, the Bonapartes. In Paris she captivated the heart of Charles DeBeriot; but, true to Count Rossi, she refused the hand of this celebrated violinist.

DeBeriot was greatly dejected at his refusal. Mme. Malibran, meeting him shortly after this event, exerted herself to arouse him from his melancholy; and, in fact, she succeeded so well that his admiration and regard turned to this beautiful Spanish singer, and he consoled himself for the loss of Sontag by marrying Malibran. In after years Malibran was a bitter rival of Sontag, as she never forgot that the latter was DeBeriot's first love.

A year or two after Sontag's marriage to Rossi the union was made public, and, as Countess Rossi, she bade farewell to the stage. Then came a period of twenty years of happy life with her husband at the different European capitals. But, in 1849, her husband having lost his property by political changes, Sontag returned to the operatic stage, where, although she had to enter the lists against the talents and popularity of Jenny Lind, she renewed her triumphs both in Europe and America. She had restored the family fortune by her income on the stage, and was about to leave it forever, when she was attacked by the cholera in our southern climate, at the City of Mexico, and in a few hours was dead.

225.—A SIGHT FOR THE BOYS.

Moscheles tells the following story of Beethoven: "One morning I went to call on Beethoven quite early, and found him still lying in bed; but he happened to be in remarkably good spirits, and jumping up immediately without dressing, placed himself as he was, at the window looking out on the street, to examine my arrangement of certain numbers from 'Fidelio.'

"Soon a crowd of boys collected under the window, and seeing them he roared out:—

"'Now, what do those confounded boys want?'

"I laughed and pointed to his slightly adorned figure.

"'Yes, yes, you are quite right,' said he, and hastily put on a dressing gown."

226.—PAGANINI IN COURT DRESS.

Musicians are like the rest of mankind. Some are sensible, others foolish; some liberal, others stingy; some foppish, others careless; some have much general education, others have none; some are broad in their views, others narrow; some are egotistical, others modest; some regular in habit, others unreliable; some just, others unjust; some prompt in meeting obligations, others never meet them if they can help it; some are respected, others forfeit respect; some pay attention to the conventionalities of life, others by their capricious actions make themselves ridiculous.

However great the musician, back of the musical skill there is but frail humanity, so why should the world expect from the musician as a man, aught save the actions, ideas, and peculiarities of the average man?

Among the great musicians who succeeded in making themselves ridiculous, not many were so successful as Paganini, the king of violinists. Several instances of his caprice might be cited, but one will suffice. The grand duchess, Marie Louise, once gave a grand fête at Paruna, and Paganini offered his services. They were accepted. Later he wished to withdraw from the programme, but was not permitted to do so. On the evening of the concert the artist was late in arriving, and when he did come, one authority tells us he wore the following costume:—

"A French coat of sky blue velvet with orange colored buttons: a long, flowery waistcoat which was longer than was fashionable, hiding the slenderness of his body; a pair of white satin knee breeches (hired, as was all the rest, from some second-hand shop) showing the bony state of his legs; his white silk stockings made hundreds of creases on his scraggy legs; and his enormous shoes ornamented with immense silver buckles, contrasted with such thin shanks.

"This ridiculous personage created great hilarity, which doubled when the strange ornaments covering his breast were observed. There was quite a variety. Decorations conferred by sovereigns, presents given by others, crosses of every description, emblems of all sorts, rings, pins, buckles, pendants, birds, fish, violins, lyres, hoops, miniature bows, all in gold, silver, and platinum. All these objects tinkled at every movement and the public continually laughed. As soon as possible silence was established and the supreme artist preluded a little and then played divinely."

227.—A GORY DRUMSTICK.

A celebrated *impresario* once had a hard battle with the tenor, Guiglini, concerning the part of "Pollio" in the opera "Norma." The tenor had taken an oath never to sing that part again, and was perfectly willing to put the manager to a great loss by his obstinacy. And all for this reason: When he had last sung that part Mdlle. Titiens was in the title *rôle*. At a certain place in the progress of the opera "Norma" has to summon, by striking a gong, an assembly which is to pass judgment on the guilt of a prisoner.

Mdlle. Titiens, in giving this gong a lusty blow, drew back the stick with such force that it came into violent contact with the unfortunate nose of "Pollio," who was behind her, and the result was that Signor Guiglini shed his life blood so freely on that occasion that he took an unconquerable hatred to the opera in question. But he was finally brought to time and made to sing his part. This little incident simply gives a hint at the whims and oddities an *impresario* has to overcome in his singers before the public can enjoy their favorite operas.

228.—GREAT MUSICAL MEMORIES.

No matter what other talents a musician may have, if he has not a very strong and retentive memory his musical genius will probably remain obscure. It is fortunate, however, that a strong inventive power or talent for composition will generally be accompanied by an adequately developed memory. For this reason, when one begins to write of the retentive memories of the great composers, there seems to be no stopping place short of the end of the list.

It goes without saying that an opera singer must be able at all times to place perfect reliance on his memory. It is hard to appreciate the task that falls to a singer taking a prominent *rôle* in some of the grand operas, Wagner's, for instance. The mere notes form only a minor part of the work. There are the words, the *nuance*, and the action; and a slip in any one of these means a failure, more or less pronounced.

Many have been the fine voices that are lost to the stage because of a lack of that vital necessity, a reliable memory. But there is this redeeming feature—memory, like all other faculties, grows with use, and especially is this true of music, where the association of words and music is a great aid for the retention of either.

Next to the operatic singer comes the instrumental executant. Among these Mozart was most prominent for his good memory. Von Bülow was another whose memory seemed to have no end. He could play almost any classic composition that might be called for. Beethoven's sonatas he could give note for note, but this is told also of Sir Charles Hallé, Rubinstein and others.

Bülow could give a piano recital every day for a month, and repeat no number, all from memory. It is related of him that his manager desired him to give certain compositions at a recital in a distant city. A telegram to this effect reached him as he was about to set out on his journey. The pieces were new to him, having been just published; but he procured the music and learned them on the train *en route*. The first time he played them was at the concert that night.

As a conductor, his memory served him equally well. His precision was such that it gave evidence of thorough acquaintance with the entire score of nearly the whole *repertoire* of symphony and opera. Most of the great conductors such as Richter, Weingartner, Nikisch, Seidl, Thomas and Paur will do a large part of their orchestral conducting without score. Especially is this true of the standard classics.

We have related how Mozart, when a boy, retained Allegri's "*Miserere*" on one hearing, and how he wrote out the whole composition on his return home from the service. This phenomenal memory stood Mozart in good stead, as the following incident shows:—

Some three years before he died he played his concerto in C before a Leipzig audience. At the proper time Mozart sat down to begin and the orchestra was all ready. The concerto had not yet been printed, and the orchestra played from manuscript. To the surprise of the audience Mozart only used a bit of paper with a few of the beginnings of the themes written thereon.

When asked about it he said, "Oh, the piano part is safely locked up in my desk at Vienna. I am obliged to take this precaution when I am traveling; otherwise people contrive, somehow or other, to get copies of my scores and print them without the least acknowledgment to me."

229.—A COMICAL REVENGE.

That eccentric *prima donna* of the French stage, Madame La Maupin, some of whose pranks we have mentioned in another sketch, after passing her prime and losing her voice and prestige, was glad to accept whatever offered as a means of earning her livelihood; and so we find her as lady-in-waiting to the Spanish Countess Marino. But that misfortunes had not broken her spirit or destroyed her sense of humor, we may see from this incident:—

Feeling that she had been ill-used and harshly spoken to on a certain occasion, she determined to have a harmless revenge. My lady was preparing to attend a grand ball, and called on La Maupin to dress her hair, as one of her duties was to assist at the toilet of the Countess. When the task was completed the Countess gave a hasty glance into the glass, and relying on her maid's skill did not make a careful examination of her coiffure. The feathers in her head-dress were tastily placed, and so, complimenting the maid, the lady hastened away.

Upon her entrance into the ball-room she noticed that she seemed to cause attention and even illy-suppressed mirth. But the reason she did not discover until she had paraded around the room, and some good friend, taking pity on her, informed her that her back hair was tastefully trimmed with little red radishes! Exit Countess! She returned home in a great rage to vent her anger on the unlucky Maupin; but the bird had flown, feeling that she had obtained her revenge by making the sharp-tongued Countess the laughing-stock of the town.

230.—SCHERZO.

It is not always that we can have from a great musician's own pen a concise sketch of his life. So we present the following one, in the line of a curiosity. In a collection of musical autobiographies we would naturally expect the "*ego*" to be rather prominent. But in the following sketch of himself which Moszkowski sent to a Boston friend, we find an admirable modesty and a ready turn of humor. In reply to his friend's request he wrote:—

"I took my first step before the public in my earliest youth following my birth, which occurred August 23, 1854, in Breslau. I selected this warm month in hopes of a tornado, which always plays so prominent a part in the biography of great men. This desired tempest, in consequence of favorable weather, did not occur, while it accompanied the birth of hundreds of men of much less importance. Embittered by this injustice, I determined to avenge myself on the world by playing the piano, while I continued in Dresden and Berlin as Kullak's pupil. In spite of the theoretical instruction of Kiel and Wuerst, a lively desire to compose was early aroused in me. I perpetrated, in time, an overture, a piano concerto, two symphonies, piano and violin pieces, songs, etc.; in short, I have twenty works in print.

"I should be happy to send you my piano concerto but for two reasons: first, it is worthless; second, it is most convenient—the score being four hundred pages long—for making my piano stool higher when I am engaged in studying better works.

"My prominence as a pianist is known to you. I have concertized in France and Germany, and soon go again to Berlin, where they are at work, day and night (by electric light), preparing my triumphal arch and a procession of virgins clothed in white.

"Besides these extensive acquirements, I can play billiards, chess, dominoes and violin, can ride, imitate canary birds, and relate jokes in the Saxon dialect. Am a very tidy, amiable man and your very devoted friend and colleague,

"Moritz Moszkowski."

231.—BUT ONE SEAT LEFT.

The public performer has frequently cause to ejaculate, "Deliver me from my friends." And there is no time when this exclamation is more appropriate than when he is pestered by his acquaintances for complimentary tickets to his concerts or recitals. If this demand came only from friends it would not be so bad; but more frequently it is the friend that pays his way and some chance acquaintance or even total stranger that unblushingly proffers his request for complimentaries.

Not every artist can keep his good humor under such provocation, or come out of the ordeal as neatly as did Rubinstein when, some years ago an old lady rushed up to him in London with,

"Oh, Mr. Rubinstein, I am so glad to meet you; all of the tickets are sold and I have tried in vain to purchase a seat to your recital. Do you not have a seat you could let me take?"

"Madame," replied the great artist, "there is but one seat at my disposal, but you are welcome to that if you will take it."

"Oh, thank you, a thousand thanks, Mr. Rubinstein. Where is it?"

"At the piano," was the smiling reply.

232.—A COMPLIMENT FROM HAYDN.

In a broad course of musical reading one is continually coming across scathing criticisms and slighting remarks made by the great musicians concerning each other's works. But it is natural perhaps, that men of so great genius should see the world through their own spectacles and not feel like allowing another man credit for seeing it through his.

But, on the other hand, we have many instances showing the thorough appreciation some have had for the works of others, and for the promise they gave of greater things. Haydn was one of the best dispositioned men, and from him we would naturally expect to hear pleasant things and gentle criticisms.

When Cherubini first met Haydn, in Vienna, in 1805, the latter was seventy-three years of age, while Cherubini was still in the forties, and just beginning to compose the works that made him famous. The old veteran handed to the younger man one of his latest compositions, remarking—

"Permit me to style myself your musical father, and to call you my son."

No greater compliment could have been paid the younger man. Encouraged and impressed by Haydn's friendliness, Cherubini could not, on parting, restrain his tears.

233.—A PARTICULAR PRIMA DONNA.

Bizet found many difficulties in the production of his celebrated opera, "Carmen." One, which gave him the most trouble, was the dissatisfaction expressed by his *prima donna* with the aria she was to sing on her first appearance on the stage. He had originally written an air in six-eight time, graceful enough, but not particularly characteristic. This would not do at all for the singer, as she wanted something which would make her first appearance effective. Bizet produced in succession no fewer than thirteen different versions of "Carmen's" *aria d'entrata*, but none of them realized the *prima donna's* ideal. Bizet's imagination was exhausted, and the lady was as dissatisfied as ever.

In despair he bethought him of an old Spanish air

which had struck his fancy while he was looking through a collection of songs years before, when his ideas of "Carmen" were still undeveloped. With the aid of this melody he composed the "*Habañera*," with which she at last professed herself contented. The singer's instinct was quite right, for not only does the famous air express the character of the wayward gypsy in a nutshell, and put it before the audience in vivid colors at the outset of the piece, but it was one of the few numbers which was praised unreservedly by the critics at the first performance, and it still remains as popular as ever.

234.—MENDELSSOHN'S KINDNESS.

Henry Chorley, an English critic and musical writer of much note, on one of his trips to the continent went to Leipzig for the purpose, among other things, of meeting Mendelssohn and hearing some of his works.

Shortly after his arrival he was taken with an acute attack of illness and confined to his room, a small apartment in a crowded German inn. He had met Mendelssohn and other musicians before his illness. It is not pleasant to be sick among strangers in a foreign land, and his feelings were not of the most enjoyable kind.

His illness had been known but a few hours when he heard a heavy tramping up the stairs. It stopped at his door.

"Who is there?" he called.

"A grand piano to be put in your room," was the reply, "and Dr. Mendelssohn is coming directly."

And soon Dr. Mendelssohn did come, with his warm smile and hearty greeting.

"If you like," said he, "we will make some music here to-day, since you must not go out," and down he sat and began to play a lot of music about which Chorley had expressed some curiosity the day before. For hours Mendelssohn stayed there delighting, as Chorley modestly said, "an obscure stranger as zealously and cheerfully as if his time could not be measured by gold, and as if his company was not eagerly and importunately sought by the 'best of the best,' who repaired to Leipzig with little purpose but to seek his acquaintance."

235.—CAMPANINI AS A SOLDIER.

Seldom do we find an operatic singer in the battlefield taking his part in his country's battles. Of those who have been delighted with the tenor voice of Signor Campanini, few have known that they were applauding a brave soldier, as well as a finished singer.

He was one of the first to volunteer to serve under Garibaldi at Marsala, and his zeal and bravery were so great that while yet little more than a youth he obtained the post of sergeant. At the battle of Capua, during the fiercest fighting, he was wounded by two sabre cuts; he still carries the scars, one on the right cheek and the other on the neck.

But this did not stop his fighting, and had it not been for a severe fever which nearly killed him, it is very likely that the brave volunteer would never have left the campaign. At this time he had never thought of such a thing as being a singer, but he soon after obtained admission to the Parma conservatory of music, where he made surprising progress. To-day he is one of the foremost tenors and has attained this enviable position of his own merit and exertion.

Of the many singers upon the concert stage we venture to say that there are few, if any, with a like record for soldiering and singing.

236.—TO MAKE A PLAYER PLAY.

When, after a life of application and artistic strivings, success crowns a composer's labors and he has reached the climax of fame and achieved a financial competence, who can blame him for taking a rest from the work of composition and the worry of conducting? This was the case with Rossini and Lulli. Each came to be regarded as the most prominent operatic composer of his time, and each after accumulating a fortune retired to private life.

Lulli was an excellent violinist, but so fatal was success upon his musical interests that he even laid aside his violin. He would not keep a fiddle in the house, nor could he be prevailed upon to touch such a thing. But a certain French noble determined to hear Lulli play once more, and hit upon the following plan. He had one of his servants take up a violin and attempt to play one day when Lulli was present. The man made more noise than music and the effect was so exasperating to the composer that he snatched the offending instrument from the servant and, to soothe his disturbed nerves, proceeded to play in his own charming manner for quite a time. The company that was present were of course delighted with the ruse.

Perhaps this plan might be recommended to those who have so much trouble in getting Mr. A. or Miss B. to perform for their friends, when upon being invited to use the instrument they proclaim their utter disability. A wish to show their superior abilities might produce the desired result, even where the spirit of accommodation and courtesy is absent.

237.—TRUE KINDLINESS.

Even Beethoven's closest friends were not always sure what mood they would find having dominion over him. But underneath the external crustiness, caused partially by the impositions to which he was subjected, and by his consequent distrust of humanity, was a vein of generosity that was not generally appreciated or realized.

When Moscheles took his brother to visit Beethoven, knowing Beethoven's aversion to strangers, he had his brother wait below while he went to Beethoven's room.

After greeting Beethoven he said, "Will you permit me to introduce my brother to you?"

"Where is he," he suddenly replied.

"Below."

"What! down stairs?" and Beethoven rushed off and siezed hold of the brother's arm, saying:—

"Am I such a savage that you are afraid to come near me?"

And Moscheles relates that after that Beethoven was kindness itself both to him and the visiting brother.

238.—VIOTTI'S INDEPENDENCE.

There was an incident in the career of Viotti, the great violinist of a hundred years ago, that parallels the little scene that took place in Cardinal Ottoboni's palace when Corelli rebuked the Cardinal for conversing during a musical performance. Viotti was, up to his time, the most polished player of his instrument that had appeared before the public. He was also a man of great independence and originality.

Marie Antoinette had commanded him to play at the royal palace at Versailles. He was in the midst of one of his finest compositions when the Count d'Artois was announced with great noise and bustle. When that haughty scion of royalty had entered, he paid no attention to the player, but disturbed the audience by his loud talking and rude behavior. Viotti's independent spirit could stand this no longer; so he took up his music, placed his violin in its case, and unceremoniously withdrew. This display of justifiable pride drew on him the displeasure of the court. This and his open expression of his democratic opinions made advisable his departure from France, and he shortly afterward appeared in London, where he gained great renown.

But here again his eccentric and independent nature

asserted itself, and he received notice from the Government that his absence from England was desired, and the quicker it came about the better for M. Viotti. So he took up his residence in Holland for some years, until this edict was revoked, when he returned to England. There he forsook art for commerce for a time and entered into the wine business. It could hardly be said of him, however, as it was of Michael Kelly, that he should be labeled, "composer of wine and importer of music." It is not surprising that an artist should be unsuccessful as a business man, and soon Viotti again turned to his art to retrieve what he had lost in business.

Going again to Paris, he became director of the Grand Opera, and was later retired to private life with a pension granted by the French Government. He then returned to London and spent his remaining days in that city, where he died in 1824.

239.—NOT THE GEESE THAT SAVED ROME.

The stories told of Hans von Bülow are legion, but the following is too good to omit:—

Bülow was a master of satire and irony, as the orchestras and choruses which came under his direction could well testify.

On one occasion he rebuked the feminine half of an oratorio chorus which he was rehearsing. While the tenors and basses were singing their parts the sopranos and altos indulged in conversation. They were called to order several times, but paid no attention. Finally von Bülow rapped upon his desk and called out, "Ladies, Rome does not have to be saved to-night," which remark produced the desired effect.

240.—THAT PATTI KISS.

An enthusiastic Missouri gentleman once showed his admiration of Patti in a way which doubtless aroused much envy in the breast of many a younger man. Here is Patti's account of the affair: " I had just finished singing 'Home, Sweet Home,' when a nice-looking old gentleman, who introduced himself as Governor Crittenden, began congratulating me. All of a sudden he put his arms around me and kissed me, saying, 'Madame Patti, I may never see you again, but I cannot help it,' and before I knew it he was kissing me. When a gentleman, and such a nice old gentleman, too, and a Governor of a great State, kisses one so quick that one has no time to object, what can one do?"

At the time this took place there was great rivalry between Mmes. Gerster and Patti, and a good deal of warm feeling was engendered on the part of each songstress, Patti going so far as to declare that Gerster was possessed of the "evil eye." Patti laid all her misfortunes at Gerster's door. When they were in San Francisco a slight earthquake took place. Patti crossed herself and ejaculated, "Gerster!"

Well, Gerster was interviewed on this Patti kiss. She told the reporter she saw no occasion for so much comment about a slight matter like that.

"What! you don't?" said the astonished scribe.

"Certainly not; there is nothing wrong in a man kissing a woman old enough to be his mother!"

241.—LONGEVITY OF MUSICIANS.

The fact that several of the more celebrated composers have died when in their prime, or in some cases even before they had reached their best years, has produced an opinion in the minds of some who have not scanned musical biography very closely, that the nervous and mental strain to which a composer or an artist is exposed is fatal to longevity. An examination of statistics does not prove this true. In fact, the burden of proof seems to be the other way.

True, some of the careers that have promised most brilliantly, and have been at the same time a fulfilment of it, have been cut short in the glory of their young manhood. So many have finished their career in their third decade of life that it has come to be known in this respect as the "fatal thirties." Pergolesi ended his short life at 28; Schubert died at 31; Bellini was 33; the brilliant Mozart was but 35; Purcell, the gifted Englishman, and Bizet, who might have been another Berlioz, 37; Mendelssohn died at 38; Chopin and Nicolai, 39; Weber, 40; Schumann, 46. In several of the above instances the untimely end was the direct result of a lack of public appreciation and support; but in few cases the end was hastened by the demands of the art itself.

Now to the other side of the matter. Out of a large list of the greatest names in musical history, I find 69 per cent. to have passed their sixtieth year, and this list included the "fatal thirties," which tended, of course, to reduce the average. But why should the musician not be long-lived? The very conditions of his work may be conducive of that result. Says a recent writer on this subject: "There is nothing demoralizing in deliberately and for a definite purpose putting one's self or others through the experience of a highly strung series of emotions. It is even a good and very healthy function of art to raise one's feelings to their highest degree of intensity. It is a part of a correct system of discipline, calculated to bring the emotions into high condition and healthy activity, and to keep them in good state—may I say?—of repair. The body is intended and suited at times to bear an extreme tension of its muscles. The athlete is perfectly aware that systematic exertion and exhaustion must be undergone in order to raise his physique to its highest form of power and health. The laws which regulate the life and health of the emotions are exactly similar, and these laws prescribe regular, steady exercise, rest, recreation, and sometimes tension. In itself the habitual exercise and discipline of the emotions in music has not an evil effect, but quite the reverse; it is the very condition of health."

But to return to our statistics. Out of the 100 most prominent musicians, composers, and performers, of all ages and countries, I find sixty-nine who have passed the age of 60, and eighty-nine who have passed 50 years. And this does not include those veterans who are still working, viz.: St. Saëns at 59, Brahms at 61, Joachim at 63, good old Verdi at 81, or Ambroise Thomas, now 83, who lately witnessed the 1000th production of his opera, "*Mignon*," the first circumstance of its kind in history.

In our select hundred, I find Hucbald reached 90 years; Auber, 89; Cramer and Fetis, 87; Lachner, 86; Zingarelli, 85; Cherubini and Dufay, 82; Matheson and Ockenheim, 83; Rameau, 81; Clementi and Palestrina, 80; Tartini, 79; Haydn, 77; Moscheles and Rossini, 76; Spohr, Liszt, and Gounod, 75; Lassus, Händel, Em. Bach, Zelter, and Pleyel, 74; Gade and Gluck, 73; Meyerbeer and Wagner, 70; Scarlatti, Czerny, and Berlioz, 66; John Sebastian Bach and Rubinstein, 65; Corelli and Raff, 60; Hummel, 59; Beethoven, 57; Paganini, 56; De Beriot, 50.

And, incidentally, we might note that some of the master works in musical composition have been composed after their authors have passed the span of life usually allotted to musicians. Händel was 56 when he wrote the " Messiah " and 61 when he wrote " Judas Maccabæus;" Gluck composed " Iphigenia in Tauris " at the age of 65; Haydn penned the " Creation " in his 69th and the " Seasons " in his 72d year; Verdi at 79 produced " Falstaff;" while Auber wrote his "*Reves d'Amour*" in his 87th (some say 85th) year.

Of these hundred musicians, the average age was

65½ years. Another compiler of statistics finds the average of several thousand musicians to be 62½ years. He finds teachers to be the longest lived; then, following in the order given, writers, vocalists, wind instrument players, composers, organists, pianists, and, lastly, players of stringed instruments.

242.—LISZT AS AN ADVERTISER.

Even modern advertisers might get a "pointer" from Liszt on advertising methods. He was once billed for two concerts in a French town. The first night the audience numbered only fifty people, of whom but one was of the gentler sex. The artists gave the most of their programme, and then Liszt stepped forward and said: "Gentlemen and madam, I think you've had enough music. We now ask you to do us the honor of supping with us." As may be expected, the audience did not decline the invitation, and they enjoyed a banquet at Liszt's expense. The next night the house was full and the pianist was more than reimbursed for his outlay on the previous evening. But the second audience "went supperless to bed," realizing that a supper did not always go with a piano recital.

243.—ARRESTED FOR TREASON.

The famous baritone, Tamburini, once had an experience which showed the appreciation in which he was held by royalty. He was passing through Venice, where he was very popular and greatly idolized, on his way to Trieste to keep an operatic engagement in that city. As he, with his lovely young wife, were seated in their gondola on the way to the ship which was to carry them on their journey, they were overtaken by a Government gondola filled with armed men, and the singer was placed under arrest. He protested that he was an opera singer simply passing through Venice, that he never meddled with politics, and that there must be some mistake. But the officer showed the order for his arrest, and the singer and his wife were transferred to the Government vessel and taken back to the city.

The gondola drew up to the heavy doors of a large building and the prisoners were conducted through a long passage-way and suddenly thrust into a brilliantly lighted room, which proved to be the "green room" of a theater. The officer then addressed him, saying, "I have the honor to announce to you the commands of his Majesty the Emperor. It is his imperial wish that you perform to-night in the 'Marriage of Figaro.' The Emperor, together with his Majesty the Emperor of Russia, will honor the performance with their presence."

The audience was one of the most brilliant that could be conceived, and Tamburini excelled himself. At the end of the last act, the audience remained to call the singer before the curtain and deluge him with wreaths of flowers. When, flushed with triumph, Tamburini returned behind the curtain, he found himself again a prisoner, and he and his trembling wife were conducted to the apartments assigned to them. While their treatment had been courteous, they knew not what was in store, nor could they obtain any information from the soldiers in charge. The answer was that "he should know on the morrow."

The next day Tamburini was conducted into the royal presence. The whole court was assembled to do honor to the illustrious guest, the Emperor of Russia. When his name was announced, the singer made his obeisance and stood awaiting the monarch's commands.

"Signor Tamburini," said the Emperor, "you stand before us a prisoner, but we understand you plead ignorance of your offense."

"I do, Sire; I am ignorant of how I have broken the laws or offended your Majesty."

"Then we will tell you. It was high treason for you to attempt to pass through this city without stopping to sing for us. You are proved guilty of a conspiracy to defraud our good Venetians of their rights in refusing them the privilege of hearing you. You lie at our mercy. But we will remit all punishment other than a few days' imprisonment with us. Moreover, we have ordered a sum of money to be paid to you in testimony of our appreciation of your performance, and, in addition, allow you to ask any favor you will."

"Sire, I simply ask to be permitted to keep my word to my friends at Trieste, who are expecting me."

"You are a noble fellow, Tamburini, and your request is granted; only to-night we must have you in '*Lucia di Lammermoor;*' and now come nearer."

The artist knelt at the monarch's feet.

"Receive at our hands this medal '*di nostro Salvatore*' and learn how much we love to honor genius," and the Emperor flung a golden chain around his neck.

Tamburini was then presented to the Russian Emperor and received the compliments and congratulation of the nobility present. The next day the artist was sent on his way rejoicing, loaded with honors and tangible marks of royal esteem.

244.—ROTHSCHILD'S MUSIC.

The difference between artistic and financial self-respect is well illustrated in Spohr's meeting with Rothschild, the wealthy banker, in London. Spohr had called to present a letter of credit. Rothschild took it, and after glancing it over said, "I have just read that you manage your business very efficiently, but I understand nothing of music. This is my music (slapping his purse); they understand that on the Exchange." As Spohr was leaving, the banker called out, "You can come out and dine at my country house." It need hardly be added that Spohr did not accept this delicately tendered invitation.

245.—THE "PRISON JOSEPHS."

Contemporaneous with Stradivarius was a family named Guarnerius, one of whom, Joseph (1683–1745), achieved great fame from the excellence of his instruments. This man, in order to distinguish his works from those of a cousin bearing the same name, generally added to his name on the tickets inserted in his instruments the cross and the letters, "I. H. S." These are supposed to be the initials of some religious society of which he was a member. From this addition to his name he is known as Guarnerius "*del Jesu.*" His grandfather, Andrew, was a pupil of Nicholas Amati, but the instruments of the elder Guarnerius, and those of three of his descendants are not particularly noticeable; the fourth, Joseph, "*del Jesu,*" whom I have mentioned above, turned out some violins which were quite the equals of those of Stradivarius when at his best.

His model is not quite so large nor the bouts quite so long as with Stradivarius, but the shape is most elegant, and no fault could be found with the wood or varnish. It is even said that some of his best specimens are more pleasing to the eye than those of Stradivarius. But during his later years there was a remarkable change. The wood became defective, the work careless, and the varnish poor. The exact cause for this decadence is not known, although a very pretty story is frequently told, which, fortunately for the reputation of Joseph, seems to be founded more on fancy than on fact.

The story runs that he was an impecunious and idle rascal, and that he was imprisoned for some unknown cause; also, that the jailor's daughter supplied him with rude tools and material and bought the varnish from various makers who were in the enjoyment of their liberty. This would have made a pretty good story as it was, but the romancers have added additional details. This fair damsel, so we are told, taking pity on Joseph's condition, took out the completed fiddles and hawked them about, selling them for whatever offered, and buying with the proceeds necessities and comforts for the prisoner, who, it should be added, was a married man. (It is best to omit this latter fact in telling the story. It sounds better.)

Unfortunately for the story, the archives of Cremona make no record of a prisoner named Guarnerius, and for an idle man he turned out a remarkable number of valuable violins. This tale has obtained so much credence that the rougher of the "*del Jesu*" fiddles are called "Prison Josephs."

It must have been a peculiar combination of circumstances that led him to send out inferior violins at this time of life, but the above story is admirably concocted to fill the niche. Another peculiar thing is, that after this poor work he made at least one violin the excellence of which has hardly been equaled. This is the one played so long and loved so dearly by Paganini, and at his death bequeathed to his native city, Genoa, where it still lies in its glass case. This noble instrument was made in 1743, and its maker died two years afterward.

246.—SCHUMANN'S FAILURE.

One of the fortunate accidents of musical history was that which occurred to Robert Schumann in his early days. Schumann had a great ambition to become a fine pianist, and had already made great strides in that direction, when his eagerness to hastily acquire a command of his instrument led him to make an unfortunate experiment. He found, as every one else finds, that a pianist is greatly hampered by the third fingers being bound down by extra tendons. This makes these fingers unwieldy and very slow of training. So Schumann, in order to more quickly acquire the necessary digital dexterity, rigged up a contrivance which should hold the unruly member quiet while he played with the other fingers. This treatment he carried to such excess that it resulted in an incurable lameness. By this, his career as a *virtuoso* was nipped in the bud.

For a while he was cast down by this misfortune, but soon determined to turn his energies to composition, and the result is that we have in his works a series of compositions second only in value to those of Beethoven.

This experience of Schumann's embittered him against all contrivances for aiding the pupil to more quickly acquire piano technic; and in his "Rules for Young Musicians" he warns all against mechanical apparatus. But because he made a failure of his clumsy contrivance is no reason why the student of to-day should be prejudiced against the contrivances which modern thought and skill have arranged to more quickly assist him toward his goal, at the same time saving him and his neighbors many hours of painful sounds.

247.—GENIUS DISCOVERED BY PUNISHMENT.

Madame Mara, one of the greatest singers Germany has produced, had her musical talent brought to light by a peculiar incident when she was a child.

Her father, besides teaching music, was a repairer of instruments. Frequently the little girl would perch herself on a high stool and gravely watch him while he mended some broken violin. One day he left a repaired instrument lying on his bench, and the inquisitive child undertook to play it and try to get from it the music she had heard others bring from the same source. But in her ignorance she broke one of the strings.

On her father's return she was roundly scolded and promised that a recurrence of such meddling would bring severe punishment. For some days this threat had the desired effect, but the wish to again produce the attractive tones made the little one forget the admonition, and again she tried her hand at playing, but this time she was caught in the act.

To punish her, the father declared he would make her learn to play the instrument she had tampered with. He expected she would shrink from this as a heavy punishment, but was greatly surprised to see her run eagerly to the violin and draw from it a series of smooth and pleasant musical tones.

Being a sensible man, he resolved to cultivate this faculty, and in due time Mara became a brilliant violinist, and later, winning great renown as a singer, the father was able to lay aside the repairing of voices and instruments.

248.—RICHARD WAGNER AND THE NUMBER "13."

If the number "13" is, as many people believe, an unlucky one, certainly the life of Richard Wagner must have been full of ill-luck; for this cabalistic set of figures turns up at all times and places in his biography. While Wagner had, during some periods of his life, a hard battle with the non-appreciation of his fellow-musicians, we would hardly like to believe, after reading the last thirty years of his biography, that his life was an utter failure! So perhaps there is not so much bad fortune in the number "13" as the superstitious Scotchmen would have us believe. But the recurrence of this number so frequently is a peculiar coincidence.

A statistically inclined writer has made the following list:—

Wagner was born in 1813 and died on the 13th of the month; there are 13 letters in his name, and the sum of the figures in 1813 equals 13. The full date of his death was the 13th day of the second month in '83; it makes 13 twice—viz., first 13, and again $2+8+3=13$. He composed 13 operas or "music-dramas." His first and determining impression in favor of a dramatic career was formed on the 13th of the month. He was influenced in his choice emphatically by hearing Weber's "*Freischütz*," and by Wilhelmine Shröder-Devrient. The latter went upon the stage on the 13th of October, 1819, and the "*Freischütz*" was completed on May 13, 1820, and first performed in Dresden, Wagner's home, in 1822 (1+8+2+2 = 13). Weber died in Wagner's 13th year. Wagner's first public appearance as a musical personage dates from the year 1831 (1+8+3+1 = 13), being at this time a music student in the Leipzig University.

The stage at Riga, where he became a director, was opened on the 13th day of September, 1837, and he there began the composition of "*Rienzi*," which he completed in Paris in 1840 (1+8+4 = 13). On the 13th of April, 1844, he completed his "*Tannhauser*," and it was performed in Paris on March 13, 1861, and on the 13th of August, 1876, he began the first presentation of his "Baireuth dramas," the "*Nibelungen Ring*."

Wagner was exiled from Saxony for 13 years. The 13th of September, 1882, was his last day at "Baireuth" before leaving for Venice. Wagner saw Liszt for the last time in Venice on January 13, 1883, and finally he died on the 13th of February, in the 13th year of the new German confederation.

249.—A LITTLE TRICK OF PAGANINI'S.

The most brilliant period of Paganini's life was from 1814 to 1818. He was in high favor in Italy and was then more free with his talent than later in life. He was poor at that time and was largely occupied with gambling and with falling in love, but at the same time he was prodigal with his music, whether it be in the palatial dwellings of the aristocracy or on the streets.

Together with an excellent guitar player named Lea, he would wander all night long playing under the windows of their friends and improvising the most fascinating duets. Then when tired they would drop into the nearest inn and refresh themselves in a way not unheard of by many other musicians.

One evening a rich gentleman begged the pair, Paganini and Lea, together with a 'cellist named Zeffrini, to serenade his lady-love. They consented. Before beginning to play Paganini quietly tied an open penknife to his right arm. Then they commenced. Soon the "E" string snapped.

"That is owing to the damp air," said the violinist, and kept on playing on the other three strings.

A few moments later the "A" broke and Paganini exclaimed, "Just see what the dampness is doing this evening!" But he went on playing. Finally the "D" snapped, and the love-sick swain began to be fearful for the success of his serenade. For what could Paganini do with only one string on his violin. But Paganini simply smiled and went on with the music with the same facility and strength of tone that he had previously used on all four cords.

The penknife was more to blame than the dampness of the air.

250.—LISZT'S COMPLETION OF THE BEETHOVEN MONUMENT.

A notable achievement of Franz Liszt was his raising of the funds for the completion of the Beethoven monument at Bonn. The enterprise had come to a standstill when Liszt became interested in it and declared he would complete it single handed. In a short time he had, by means of concert giving, raised the required amount, and the commission for the statue was in the sculptor's hands.

A great Beethoven festival was arranged for the dedication of the monument. After meeting with all kinds of difficulties and overcoming them, it was discovered there was no hall in Bonn large enough for the huge audience that would be gathered there at that time. The committee of that city were afraid to build one, fearing they would be put to some expense. Liszt settled the matter by himself guaranteeing the necessary amount, and the "*festhalle*" rose as if by magic. The exercises incident to the unveiling of this monument were attended by many royalties of Europe, among them being King William, of Prussia, and Queen Victoria, of England. The whole affair was a great triumph for Liszt as well as a memorial for Beethoven, and was a fine exemplification of this great pianist's energy and versatile abilities as business manager, conductor and pianist.

251.—DELAYED APPRECIATION.

At a recent auction sale of autographs and original manuscripts in Berlin, the sixteen-page score of a cantata by J. S. Bach sold for £80, and two others by the same composer for £70 and £65, respectively. For the three manuscripts £215! During his lifetime Bach hardly received so much for all the compositions he disposed of. In fact many were never printed at all.

So slight was the recognition given him that the publishers would issue but few of his works. In order to save some of them from oblivion, Bach engraved them with his own hands, and the extra strain this made on his eyes caused him to lose his sight. His "Art of Fugue," which appeared two years after his death, *i. e.*, in 1752, though having a flattering preface from Marpurg, then the foremost critic of Germany, did not meet with sufficient sale to cover the cost of the plates on which the music was engraved; and as there seemed to be no chance of more income from the work, the plates were sold by his heirs for old copper.

Posterity is atoning for this neglect of genius. The Bach Society is issuing in large handsome volumes all of his works. He is now regarded as the fountain head of instrumental music. To have the firmest foundation, a musical education must be based on the study of his compositions.

This revival of interest, or, rather, creation of interest in Bach, must be largely accredited to Mendelssohn, who admitted that his own fluency and versatility in composition, especially in contrapuntal forms, had much of its origin in a careful study of the scores of the old Leipzig cantor. Mendelssohn was also very prominent in bringing the music of Bach before the public of his day, and securing for it its proper recognition by the musical world.

Bach was a very religious man, and is doubtless enjoying the reward of a well-spent life. But while the recognition of to-day cannot save him the poverty and trials of his years of painstaking composition, who can say that it may not even now afford him pleasure to know that the century succeeding the one in which he lived has awarded him the olive wreath which was then withheld.

252.—OVERFED COMPOSERS.

While some of the men whom we have to thank for our best music had to struggle hard for the necessities of life, and then were not always successful in obtaining them, others have lived in luxury and have even been famous as gourmands.

Rossini, for one, was quite an epicure. It is told that he once gave his picture to his provision dealer with the words "To my stomach's best friend" inscribed on it. The merchant thought this too good an advertisement to lose and so had the whole thing engraved on his bill-heads and circulars.

Dussek was a notorious glutton, in fact, over eating and drinking brought him to his death-bed. His patron, Prince Benevento, besides paying him a good salary furnished him seats for three at his tables, and it was no infrequent thing that Dussek "got outside of" the provisions at all three places.

Many a time was Händel caricatured in England as an overfed glutton. In one fanciful engraving he was pictured as a huge hog sitting on the organ bench surrounded with cabbages and strings of sausage. There was some cause for this, as witness the following: Intending to dine at a certain inn, Händel ordered dinner for three. He waited a while, and, as the dinner did not put in an appearance, he asked why the delay. The waiter replied,

"It shall be sent up, sir, as soon as your company arrives."

"Den bring up de tinner *prestissimo*. I am de gombany!"

253.—NASAL.

A peculiarity about the singing of French artists is a tendency toward a nasal quality of tone. This probably owes its origin to the language and, perhaps, somewhat to the French school of singing. So whenever Frenchmen condemn a singer for using a nasal quality we may be sure the peculiarity was quite pronounced. Such was the case with a singer of the last century named Larivee who sinned so much in this nasal respect that when he appeared he was frequently greeted with the remark, "That nose has really a fine voice."

How many noses we may listen to in the average congregation that can hardly be said to have good voices; or, perchance, we might put it, how many voices which have defective noses.

254.—A BOLD PUPIL.

It is to Ferdinand Ries that we are indebted for many particulars as to the life and habits of Beethoven. This great master lived a solitary life, and for this reason our records of him are not so complete as to details as are the accounts of some of the other great composers. It is said that Ries, who, by the way, was a pupil of Beethoven, gave way to the temptation to "draw the long bow" occasionally, and that some of his statements concerning Beethoven are more or less tinged by his imagination.

However, here is one little story that probably may be accepted: "Upon Ries' first appearance in public as Beethoven's pupil, he was to play the C minor concerto from manuscript. This was the first performance of a work which has since become a general favorite with concert pianists, though it is not so great as the E flat concerto. Ries asked his teacher to write a cadenza for the work, but Beethoven, in a particularly genial mood, told the young man he might compose one himself and insert his own cadenza.

This was a high honor. Ries wrote his cadenza, but, on presenting it to Beethoven, the latter objected to one passage which was so difficult that its correct performance was doubtful, and advised the substitution of an easier passage. This Ries did until the time of the concert. When he came to the cadenza, instead of playing the easier passage he dashed into the forbidden one and completed it with great success.

"Bravo," cried Beethoven, and the audience took up the applause. After the performance Beethoven, remembering the disobedience said to Ries, "You are always obstinate. I would never have given you another lesson had you missed one note of that passage," and we may well believe Beethoven would have kept his word.

255.—WAGNER'S ACTIVITY.

Richard Wagner was a merry little man, and retained his health and spirits till his last years of life. The two incidents here given show his quick judgment and prompt action, as well as his eccentricity. He was once climbing a precipitous mountain in company with a young friend. When some distance up and walking along a narrow ledge the companion, who was following, called out that he was growing giddy. Wagner turned round on the ledge of the rock, caught his friend and passed him between the rock and himself to the front, where he was safe.

Ferdinand Praeger, relates an incident of a visit to Wagner at his Swiss home. The two men sat one morning on an ottoman in the drawing-room, talking over the events of the years. Suddenly Wagner, who was sixty years old, rose and stood on his head upon the ottoman. At that moment Wagner's wife entered. Her surprise and alarm caused her to run to her husband, exclaiming: "Ah! Richard! Richard!" Quickly recovering himself, he assured her that he was sane, and wished to show that he could stand on his head at sixty, which was more than Ferdinand could do. Perhaps Wagner wrote some of his music while standing on his head. It certainly reverses many old-time ideas of composition.

256.—AN OPERA SACRIFICED.

The pages of manuscript that lie on the composer's desk may represent to him the thoughts, ideas, aspirations of years. It is no wonder, then, that his first thought should be for his beloved score, and that he should be ready to risk a good deal in order to preserve it from destruction. Lulli once ran a terrible risk to save the score of his best opera, no less a risk than that of incurring eternal damnation—according to his father confessor.

It happened this way: Lulli was ill, so ill as to fear death. He hurriedly sent for a priest and asked for absolution, but the priest would not grant it unless he would promise to destroy the score of his latest opera. It seems the church did not regard his operas as being conducive of a rapid moral growth among the people.

Finally the composer gave in, and pointed to his desk where the lately finished work lay in rough score. The priest secured the doomed manuscript, burnt it, and then granted the desired safe conduct to paradise. But Lulli was not so sick as he thought, and proceeded to get better. Some time after, he was visited by one of the young princes, who, when he heard of the destruction of the opera protested vigorously.

"What," said he, "you have burnt your beautiful opera. You are a fool to have given way to so gloomy a priest and to have destroyed so much music!"

"Don't get angry," whispered the sick man, "I knew what I was about; I have another copy of it laid away."

Unfortunately, the recovery was not permanent and Lulli suffered a relapse. He was now told that it was impossible for him to recover. Again he sent for the priest and this time delivered to him the remaining copy of the opera and begged forgiveness for his deceit.

The priest prescribed as penance that he should be laid on a heap of ashes with a cord around his neck! Lulli gladly submitted and died happy.

257.—AN ERRATIC PRIMA DONNA.

One of the "freaks" of the operatic stage was a lady who was before the public in the time of Lulli, and who bore the name of Madam La Maupin. This versatile lady was given to all sorts of questionable pranks, such as would hardly be tolerated in the present century.

Having secretly learned the art of fencing, she proceeded to seek an opportunity to put her skill to use. She declared a certain opera singer had insulted her; and, donning male attire, she lay in wait for him as he left the theater one night, and challenged him to draw his sword and defend himself. But the fellow was a coward and refused to fight; so she demanded his money and jewelry and then gave him a sound thrashing. The next day when this brave gentleman was boasting to some friends how he had been attacked by three robbers and how he had put them to flight, she coolly produced the plunder and told the whole story.

When only sixteen, this adventuress ran off from her husband and proceeded with a new admirer to Marseilles, where she appeared on the stage in masculine attire; and so good a looking man did she make that one young lady in the audience fell violently in love with her. La Maupin, keeping up her disguise, encouraged the love smitten damsel, and the affair grew so serious that the girl's parents placed her in a convent to remove her from the influence of this captivating suitor.

But La Maupin was not so easily frustrated. Donning her proper attire, she applied at the convent for admission and finally was received as a novice, and thus kept up her intimacy with her admirer, who thought her assumption of feminine attire a disguise. But convent life soon lost its attractions for this uncertain person and she quickly hit on a scheme that permitted them both to escape. One of the nuns having just died and having been buried on the grounds, La Maupin, disinterred the poor lady, placed her remains in the infatuated girl's bed; then she set fire to the dormitory and in the confusion which followed they both made their escape. Then tiring of the part she was playing, she discovered her sex to her admirer and sent her home to her mother, sadder, and perhaps wiser.

258.—WHEN THEY BEGAN.

It is generally thought that a man must begin his career before the public at a very early age if he is to reach a high point in the world's list of celebrities. But the perusal of the following list shows that some have begun their musical career late in life. In this list we do not refer to the date of the first entrance of the musician into the field of composition or of his first public appearance, but give the age at which he stepped out into earnest work, his preliminary studies being completed.

Mozart began his career at the age of 12; Weber at 14; Rossini at 18; Händel, Cherubini, and Donizetti at 20; Scarlatti and Meyerbeer at 21; Bellini and Wagner at 23; Grétry and Massenet at 25; Thomas and Verdi at 26; Gluck at 28; Gounod at 33; Lulli at 39; and Rameau at 50.

259.—SARCASM.

Porpora, the most celebrated singing master of all time, lived and flourished in the last century. He it was who had no less a person than young Haydn as pupil, and Haydn paid for his tuition in acting as valet for the tyrannical old teacher. How many students of to-day would black their teacher's shoes to pay for their tuition?

Porpora was very quick of tongue, and he did not spare even his intimate friends and his best pupils. As a specimen of his sarcasm we may quote the following:—

He one day visited a certain German monastery, and the monks, being proud of the skill of their organist, begged him to stay to service and give them his verdict. He remained, and at the close of the service they were eager to hear his testimony as to the organist's ability.

"Well—" began Porpora.

"Well," interrupted the prior, "he is a clever man, isn't he? and likewise a good man, quite pure and simple."

"Oh! as to his simplicity," Porpora hastened to remark—" as to his simplicity, I readily perceived that; he even carries it so far that his left hand knoweth not what his right hand doeth!"

Alas, poor anecdotes! How many times they have to do duty in the world. It is not enough to pass through one life, but they must be reincarnated by succeeding story tellers, generation after generation. Or are the musicians to blame? Is it their lack of originality? Witness the following from a late paper:—

"The French composer, Massenet, had accepted an invitation to dinner; the hostess begged him to listen to her daughter's playing. When she had finished, he was, of course, asked for his judgment; and he, with the earnest face of a weighty critic, declared that the young lady was a perfect Christian. 'Why?' 'Because she follows strictly the teaching of the New Testament: 'Let not thy left hand know what thy right hand doeth.'"

260.—A PRIMA DONNA'S PETS.

The operatic ladies with high voices—and higher salaries—are credited with having more whims and peculiarities than other mortals. But along with them must be ranked the gentlemen with the high "C." The *prime donne* and the *primi tenori* are the plague of the operatic manager's life.

Nearly all of the great sopranos and contraltos have some pet animal that they continually carry with them and on which they lavish their surplus affection. It may be a parrot, a dog, or a monkey, but all the same, it must have the best of care and accommodations.

Generally the ladies are satisfied with one or two traveling companions of the animal kind, but Ilma di Murska was not content with less than a number which would be considered a fair start for a zoological garden. First, there was an immense Newfoundland, who regularly had his plate placed at the *prima donna's* table and dined at her side.

Then there was a monkey; and in order that the proverbial "time" could be had, there were also two parrots. The last member of the aggregation was an Angora cat, and it was between this long-haired beauty and the monkey that the enmity was greatest. The expression "to make the fur fly" could literally be applied to di Murska's caravan. But in spite of the annoyance, the expense, and the trouble with hotel-keepers, she was willing to have it all rather than part, even temporarily, with one of her beloved pets.

261.—PAGANINI'S METHOD OF STUDY.

We can hardly realize at this day of the world the furore created by the marvelous performances of Paganini. The gaunt, cadaverous figure, the eccentric poses, the bewitching music, the undreamed-of technic, seconded by the terrible tales which had been circulated about his selling his soul to the devil in exchange for his wonderful powers—all this created such an interest and excitement as has hardly been paralleled in musical records.

Various fiddlers whom he put sadly in the shade would have almost sold their souls to have captured the secret of his abilities. One of them went so far as to follow him from place to place, hoping to get an inkling of the magic that Paganini used. This man would even engage an adjoining room at the hotel where Paganini was staying, and kept up an unceasing espionage over the *virtuoso*, even going to the length of peering through the keyhole of the latter's room. On one occasion, when so engaged, he saw Paganini take up his instrument and place it in position as though about to play, but, greatly to his disappointment, not a sound did the player make. He simply moved his left hand up and down the neck for a few moments, as though studying positions, then laid it aside, and that was all.

During his youth Paganini was made to practice many hours per day, and the severe training that he was put through at that time, together with his phenomenal genius for his instrument, so settled his technic that it was not necessary for him to keep a severe and arduous course of practice with fixed regularity. Even when rehearsing with the orchestra, beyond a few isolated snatches, more often than not played *pizzicato*, he rarely ever played through those compositions which, at his concerts, delighted and astonished his audiences.

But while his technical practice was largely finished

in his youth, he was throughout his whole life an earnest student.

The works which he performed were such as to demand constant study, for he constantly added new compositions to his repertoire, all of which he memorized. He studied them as one would study a poem, committing them to memory line by line and stanza by stanza, thus relieving himself of constant repetitions. He would so impress the notes, dynamic marks, and bowing upon his memory, that when he came to give the work audible expression, it remained only to apply the physical machinery he could so well control to its demonstration. At the proper moment every note appeared in its place with fitting finish and expression, although the artist may not previously have traced the combinations upon his instrument. An active and discriminating intelligence was at the root of all of his musical performances.

262.—GOAT HAIR FOR HERO WORSHIPERS.

Notwithstanding his gruffness, which frequently became out-and-out rudeness, Beethoven was a favorite with such ladies as happened to know him intimately, and many who were deprived of this privilege worshiped at a distance.

He frequently received requests for a lock of his hair; in fact, so numerous were they that his tangled locks would have showed a sad decimation had he granted all these requests. Some of his intimate lady friends and pupils were thus highly favored, but others were not so well treated, as the following incident will show.

The wife of a Vienna musician, desiring very much to possess one of his shaggy locks, one day induced her husband to ask a friend of the great composer's to intercede for her, and procure her the relic she desired.

This friend told Beethoven of her wish, but persuaded him to send her a wisp of hair from a goat's beard, which Beethoven's coarse gray hair nearly resembled. Some time later, when the lady was exhibiting this peculiar souvenir as a lock of Beethoven's hair, another friend, who was a party to the joke, acquainted her with the deception.

The husband of the hero worshiper wrote a letter to Beethoven charging him with discourtesy and unkindness; and Beethoven, feeling ashamed of the trick, wrote a letter of apology to the aggrieved lady, enclosing in it a real lock of his hair, and refused to receive further visits from the gentleman who had prompted the deception.

263.—STAGE CENSORSHIP.

It seems strange that at this age of the world a composer should have to ask the police what characters and incidents he may use in the plot of his opera. Yet within a short time the Italian, Leoncavallo, in putting his "*I Medici*" on the stage in Vienna, has had to make serious alterations in the text at the "suggestion" of the censor of that city. He had to change a scene in the last act because two priests are there depicted as murderers of Giuliano Medici. The composer, unwilling to have his work forbidden, replaced the priests by two young courtiers. Also the Credo sung in Latin in a church scene was given with German words, and each time the name of the Pope had to be uttered during the course of the piece a nobleman's name was to be substituted.

This reads like the days in 1847, when republican sentiment was rampant in Italy, and the supervision of what was given to the public in print or on the stage was very strict. When, at that time, Verdi brought out "*I Masnadieri*," Schiller's great tragedy of "The Robbers" arranged to a string of Italian melodies, he was obliged to cut and slash his libretto in all directions at the bidding of the police authorities for fear there would be allowed to remain in the work some reference to liberty or republicanism.

The "Masked Ball" was not at first permitted a representation because it dealt with the assassination of King Gustavus III, of Sweden; so Verdi offered to turn his king into a duke; but finally, to give satisfaction, he metamorphosed the monarch into the "Governor of Massachusetts" and allowed him to be killed in sedate old Boston! The tenor, Mario, was to appear in this first presentation, and when he came to don the sombre garb of the Puritan governor, he decidedly objected to its lack of color and ornamentation. So Verdi obligingly allowed the sober Puritan to strut the stage in Spanish mantle, high boots, spurs, and a helmet with waving plume!

Rossini's "William Tell" has also come under the ban of governmental displeasure in monarchical Europe. At various times the libretto has undergone change for political reasons.

At the Royal Opera, Berlin, in 1830, for example, the title "William Tell" was altered to "Andreas Hofer," the hero of the Tyrolese insurrection against the French and Bavarians, who was shot at Mantua in 1810; while the tyrant Gessler was, of course, replaced by a French general. In Russia the piece was some sixty years ago rechristened "Charles the Bold," and instead of William Tell another hero was invented, called Rodolphe Doppelguggel.

264.—FALLIBLE.

Here is a little incident that illustrates how great composers are not above the slips made by common mortals, and how human ears are not always as infallible as their owners would pretend them to be.

Meyerbeer once went to Stuttgart to conduct the first performance of one of his operas at the court theater. During the rehearsal of the work, he found fault with the clarinet player because he played a certain melody on the B flat clarinet when it was written for a clarinet in A. He requested the player to substitute an A clarinet. The clever performer bent forward and placed the instrument on the rack at his feet, then took it up again, blew through it, as if to warm up another clarinet, and began anew on the same B flat instrument. "Listen, gentlemen, listen," cried Meyerbeer; "there is the A clarinet tone color I had in mind!"

265.—A DRESSING-ROOM WAR.

A disturbance took place among some of the prominent singers of the Mapleson company at Chicago, in the season of 1879, that shows the lengths to which selfishness and spite may be carried at the risk of reputation.

The season was opened by Madame Gerster. On each side of the stage were dressing rooms, and though they were alike in every respect, Gerster happened to choose that on the right-hand side. From this fact that room came to be called the "*prima donna's* room."

On the second night the opera given was Mozart's "*Le Nozze di Figaro*," in which Mme. Roze and Minnie Hauk took prominent parts. Thinking to secure the *prima donna's* room for herself, Miss Hauk went to the theater at three o'clock in the afternoon and had her trunks and dresses placed in it. But at four o'clock Mme. Roze's maid, discovering what had been done, told Roze's husband, and he had Hauk's trunks taken to the opposite room, and his wife's belongings placed in the coveted apartment.

An hour or so later, Minnie Hauk's agent happened in to see if things were all right, and found Roze's costumes where Hauk's were supposed to be. So he ordered the baggage reversed and had a padlock put on the door.

When, at six o'clock, Mme. Roze put in an appearance at her dressing-room and found it locked, she secured a locksmith, had the door opened, and ousted Hauk's belongings and proceeded to personally occupy the *prima donna's* room. On Minnie Hauk's coming early, as she supposed, to steal a march on her rival, she found Roze had outwitted her.

But one thing was left the fair Minnie to do, and this she did. She went back to her hotel and declared she would not sing a note that night. It was only after the manager and his lawyers had labored with the irate songstress for some two hours that she was finally persuaded to go back to the theater and assume her part, after the opera was one-third finished.

266.—ARISTOCRATIC PATRONAGE—HAYDN'S FAREWELL.

The composers of previous centuries were largely dependent on the patronage of the titled aristocracy for their support. In those times class lines and distinctions were drawn closer than to-day. The lower and middle classes were more deficient in education and culture. If a composer did not secure the good will of one or more titled patrons, his works went unperformed and he remained unknown and unappreciated.

It was fortunate that the nobility patronized art in the seventeenth and eighteenth centuries, for, had it been otherwise, many a masterpiece would never have seen the light of day. What the Church did for the arts in the dark ages the nobility did in later times.

To-day the artist asks protection of neither Church nor aristocracy. The greatest artists come from the common people—the middle classes—and these same classes do the most to support the artist by admiring, appreciating, and paying for his works.

In Europe painters and sculptors still depend to a great extent on the nobility for patronage, as the nobility holds the preponderance of the wealth of that continent. This will be true as long as the poorer classes are kept poor by paying to crowned heads such sums as £5,000 per day, the expense of the Czar of Russia, or £1,200 per day, the salary of the German Emperor.

But it is not so with music. The musician works for the people. The people of all classes flock to hear his music and appreciate it. It matters not whether the nobility attend. The people see that the composer gets what is due him.

In the last century things were different. Händel, Haydn, Mozart, Gluck—all engaged in a scramble for the favors royalty had to bestow. The very constitution of things made this necessary. The composers were poor. The prince was wealthy. Securing the prince's favor meant a pension, a home, an orchestra, a hearing. Without aristocratic patronage all this was lost. Be it said to the credit of good old John Sebastian Bach that he remained true to his allegiance to the Church and its music and sought no favor from king or prince. But Bach died almost a pauper, while his son flourished at court.

Even the present century has seen a patronizing monarch and a fawning musician. Wagner received uncounted favors at the hands of the mad King of Bavaria, until he almost thought himself a king, and treated his royal patron with base ingratitude.

Haydn was for many years at the head of musical matters at Prince Esterhazy's establishment. This liberal and highly educated Hungarian Prince gave him every opportunity for composition, and placed him in a comfortable position of ease and freedom from care or want.

But a period of retrenchment set in, and, as usual, it began to be felt first in musical matters. Haydn was informed that the Prince felt he must give up the orchestra which he had long maintained. We can imagine that to entirely support a body of twenty-five or thirty men required no small sum. But the cost was much less in that day than in ours.

So Haydn set about composing a symphony which was to be played before the Prince and his guests at the last appearance of the orchestra. A brilliant company had assembled. The symphony began. At first the strains were merry; but ere long they grew more sad and plaintive. A player back in the rear of the band was seen to blow out his candle, take up his instrument, and leave. Soon another did the same. This was unheard of. Had all discipline come to an end? But the plaintive strain wails on. More players leave. Finally there remains only the first violinist. His sorrowful cadences continue for a few moments; then he, too, follows his brethren.

Haydn turns to the Prince, bows his head on his breast, and lays down his *baton*.

This was the " Farewell Symphony."

Cried Prince Esterhazy, " What does all this mean ? "

" It is our sorrowful farewell," replied the composer.

The Prince was overcome, and promised to reconsider his decision. He kept his word; and Haydn and his whole orchestra were reinstated and remained in the service of this generous and appreciative friend of art to the day of his death.

267.—THE HEBREW IN MUSIC.

Prior to this century we find in musical history no great names of Jewish origin. Doubtless there were many professional musicians of Hebrew origin before the times of Mendelssohn, Meyerbeer, and Moscheles, but the fact remains that they are the first with Jewish blood in their veins to make a name in the musical world. After these three great " Ms" we find the number continually increasing, and if we subtract from musical literature that which Jewish blood has added, we leave the world much poorer. A brilliant array of Hebrew names is there upon the page of modern music, —Goldmark, Jadassohn, Rubinstein, Cowen, Joachim,

Wieniawski, Damrosch, Ernst, David, Costa, Hiller, Halevy, and even Offenbach. Truly, an array to be proud of. Among these we find men that have been in the very first rank as composers of symphony, opera, and all other musical forms; and we also find conductors and performers of almost unexcelled merit. The two great faiths, the Catholic and the Hebrew, have done more for the art than the world is willing to acknowledge.

268.—THE STORY OF MOZART'S REQUIEM.

Not long before Mozart died he was visited by a tall and dignified stranger, who said he came from a person who did not want his name to be known, but who wished that Mozart should compose a requiem for the soul of a friend recently lost, and whose memory he was desirous of commemorating by this solemn service. Mozart undertook the task, and engaged to have it completed in a month. They arranged the price that was to be paid for the composition, and the stranger paid Mozart a hundred ducats in advance.

Mozart was at that time in ill health, and was affected frequently with a deep melancholy. The mystery of this visit seemed to produce a profound effect on his mind, and he brooded over it for some time, and then set to work earnestly at composition. So intense was the ardor of his application that he was taken with fainting spells, and was finally obliged to suspend his work. "I am writing this requiem for myself," he said one day to his wife; "it will serve for my own funeral service."

At the end of the month the stranger appeared and asked for his requiem.

"I have found it impossible," said Mozart, "to keep my word; the work has interested me more than I expected, and I have extended it beyond my first design. I shall require another month to finish it." The mysterious stranger made no objection, but, saying that Mozart should be compensated for his extra work, he laid down fifty ducats on the table and departed, promising to return at the end of another month. Mozart sent a servant to follow his visitor and, if possible, to find out who he was, but the servant lost sight of him.

More than ever persuaded that his visitor was a messenger from the other world sent to warn him that his end was approaching, Mozart applied himself with fresh zeal to the requiem, and, in spite of his exhaustion of body and mind, he completed it before the end of the month.

At the appointed day the stranger came for the work and received it, but the composer's work on earth was finished.

Later investigation proved that the visitor was the servant of a certain nobleman, who wished in this manner to obtain a composition which he could pass off as his own work, written by himself, and dedicated to his wife's memory; and for many years the fraud remained undiscovered.

269.—LISZT'S REPLY TO LOUIS PHILIPPE.

In Liszt's essay on "The Position of an Artist in France," he scored King Louis Philippe and his administration quite severely on their niggardly appropriations for music. Ever after that he avoided meeting the king and declined to play at the Tuileries. But some time afterward he came face to face with His Majesty at an exhibition, and the king engaged him in conversation. Liszt could not escape, but only answered with a bow and "Yes, Sire."

"Do you remember," said the king at last, "that you played at my house when you were but a boy and I Duke of Orleans? Much has changed since then."

"Yes," Liszt burst forth, "but not for the better."

The result of this reply was that when the roll of

names for the cross of the Legion of Honor was sent to the king, he drew his pen through the name of Franz Liszt.

270.—JENNY LIND'S GENEROSITY.

During Jenny Lind's wonderful career, her name became a synonym for generosity. This most talented singer probably gave more money to the cause of charity than any other two singers on record, and the singers of all ages have been proverbially lavish with their gifts.

In 1849, while singing in Germany, she signed a contract with P. T. Barnum, the great showman, for a series of one hundred and fifty concerts in America, at a rate of one thousand dollars per night and all expenses. The tour was to begin the next year. The intervening time she spent in England and on the Continent, and the proceeds of all the concerts given that year she devoted to charitable uses.

When she arrived in New York in 1850, the people were crazy to see and hear this wonderful "Swedish Nightingale." Mr. Barnum had stirred up curiosity in the manner for which he was celebrated, and the "Lind fever" raged as strong in this country as it had previously in England. On her arrival she was greeted by a crowd of thirty thousand people and serenaded by a band of one hundred and fifty instruments. On the day of her first concert, five thousand people stood in the rain to buy tickets, and the first one was sold to an enterprising hatter for six hundred dollars. The proceeds of this first concert, which was attended by seven thousand people, were twenty-six thousand dollars. It is said that her share was ten thousand dollars, every cent of which she gave to benevolent societies of New York city. Her charitable gifts on this American tour were numerous, amounting to fifty thousand dollars. In Germany she had previously scattered thirty thousand florins and in England some sixty thousand pounds in charity.

Having a difficulty with Mr. Barnum, she paid a forfeit to him of thirty thousand dollars and gave the last sixty concerts of the series on her own management. In 1852, in the city of Boston, she was married to Otto Goldschmidt, her accompanist, and the same year they returned to England, where this famous singer retired to private life.

Besides the fifty thousand dollars given in charity, she had received in America one hundred and fifty thousand dollars, and this latter sum she devoted to charities and educational uses in her native country of Sweden. The whole sum of her beneficences has been estimated at one hundred thousand pounds.

271.—BEETHOVEN, BRAIN-OWNER.

Beethoven's relatives have not come down to us lauded as examples of sobriety or kindliness. His brother, Johann, was in many ways the opposite of the composer. Ludwig van Beethoven was possessed of genius, Johann had none; Ludwig had little of this world's goods, Johann had considerable; Ludwig had knowledge instead of business talent, while Johann could turn what he touched into gold and despised his brother's lack of money making. But with all this, the world worships at Ludwig's shrine and has no cause to remember that Johann ever lived.

Johann used to delight in refreshing his brother's memory as to his success in life—a proceeding which we may imagine did not add to the musician's sweetness of temper. On one occasion, however, Ludwig rather got the upper hand of his purse-proud brother, but we may question whether the latter saw the point. Johann having purchased a piece of land, felt rather elated at being a landlord, and sent to his brother on New Year's a card with his name inscribed:—

" Johann van Beethoven, Land-owner."

On receiving it, the composer snatched it up and hastily wrote on the back of the card:—

"Ludwig van Beethoven, *Brain-owner*," and sent it back to his proud relative.

272.—SCHUBERT'S MODESTY.

True worth is always modest. This was especially seen, among the great composers, in the case of Franz Schubert. A characteristic bit of his modesty we find in the account of his first meeting with Beethoven. Grove tells us of this meeting in these words:—

"Beethoven was at home, and we know the somewhat overwhelming courtesy with which he welcomed a stranger. Schubert was bashful and retiring, and when the great man handed him paper and pencil provided for the replies of visitors, Schubert could not collect himself sufficiently to write a word. Then Schubert produced some variations which he had enthusiastically dedicated to Beethoven, and this added to Beethoven's good humor. The master opened them and looked through them, and seeing something which startled him, naturally pointed it out. At this Schubert's last remnant of self-control deserted him and he rushed from the room. When he got into the street and was out of the magic of Beethoven's personality, his presence of mind returned, and all that he might have said flashed upon him, but it was too late."

273.—OUR MUSICAL ADVANCEMENT.

But few of the great composers have heard their works given with such completeness and skill as they can be given to-day. Wagner was of course an exception to this rule. In our day, while the voices may not be better they are used in more massive combinations, and the orchestral instruments have been improved by modern skill. But of course the stringed instruments are an exception to this rule. The organs of to-day are larger and have a more flexible action and greater varieties of tone color than in the time of Bach. The piano of to-day has a much greater volume of tone and an increased compass over the piano of Beethoven's time. In the field of choral music the choruses have been largely augmented, though, to be sure, a large chorus does not always promise the best results in shading and promptitude.

Händel heard no such choruses give his oratorios as we may hear sing them to-day.

When "The Messiah" was first given in Dublin the chorus consisted simply of the choirs at the two cathedral churches. And if Dean Swift had been sane in 1742 it is doubtful whether Händel would have been allowed the use of St. Patrick's choir, for in 1741 the great Dean addressed an exhortation to the Sub-Dean and Chapter, commenting on the conduct of certain members of the choir for "singing and fiddling at a club of fiddlers." The choruses that took part in the performance of Händel's oratorios during his lifetime numbered less than 100 singers. The chorus brought together for the great commemoration performances in Westminster Abbey and in the Pantheon in 1784 was made up of about 275 singers, and yet its size was the astonishment of the contemporaneous musical world.

What would the musicians and public of that day have said to a chorus of five or six thousand singers, such as are now frequently gathered together?

274.—HONEST OPINIONS.

Professional musicians often have questions propounded to them that are quite hard to answer, and occasionally some to which, were the truth answered, the reply would not be particularly enjoyed by the questioner. Very frequently some fond mamma brings her aspiring daughter, who, by the way, hardly knows the difference between the manipulation of the piano and that of the bass drum, and seeks to be told that her fair offspring is an incipient Clara Schumann or Fannie Bloomfield, and only needs a few suggestions from a teacher to be ready to take the concert stage. Or, perhaps the fair damsel has succeeded in singing the first ten bars of "Bel Raggio" and can sing "Home, Sweet Home" (*à la* Patti) without getting off the pitch more than five times. The aspiring *mater* insists that the daughter has a heavenly voice and remarkable talent, and will surely be able to graduate next year, and possibly this year, if the teacher is propitious. And she feels personally insulted if the teacher ventures to offer the information that even the first principles of correct breathing are unknown,—that the tones are throaty and not "placed" at all,—that her daughter has to have a thing taught to her by hearing it (like a parrot), and cannot read two consecutive measures correctly,—and that it is necessary to have at least a majority of the notes in tune; but when he adds that it will take two or more years to complete the purely theoretical part of the musical education, the pair take their departure in angry haste and declare that they will go to some teacher who knows a little something about music, and who will at least not insult defenseless ladies who call upon him with the most honorable of intentions.

It would save trouble, though it might lose the teacher an occasional pupil, if he were always to be as honest as was the great French teacher and composer, Cherubini.

One day he was appealed to by a singer, a man with a tremendous voice, to tell him what art he had better follow,—if he had not better become a singer. Cherubini at once asked him to sing, whereupon he opened his mouth and the foundations well nigh trembled with his bellowing.

"What shall I become?" he asked, when he had finished.

"An auctioneer," laconically answered the master.

The singer fled.

275.—THE MODERN TENDENCY.

The modern tendency is to do away with the lengthy repetitions which characterized the music of the old classic school. Quite a number of the standard compositions of that epoch are subject to a pruning-down process when given a modern hearing. Whole acts of some of the longer operas are frequently omitted, such as "*Roberto*" and "*L'Africaine*" of Meyerbeer, and in others some of the longer-winded parts are excised in performance. Wagner's "*Lohengrin*" is treated to this kind of a pruning, and the day will doubtless come when this same process will be used in his later works. The general opera-going public, outside of a certain circle of enthusiasts, do not care to hear operas four and five hours long, or a series of operas that, to complete, one must hear three or four presentations. The day of the bulky three-volumed novel is past.

The "Messiah" is so generally "cut" that we might say it is never given in its entirety. Even with a dozen numbers omitted it takes some two hours to give this great oratorio. In it, also, a majority of the long repeats are omitted.

Beethoven felt this spirit dawning even in his day and was inclined to meet it half way. To the opera of "Leonore" he wrote four different overtures before he was satisfied. In the second of these, of which there are two manuscripts in existence, there are many excisions, some of them being ten, fifteen, or twenty measures in length. Had some other and lesser lights submitted their music to this same pruning operation, their works would be more frequently heard and stand higher in the estimation of the musical public.

276.—FUGUES AND CHESS.

Many are the musical prodigies who come before the public, though but few of them reach the great heights of musicianship of which they, in their youth, give promise. Händel, Mozart, and Liszt fulfilled the expectations aroused by their youthful feats.

Among those whose fame was not so great was Walter Parratt, who was knighted by Queen Victoria. He played the organ in a Yorkshire church when only seven years old. At ten he performed all of Bach's forty-eight preludes and fugues without the music before him, and in later life he accomplished the extraordinary feat of playing, blindfolded, three games of chess and one of Bach's fugues at the same time, manipulating the keys of the organ and calling out his moves on the chess-board simultaneously.

277.—FORTUNES IN FIDDLES.

The prices set on their instruments by the makers of them, the appreciation in value, and the immense sums now demanded for the works of the old masters, forms a most interesting topic, to which, however, we can give but short space.

Stradivarius received for each violin four *Louis d'or*, and these same instruments would to-day mount into hundreds of pounds in value. His violoncellos he sold for a larger sum. Stradivarius' instruments were not appreciated in their earlier days in England, for it is related that a merchant named Cervetto took some "Strad" 'cellos to England and put them on sale, but not being able to get five pounds apiece for them he sent them back to Italy as a bad investment. They would now bring several hundreds of pounds each. While his 'cellos were thus lightly valued in England in those days, we find a Cremona violin selling in 1662 for £20.

A "Strad" 'cello which had been played by three generations of the Servais family, brought £5,000 when placed on sale a few years ago in Vienna.

The phrase, "worth its weight in gold," may well be applied to such transactions. On weighing a Stradivarius violin sold in 1856, it was found to have brought £40 an ounce. The great bass player, Dragonetti, had a celebrated Stradivarius double-bass which he valued at £1,000. It would now probably bring three times that amount.

In 1716 Stradivarius made a violin, which in 1760 he sold to a Count Salabue, after whose death in 1824 it was purchased by Tarisio, the peripatetic violin collector. He kept the treasure hidden, but after his death it was ferreted out by Viullaume who, in turn, on his death, left it to his son-in-law, Alard, the violinist. A few years ago it was sold to a Scotch violin collector for £2,000. Madame Norman-Neruda gave £2,000 for one "Strad" which had belonged to Ernst, and Wilhelmji paid £3,000 for another, for which he was afterward offered £5,000.

Stradivarius' is not alone in bringing high sums. Amati's and Guarnerius' instruments have had a similar appreciation in value. In 1790 Foster, the English instrument dealer, sold a Nicholas Amati for £19, and in 1804 another for £30. These would now bring from £200 to £300 each. In 1827 one of his 'cellos sold for £280, and in 1859 a violin by the brothers Amati brought £140. It may be imagined that some of the fiddles of Guarnerius "del Jesu" brought him originally but a pittance; but in 1826 we hear of one of his 'cellos bringing £120. Wieniawski's Guarnerius was sold to Hubey, of Brussels, for £3,000, and Ferdinand David's favorite instrument, a Guarnerius, was bought by Zajic, of the Strasburg Conservatory, for £4,000.

General Morgan Melville, of Cincinnati, related that his father, who, by the way, was an *aide-de-camp* to La Fayette, gave 1,500 acres of land, then valued at a dollar per acre, for a Stainer violin that took his fancy. This was quite a fair price in those days, but the value of the payment would be somewhat enhanced now by the fact that this land is at present covered by the city of Pittsburg. As Stainer rarely received large sums for his violins, that one would have been a good investment could the original purchaser have waited two hundred and twenty-five years to realize on his investment.

278.—ONE KIND OF CRITICISM.

Cherubini was able to make use of a species of criticism that was pointed enough, and yet was of a kind that could give no one excuse for blaming his sharpness of tongue. When a disagreeable topic was introduced or when that was brought to his notice that he felt deserved his condemnation, he retired into silence and could not be persuaded to open his mouth on the subject.

Halévy was a favorite pupil of this celebrated French composer, and on one occasion asked the old master to go with him to hear one of Halévy's operas. At the end of the first act he asked Cherubini how he liked it.

No reply.

At the end of the second act he repeated his question with more emphasis. Still no reply.

"Will you not give me an answer?"

Cherubini was still silent.

Halévy then became so enraged that he got up and left the box, muttering indignation at his teacher's sitting there for two hours without deigning to say a word.

Afterward a reconciliation was effected and Cherubini was prevailed upon to point out those points in the opera that caused him to make such a severe, though such a silent, criticism. Cherubini might, in this respect, serve for a model for the numerous musical critics who afflict their friends and the public with their uneducated inanities. He was silent because he knew so much. They are verbose because they know so little.

279.—MUSICAL COOKS.

Curious stories have come down to us as to the idiosyncrasies of many a noted musician; but we have not elsewhere had occasion to note one peculiar enjoyment that several of them have taken in an occupation that is not generally supposed to give great pleasure to the average man. We refer to the art of cooking. Not a musical art, certainly, but one deprived of which we might hardly relish even a Beethoven symphony.

Lulli was an accomplished cook and used frequently to return to the instruments of his early days, *i. e.*, pots and kettles. For his original occupation was that of cook's assistant. From him, considering his early training, we might certainly expect musical *pot-pourris*.

Then there were the Italian musicians Rossini and Paganini. They each enjoyed dabbling in the regions where the cook is supposed to have full sway. The violinist especially was fond of this occupation and turned it to good account when in later years he became so miserly. We may well suppose that neither of them (being Italian) was forgetful of the odoriferous little plant called garlic, in the preparation of their artistic dishes.

And then the greatest musician to cook, if not the greatest cook among musicians, was Beethoven. He had an idea that no one could prepare his food quite as well as he could himself. It is probable that he had a good deal of experience at it, perhaps more than he really wanted at times. For his treatment of his servants was so peculiar that it was seldom one would stay with him for any length of time. Part of his culinary arrangements Beethoven determined with mathematical accuracy A friend once found him counting coffee grains, and on inquiring the reason for the seemingly absurd occupation he was informed that sixty grains was just the right number to produce the best possible cup of coffee.

280.—ARTISTIC PRIDE.

Musical artists have a proper pride as to circumstances and surroundings in their public appearances. In former days the musician was content to be a servant, to eat at second tables, and to be railed off from the aristocracy that boasted money instead of brains. Nowadays things have changed and a musician's art is the "open sesame" to the high places of the earth. There is an aversion on the part of a true artist toward appearing amid other than dignified surroundings.

This was shown not many years ago in Vienna, where there were being given a series of symphony concerts at popular prices; the listeners were seated at tables where refreshments, solid and liquid—more particularly the latter—were served. At each of these concerts some well-known composer has conducted one or more of his own compositions. Tschaikowsky was also invited to direct one of the series, but hearing that popular prices were charged and the hall resembled a restaurant he refused to assist at the concert, for which the celebrated Russian pianist, Sapellnikow, was also engaged to play. So, after having traveled for these concerts all the way from St. Petersburg to Vienna, he packed his valise and returned to Russia.

281.—BEETHOVEN'S FRIENDS.

Beethoven was fortunate in finding friends during all of his career who would humor his caprices and could understand his whims.

When quite young he lost his mother, and this was a great blow to the loving son. Beethoven looked upon his mother as his dearest and best friend. After her death he wrote: "Who was happier than I while I could yet pronounce the sweet name of mother? There was once some one to hear me when I said 'mother.' But to whom can I address that name now? Only to the silent pictures of her which my fancy paints." Fortunately he found a second mother in Mrs. Breuning, in whose house at Bonn he soon came to be regarded as one of the children. He spent the greater part of every day with the Breuning family, who were, as Schindler says, his guardian angels, and his friendship with whom was never interrupted for a moment during his whole life.

Soon after his arrival in Vienna Beethoven was fortunate enough to make the acquaintance of the Prince and Princess Lichnowsky, who seem at once to have taken the young musician to their hearts, and who treated him almost like an adopted son. The Prince gave him an allowance of 600 florins, while the Princess did her best to spoil him—finding everything that the young man did or left undone, right, clever, original, and amiable. In later years Beethoven, when speaking of these good friends, said: "They would have brought me up with grandmotherly fondness, which was carried to such a length that very often the Princess was on the point of having a glass shade made to put over me so that no unworthy person might touch or breathe upon me." The Lichnowskys do not appear to have been alone in this treatment of the young composer, for we are told that his eccentricities met with indulgence and even admiration from high and low, and that there was a time when the name Beethoven had become a general password to which everybody gave way.

But Beethoven's friends had much to suffer from his suspicious disposition. When the Ninth symphony was produced, in 1824, it was given with great success, but the receipts were painfully meagre. Beethoven, as usual, accused his friends of defrauding him. Six months later he saw his error and begged Schindler and Duport to forgive him. He was extremely suspicious, and at times would not trust his best friends. But when convinced of his wrong, he would try to make peace in so hearty a manner that they would forgive every insult and vexation they had received at his hands. In a repentant note to Schindler, after one of these outbursts, he says:—

"What an abominable picture of myself you have shown me! I am not worthy of your friendship. I did not meditate a base action; it was thoughtlessness which urged me to my unpardonable conduct toward you. I fly to you, and in an embrace ask for my lost friend; and you will restore him to me,—to your contrite, faithful, and loving friend, Beethoven."

282.—PROLIFIC COMPOSERS.

If it is true that of the making of books there is no end, it would seem to the student of musical history that the same might be said of operas. Nearly every young composer, at one time or other in his career, feels called upon to inflict an opera on an already long-suffering world. But we should not object to this, for it does the composer "a power o' good," and doesn't harm the world any, for but a small percentage of the operas ever reach the point of a public presentation.

It will be noticed in the following list that the composers most celebrated for the value of their operas are not those who turned out the largest number. A great work must naturally represent a great brain, and long and intense application of it. It is not to be expected that he who does twenty things should do them as well as he who does two. So, other things being equal, we would naturally expect greater works where there has not been such a continuous flow of them.

Perhaps the composer most prolific of operas was Reinhart Keiser, who has 120 to his credit, although one authority claims that Piccinni wrote 133 operas. Alessandro Scarlatti composed 115; Pacini and Piccinni each 80; Donizetti, 70; Mercadante, 60; Auber, 50; Händel, 43; Coccia, 40; Rossini, 39; Halévy, 32; Verdi, 29; Ricci, 28; Haydn, 24; Mozart, 23; Meyerbeer, 15; Gounod, 13; Wagner, 13; and Bellini, 10; while from Beethoven's colossal mind there came but one lone opera.

283.—MUSIC FOR THE EYE.

Composers get queer ideas into their heads sometimes. Some think they can represent storms and battles in music; but they always take pains to tell one in plain type just what is supposed to be going on, thus showing the inadequacy of music to depict concrete ideas. One old composer, Kuhnau, undertook to illustrate the Bible by clavichord sonatas, but it is not recorded that he made any converts to religion thereby or that his exegesis was satisfactory to the theologians. Another, Matheson, Händel's rival, undertook to represent a rainbow when setting music to the words, "And there was a rainbow round the throne." He made the notes on the full score look like an arch beginning and ending in the low double bass notes, the apex being in the piccolo part. While this might give a faint idea of a rainbow to the eye, we doubt if it would to the ear.

284.—SCHUMANN'S MADNESS.

The border-land between great genius and insanity is narrower than we sometimes realize. Some of the great minds in the music life have passed over the dividing line; some have come back to a correct mental balance, but others suffered this mental affliction until relieved by the Grim Reaper.

It is not generally known that Hans von Bülow spent some time in an asylum. But such was the case, and the rest and quiet restored his tired and slightly unbalanced mind to its usual strength.

Next to Beethoven in intensity of thought and feeling, stands Robert Schumann. It was perhaps the continual habit of mental concentration and overtaxing his physical and mental energies that hastened the painful malady that caused his death. Some twelve years before this occurred, he began to be afflicted with excruciating pains in the head, sleeplessness, and other troubles caused by a disarrangement of the mental and nervous systems, such as fear of death and strange auricular delusions.

A visit to Italy and its relaxation from work gave him some relief and he returned to Germany; and during the three years that followed he penned some of his finest works, such as his Second symphony, "The Rose's Pilgrimage" and music to Byron's "Manfred." For eight years after this Italian journey Schumann was continually occupied with composition and directing concerts, but during the latter part of this period the pain in his head had so increased as to make him unaccountable for his actions. In fact, at one time in 1854, he attempted to end his life by jumping into the river Rhine. The malady now seized him with a grasp that was loosened only for short intervals.

In spite of the loving care of Madame Schumann, who was a celebrated pianiste and one of the ablest exponents of his works, this great composer was obliged to end his days, in 1856, in a private insane asylum near Bonn, the birth-place of Beethoven.

285.—HUMOR IN COMPOSITION.

We are told that "all work and no play makes Jack a dull boy," or something to that effect. The famous composers evidently believed this, for not only do we find in some of their serious works comical touches, but several of them, and those the greatest, too, have written works that are entirely humorous in their character.

Of the comical touches we might mention the three bassoon notes in Beethoven's Sixth, or Pastoral, symphony. Here we might imagine some old bassoonist seated on a cask, playing the only tones that can be gotten out of his dilapidated instrument, while the village rustics join in a clumsy dance. Then, too, there is that unmistakable bray which Mendelssohn associates (a good word in this case) with "Bottom" in his "Midsummer Night's Dream" music, and there are also the antics of the music to accompany the entrance of the clowns in the same composition.

We would hardly expect to find anything humorous coming from that old periwig, Sebastian Bach. Yet Bach has left us two cantatas, entitled "The Peasant's Cantata" and "The Coffee Party," in which he is supposed to be very funny. But the humor is so artistically concealed—shall we say—in florid counterpoint that to our non-appreciative ears it would sound more like a fugue from the "Well-Tempered Clavichord" than a side-splitting farce. But then perhaps the humor of that day had to have its *canti fermi*, counter subjects and episodes.

Haydn's humor was more pointed and sudden, especially in the "Surprise" symphony, when an explosive *sfz—fortissimo* occurs in a *pianissimo* passage. The "Toy" symphony, too, has a decided humorous side. Then there is a composition for instruments called "A Musical Joke," wherein he parodies the attempt of an uneducated composer to write a symphony.

We may once find even Beethoven writing a comic song. He must then have been in a thoroughly "unbuttoned" mood, as he used to express it, especially as the song had fourteen verses. In his Op., 129, Beethoven vents his "fury over a lost groschen" in a beautiful rondo.

Wagner used many a comic touch in his "Mastersingers of Nuremburg," but it is done with the most artistic musical means and the deftest of touch, forming some of the most delicious musical humor ever written. He also wrote a burlesque work entitled "A Capitulation."

An instance of neat humor is Gounod's popular little

"Funeral March of a Marionette," too familiar to require any explanation further than to say it depicts the breaking of a Marionette and the subsequent lamentations of the troupe as they bear it to the grave. It is, after a fashion, a musical Humpty-Dumpty. Another instance is the chorus of students in Berlioz's "Damnation of Faust," who sing an elaborate chorus in the form of fugue, the entire development being wrought out on the word "amen." It was Berlioz's idea in this to ridicule the method and pedantry of the old school, just as Wagner had done in his "Meistersinger." In Schumann's "Children's Album" there are several charming instances of musical humor, the "Don't Frighten Me" and "The Bear Dance" recalling themselves to our memory specially. Indeed, with only a little investigation into musical literature, one might make out quite a long list of examples of this kind.

A modern example of real humor is a composition by Dr. J. K. Paine, America's greatest native composer. In this he exploits the virtues of a certain patent medicine, prominent before the public some years ago, and tells all about the virtues of Radway's Ready Relief to a musical setting that is of the most musicianly character. The text is simply an old newspaper advertisement of the patent medicine. These utterly prosaic words are set for four-part male chorus and bass recitative.

The certificate from the rheumatic sufferer is given to a dramatic *agitato* movement, and the price of the medicine is heralded in learned counterpoint. The music cleverly takes off both the Händelian contrapuntal and the modern romantic styles, the burlesque solemnity of the writing being infinitely comic, the whole ending with a sidesplitting parody on the Finale to "Egmont," and not forgetting the little shrieks of the piccolo (the only instrument employed). The very excellences of the writing and the purity of the musical form add an element of ludicrousness to what altogether affords one of the best instances of the composer at play, but not forgetting his erudition in his humor.

286.—HAYDN'S LAST APPEARANCE.

Haydn was a very religious man, and at the same time conscientious and modest. That he recognized the source of his musical talent and rendered unto God the things that are God's, is shown in the following incident:—

In 1808, shortly before Haydn's death, a grand performance of his oratorio of the "Creation" took place in Vienna. Haydn was present, an old man of seventy-six years. He was so feeble as to be wheeled into the theater in a chair. This was the last time that the venerable composer made his appearance in public, and then it was only as a listener, his age and state of health precluding any active performance.

The audience greeted the old man with great enthusiasm, and when, in the course of the work, the orchestra and chorus arrived at the place where there is a sudden change from the minor to the major, at the words "And there was light," they created a tumult of applause.

The old composer struggled to his feet, and mustering up all his strength cried in reply to the applause of the audience, in as loud a tone as he was able:—

"No, no! not from me, but from thence, from heaven above, comes all!" at the same time pointing upward.

He fell back in his chair exhausted by the excitement, and was hastily removed to his home, never again to come before his beloved Austrian public.

287.—THE HEROIC IN MUSIC.

Beethoven recognized in Napoleon Bonaparte some traits of character that were natural to his own rugged and world-defying disposition. In order to testify to his admiration for what he considered the heroic elements of Napoleon's character, the great composer dedicated to him one of his greatest symphonies.

This symphony, Number 3, Opus 55, has been regarded by some as "an attempt to draw a musical portrait of a historical character,—a great statesman, a great general, a noble individual; to represent in music, Beethoven's language, what Thiers has given in words, and Delaroche in painting."

One writer has said of this symphony: "It wants no title to tell its meaning, for throughout the symphony the hero is visibly portrayed." Such views as these concerning any music are rather far-fetched. We doubt if this same writer would have associated a hero with this symphony on his first hearing of it if he had not previously been educated to the fact that it represented the heroic in music. If a hero can be pictured in music, so can a scoundrel; if these, then a saint, a sinner.

However, if the hint is given, then we can see massiveness and strength in the music that we may parallel in our own minds to our ideal of a hero. But without this hint, this massiveness and grandeur may just as well portray a chain of lofty mountains rearing their snow-capped tops in majesty above the surrounding scene.

We doubt if Beethoven intended or expected his music to represent to the hearer a concrete hero. When he wished concrete images to come to the mind of his hearers he did not depend on music to fulfil this errand, so foreign to its mission, but wrote, in so many words, the scene or idea that he wished to be in the listener's mind as he heard the music. For proof of this see the annotations affixed to the various movements of the "Pastoral" (sixth) symphony, and, somewhat similar, the "Farewell, Absence and Return" sonata.

But, undoubtedly, as much of the heroic as can be expressed in music, Beethoven has given us in this "Heroic" symphony. It is not a hero, but the heroic, that he portrayed, that he could portray in music; the large, the grand, the massive.

Then, the natural thing to do was to dedicate it to the man that filled in his mind at that time the niche of hero. That happened to be Napoleon I.

The original score had been sent to the French ambassador to be forwarded to France (and much Napoleon would have cared for it had he ever received it!), when one day in came Ferdinand Ries, a pupil of Beethoven, and told the news that Napoleon had taken the title of "Emperor" and had crowned himself Emperor of the French.

When Beethoven heard this, he started up in a rage, seized his copy of the "Heroic" symphony and, tearing off the title page with the dedication thereon, he threw it on the floor, exclaiming: "After all, he is nothing but an ordinary mortal. He, too, will trample the rights of men under foot!"

From that time till Napoleon's death at St. Helena Beethoven never spoke of his hero; but when that event occurred he said: "I have already composed music for this calamity," referring to the "Funeral March" in this symphony. Meanwhile he changed the dedication of the work, making it read "HEROIC SYMPHONY, composed to celebrate the memory of a great man. Dedicated to His Serene Highness Prince Lobkowitz, by Louis van Beethoven."

288.—A PECULIAR VISITING CARD.

In Haydn's old age he resided in quiet repose at his villa at Grumpendorff, near Vienna. When he wished to remind some old friend of his uncertain health and of his still lingering on this planet, he would send him one of his cards, on which was engraved a passage from the close of his last quartet. The music consisted of but a dozen notes of melody; but the rhythm was halting and the ending had no cadence. It was well suited to the words he had added underneath, which ran:—

"Hin ist alle meine kraft,
Alt und schwach bin ich."

Which may be translated,

> "All my strength has left me,
> Old and weak am I."

289.—ORIGIN OF THE NAME "KREUTZER SONATA."

The great composers frequently dedicated their works to friends or patron princes whose names are known to us only by this fact of their appearing on the title pages of some masterpiece.

Sometimes, musicians who were famous in their own day have had their very names forgotten in our times, were it not that some such dedication keeps their memory alive.

So it was with Rudolph Kreutzer, once a famous violinist and composer. To him Beethoven dedicated his great sonata for violin and piano, Opus 47, the sonata universally known as the "Kreutzer Sonata."

But it was only an accident and a whim of the composer's that gave Kreutzer this celebrity. Beethoven had intended to dedicate this sonata to Bridgetower, a young violinist of his day, and, by the way, a native of Africa. But before the sonata was published Beethoven and Bridgetower quarreled over a very commonplace subject, *i. e.*, a young lady.

As a result, the friendship was broken off and Bridgetower's name erased from the title page and that of Kreutzer substituted. But the peculiar part of it is that Beethoven is said to have known Kreutzer but slightly, and more than that, never to have seen him!

290.—ROYAL MUSICIANS.

Music has had its votaries among the crowned heads of all ages. None of them have achieved great fame, however, as composers or performers, as distinct from their royal positions. Were it not for their exalted station, we should never have heard of their accomplishments.

It is fame enough to be a prince or king without being a musician!

If we delved among the records of the ancient Greeks and Romans we might find many a monarch who was celebrated for his flute playing or his singing. We know that these personages were excellent performers, for did they not win all the contests into which they entered, even when their opponents were the principal musicians of their countries? In fact, the continuation of the good health of the opponent required that the emperor should be victor.

We have all read the old story of how Nero fiddled while Rome burned. This is a very respectable and antique myth; for there are no records of any kind to show that the Romans knew or practiced the use of the bow—save to slay their enemies. No doubt the fiddle that Nero played on was a flute, that is, if he played at all on the occasion of that historical illumination.

Coming down to more modern times and less sanguinary musicians, we find the Emperor Charles the Fifth, of France, to have been quite a music critic (though that does not necessarily imply great musical erudition). His namesake, the Emperor Charles the Sixth of Austria was endowed with musical abilities of a very high order. So discriminating was his knowledge of musical worth, that Farinelli, the greatest singer of all Europe at that time, said that the Emperor gave him musical instruction that was "of more use to him than all the precepts of his masters or the examples of his rivals." The idea that this royal teacher advanced was that a more simple and less exaggerated style would reach the heart quicker than all the long notes, roulades, and *tours de force* that the singer could use.

King Henry VIII, he of frequent marriages, was regarded in his day as " extremely skilled in musical art " and as " acquitting himself divinely." He was quite a singer and played the organ, harpsichord, and lute. Besides this, he was a poet, and frequently set his verses to music. There are still in existence two services of his composition for the royal chapel.

Good Queen Bess and the unfortunate Mary, Queen of Scots, were both excellent performers on the virginal. Mary's ambassador at the court of Elizabeth one day heard her playing, and the Queen, discovering him, required his opinion as to which was the better player, she or his royal mistress. This inquiry placed the poor fellow " 'twixt the devil and the deep sea," as Queen Bess's temper was none of the most pacific, and of course he must not disparage his own Queen. But, courtier-like, he complimented them both and came out with flying colors.

Leopold I, of Germany, was an ardent lover of good music and kept up an orchestra that was regarded as being remarkable in its general *ensemble*. His love for music manifested itself up to the hour of his death. Feeling his end to be near, he sent for his band of players and ordered them to play a symphony. They obeyed, and the monarch expired with a full orchestral accompaniment, *à la opera*.

Frederic the Great was a fine flute player as well as having a large collection of harpsichords, spinets, and the like. So many flutes did he have that it required one man's time to keep them in good condition. This royal amateur had one good point. He considered it a disgrace to play a wrong note, and would never undertake a composition till he had shut himself up alone and practiced it for hours. Oh, for more of the kind! Emanuel Bach held the position of accompanist to Frederic the Great, and his especial duty was to accompany on the harpsichord as the king played his beloved flute. This monarch combined a musical appreciation with the strictness of a military martinet. He would station himself in the pit behind the conductor, so as to have a full view of the score. In this position he would frequently usurp the conductor's duties; and if a mistake were committed on the stage or in the orchestra, he would rebuke the offender on the spot. And if any of the singers ventured to alter a single passage he was reminded that he changed the notes at his peril, and that he had better adhere to the composer's intentions.

Queen Victoria was, in her youthful days, an excellent pianiste and vocalist. Mendelssohn relates that on visiting England he was entertained by the Queen and Prince Consort at Buckingham Palace, and that the Queen sang some of his songs with charming expression and feeling. Says he, "I praised her heartily and with the best conscience in the world." Prince Albert was himself an excellent organist and Mendelssohn leaves record that "his playing would have done credit to any professional." He was also a composer of no mean ability.

The Duke of Edinburg and Saxe-Coburg-Gotha has inherited his father's talent and is quite proficient as a violinist. He has appeared frequently in public both as a violinist and as an orchestral conductor. He is really possessed of much talent, although some of the Liberal papers delight to speak in a sneering way of the "royal fiddler."

The present Princess of Wales has had the degree of Doctor of Music conferred upon her by one of the great English universities, although it was evidently a matter of honoring royalty more than one of honoring a musician.

The royal family of Germany is also quite musical. The recent emperors have had considerable musical training and old Emperor William had been known to take the baton and conduct a military band, in this way securing a performance to his liking. The present Emperor, William II, is much of a musician and has even published a few compositions in march and song style. In one of his recent compositions both words and music are from the royal pen.

291.—A CHARITABLE TRIO.

One night near the middle of this century, three lively young students were strolling along a Paris boulevard in quest of exercise and recreation. In the course of their walk they came across an old man who was trying to play a violin he was almost too feeble to manage. The generous young fellows went down in their pockets, but the whole trio could only raise a few cents and a piece of rosin.

Thereupon one of them proposed to take the old man's violin and accompany the voices of his companions. No sooner said than done. Commencing with a solo upon the theme of the Carnival of Venice, a large concourse of listeners was soon attracted. Then came a favorite cavatina from "La Dame Blanche," sung in such a manner as to keep the audience spell-bound; and yet again the trio from "Guillaume Tell." By this time the poor old man was galvanized into life and activity by the artistic performance. He stood erect, and with his stick directed the concert with the authority of a practiced leader. Meanwhile contributions of silver and even gold rained into the old man's hat.

To his astonished and grateful demand to know who were his benefactors, he received from the first the name of Faith, and from the others the response of Hope and Charity. "And I," said the poor old fellow, "used to direct the opera at Strasburg. You have saved my life, for I can now go back to my native place, where I shall be able to teach what I can no longer perform."

The young violinist was Adolph Hermann, the tenor was Gustav Roger, and the originator of this charitable scheme was Charles Gounod.

292.—BEETHOVEN'S FORGETFULNESS.

Numerous stories are told of Beethoven offending those with whom he came into contact by his gruffness; but their number is almost equaled by the records of his seeking pardon from the people he had unintentionally offended. While he was forgetful in most matters of a non-musical nature, it was rarely that he was led into such a blunder as is here related.

When he brought out his Fantasia for the first time with an orchestra and chorus, he directed, at the usual hasty rehearsal, that the second variation should be played through without repeat. In the evening, however, completely absorbed in his own creation, he forgot the order he had given, and repeated the first part, while the orchestra accompanied the last, a combination not productive of the best effect.

At last, when it was too late, the composer suddenly stopped, looked up in amazement at his bewildered band, and said dryly, "Over again;" the leader unwillingly asked, "With the repeat?" "Yes," was echoed back, and this time things reached a happy conclusion.

That Beethoven had, to a certain degree, affronted these excellent musicians by his irregular proceeding, he would not at first allow; he contended that it was a duty to repair any previous error, and the public had a right to expect a perfect performance for their money. Nevertheless, he readily begged pardon of his orchestra for the unintentional offence, and was generous enough himself to spread the story abroad, and to lay the blame upon his own abstraction.

293.—ROSSINI'S ARROGANCE.

Royal patrons have often been overbearing, but, on the other hand, the patronized musician has frequently proved himself an insufferable bore.

The following incident would probably not have occurred had not music already broken away from royal patronage and become, as we might say, self-supporting.

Rossini was once the principal musical figure at a party given by King George IV, at St. James Palace, London. During the evening the king paid particular attention to the Italian composer, and was much pleased with his compositions. As the company was about to break up His Majesty said: "Now, Rossini, before we stop, let us have one piece more, and that shall be the *finale*."

But Rossini, insensible to the honors that had been bestowed upon him, arrogantly replied, "I think, Sire, we have had enough music for one night," and took his departure.

294.—TO A PAUPER'S GRAVE.

Poor Mozart! In life pushed from pillar to post; in sickness working to the last moment to bring bread to his family; in death occupying an unknown grave!

After Mozart's death, that night of December 4, 1791, the little house on Roughstone Lane, in Vienna, was almost deserted. Only two or three callers came. The men who made money by the dead master's genius stayed away. The widow was left almost destitute, as Mozart's fortune amounted to five pounds in money and his effects were valued at about twenty-six pounds more. A heavy draft on this was made by the undertaker's and doctor's bills, which amounted to perhaps twenty pounds.

The cold rain and sleet pounded down, that gloomy day when the little group left the house. After the services at the church the mourners dropped off, and when the hearse reached the cemetery no one followed the remains of the composer of "*Don Juan*" and the "Jupiter" symphony.

Two paupers had been buried that day; and, as it was

late, Mozart's coffin was hastily thrust into the pauper's grave—being the last for the day it was uppermost,—the earth was hastily thrown in, and the great composer lay at rest in a pauper's grave.

But a stranger thing happened. After some years the grave was opened to receive more bodies of the unfortunate poor. The grave-digger remembered which was Mozart's grave and, having been an admirer of Mozart's music, he preserved the great composer's skull. This man sold it to a certain official, who in after years bequeathed it to his brother, and it was he who made known to the world the fact of this gruesome possession.

Be this as it may, Germany can by no admiration for Mozart's works at this day atone for her neglect of their author at the time of his need and distress. It will always be a blot on the good name of Vienna and the Fatherland.

NOTABLE MUSICAL ANTAGONISMS.

295.—HÄNDEL—BUONONCINI.

Musical history furnishes some notable instances of contest for public favor. Such rivalries have not been confined to the petted favorites of the footlights, the operatic stars; we find the strongest antagonisms between some of the prominent composers, or rather, their followers; the principals did not, as a general thing, share in the anger and denunciations of their partisans.

The first notable rivalry in the history of modern music was that between Händel and Buononcini, in 1720. The latter was an Italian composer, who had been invited to England to give prestige to the Royal Academy of Music, of which Händel was at the head. Händel was patronized by King George I, and for this reason his rival was taken up and supported by the titled houses of England; for the German Elector who had inherited the British throne did not meet a warm reception at the hands of the English aristocracy. Though the nobility favored Buononcini, the people favored him who gave them the best music, and in spite of the titled opposition, Händel was for some time in the ascendancy.

Finally it was arranged that these two composers, together with a third, Ariosti, should conjointly compose an opera, and from it the public was to decide which was the greater composer. As it happened Händel had met both of his opponents before, when he was a mere boy. At that time, Buononcini, fearing a dangerous rival in the talented youth, had treated him with supercilious contempt; but Ariosti had warmly recognized his genius and had extended to him the courtesies that one artist should award another.

In this competition each wrote one act and an overture. Händel was on all sides proclaimed the victor. But he had, by his independence, made so many enemies among the aristocracy and even among his own adherents, that, some years later, popular tide had turned against him so completely as to drive him into bankruptcy. Many were the squibs and lampoons that were issued during this rivalry. One of the epigrammatic verses ran as follows:—

> "Some say, compared to Buononcini,
> That Mynheer Händel's but a Ninny;
> Others aver that he to Händel
> Is scarcely fit to hold a Candle;
> Strange all this Difference should be
> 'Twixt Tweedle-dum and Tweedle-dee!"

296.—GLUCK—PICCINNI.

Another contest in which the competitors were more evenly matched, was that which took place in Paris, about 1780, between Gluck and Piccinni (or Piccini). Gluck had as his patroness no less a personage than Marie Antoinette, who had been his pupil in Vienna.

He was introduced into Paris under the best auspices and received a warm welcome; but the very excellencies of his operas, his dramatic truth and rugged harmonies, grated harshly on ears used to the pleasant and flowing French and Italian tunes; and soon Piccinni, an able Italian composer, was imported and pitted against the progressive Gluck. Then the battle waxed hot; and every person of any consequence took sides either with Gluck or Piccinni. The operas of each were greeted with much success and it was not until the subject, "*Iphigenie en Tauride*," was given to them, to which each wrote an opera, that the conflict was decided in Gluck's favor. The Italian was conservative and dealt more with graces and ornaments than with dramatic proprieties; the German was progressive, was the Wagner of his day; in fact, it was on his reforms that many of Wagner's innovations are based.

Meanwhile, all Paris was in a ferment over the rival schools of composition; pamphlets and lampoons by the score were published. One was met on all sides with the question. "Are you a Gluckist or a Piccinnist?" Society was divided and friends estranged over the all important question, until it was finally decided by the triumph of progress over conservatism. This was undoubtedly the foremost rivalry in musical history, when we consider, not only the intensity of the partisanship displayed, but also its far reaching results in the field of operatic composition.

297.—CUZZONI—BORDONI.

The animosities of the public's vocal favorites have been more numerous than those of the composers. And while not of so serious a nature as these latter, they are certainly ornamented with a wealth of striking detail. Händel's time of life was fraught with musical dispute, one of the most prominent battles being fought between Francesca Cuzzoni and Faustina Bordini, afterward wife of the composer, Hasse. Both of these singers were brought to England by Händel, Cuzzoni being first on the ground. Although she was lacking in beauty of face and form, and was of a capricious and obstinate temper, she was flattered and petted until she developed a remarkable amount of conceit and insolence.

When Händel brought over Faustina, Cuzzoni found in her a dangerous rival; for this latter importation was fair of figure and face, intelligent and amiable. Cuzzoni excelled in the expressiveness of her singing and Faustina in skill and agility. As might have been expected, Cuzzoni's fiery temper and envious jealousy would not allow her to keep the peace with her rival, and soon there was open warfare.

The attendants on the theater sided with one or the other of the ladies, and quickly those in high places began to take part. The Countess of Pembroke headed the faction of Cuzzoni and the Countess of Burlington, that of Faustina. The fair songstresses even came to blows on several occasions; while their followers wrote epigrams, libels, and fought duels to their hearts' content. A contemporary of Händel's wrote, "These costly canary birds contaminate the whole body of our music-loving public with their virulent bickerings. Ladies refuse to receive visits from friends who belong to the opposite musical party. Cæsar and Pompey did not excite the Romans to more violent partisanship than these contentious women." The culmination of the affair was at a concert where both cantatrices took part. Their followers kept up an uproar of shouts, cat-calls, shrieking and stamping, fair ladies taking part in the *melee* with the sterner sex. A performance was almost impossible. Soon after this, the directors of the opera house permitted Cuzzoni to break her engagement, and she quickly left London and the field to her rival.

298.—SONTAG—MALIBRAN.

Another rivalry between vocalists of note was that which for some years existed between the *prima donnas*, Sontag and Malibran. It was hard to determine which of these ladies was the greater artist, so equally were they matched. Sontag possessed the greater power of vocalization, but Malibran gave to her singing a passionate warmth that touched the hearts of her auditors more than the perfect execution of her rival. Although the antagonism between them was personal as well as artistic, they did not descend to the vulgar displays of temper and envy that characterized the Bordoni-Cuzzoni feud.

It seemed that Sontag had fallen in love with and become engaged to, a scion of French royalty, a Count Rossi; but in spite of this, her hand was sought by De Beriot, the great violinist. It is needless to say that he was rejected. At this turn of affairs, De Beriot became much depressed and sought solace at the side of Malibran, who was a captivating brunette. Her quick sympathy caused a recovery from the Sontag rejection, and his affections naturally became centered on this consoling angel to such an extent that Madam Malibran afterwards became Madam De Beriot.

The rivalry that took place between Sontag and Malibran at the time we mention, was thought to have much of its origin in the fact that the Spanish brunette never forgave the fair German for having been the first loved of the French violinist. This quarrel was amicably settled, however, when, in 1828, they met in London and appeared in public together in several operas that required *prime donne* of great power and scope of voice. They then declared great admiration for each other's abilities and professed mutual friendship.

299.—LISZT—THALBERG.

Leaving the rivalries of vocalists with a number of incidents entirely out of proportion to the frequency of such animosities, we will cite one case in the ranks of the instrumentalists which was remarkable not only for the intensity of the partisanship it inspired, but for the artistic interests and principles it involved. We refer to the contest that took place in Paris, in 1836, between the pianists, Thalberg and Liszt.

Prior to this time, Liszt had been undisputed master of the pianistic world. We have not the space to dilate on his wonderful career further than to say that it reads like a romance of the imagination. He had seen all Europe at his feet and had retired to Geneva for rest and study, when there came the word that a new star had appeared in the firmament, and wonderful tales were told of this mighty rival. And truly, Sigismond Thalberg, the son of an Austrian prince, was a rival not to be despised. He was highly talented and every advantage of education was his. Liszt recognized in him a formidable antagonist, and hastened back to Paris to defend his title of "King of Pianists."

Quickly the mercurial Parisian public was arrayed on one side or the other. To be neither a Lisztian nor a Thalbergian was to admit that one had no standing whatever in society. Thalberg's playing was the acme of elegance and grace. In velvety smoothness he was held to be the superior of his fiery antagonist. On the other hand Liszt was full of brilliancy and startling effect.

Schumann said that Thalberg's playing "kept him in a tension of expectancy, not on account of the platitudes which were sure to come, but on account of the profound manner of their preparation. He deceives one by brilliant hand and finger work in order to pass off his weak thoughts."

Concerning Liszt's playing we may quote the remark

made to him by Chopin: " I prefer not to play in public; it unnerves me; you, if you cannot charm the audience, can at least astonish and crush them."

This contest was not only concerning the merits of the contestants as performers; their compositions and their artistic ideals were placed before the world for judgment. Thalberg was the personification of elegance and of the aristocratic—the conservative element. Liszt, *per contra* was imbued with high ideals of the mission of musical art, and was inspired with an enthusiasm for that which he considered true art and a hatred for the shallow inanities as poured forth by the school of which Thalberg and Herz were the chief exponents. How overwhelming was the triumph of Liszt, his great popularity in the succeeding years of his life can best answer. But through all of this artistic warfare the contestants were above malice and remained personal friends.

In the matter of personality, the advantage, so far as popularity was concerned, was with Liszt: for he was a man of much personal magnetism and his autocratic manner and his very eccentricities had a captivating effect on the public mind. But, while this was true, Thalberg was really the more dignified of the two artists. His manner was quiet and reserved, and he disdained the restless movements which characterized Liszt when at the keyboard. Nor did he lend himself to sensational occurrences in order to attract attention to his abilities as a *virtuoso*.

With two such strongly marked individualities in opposition, and with the lusty partisanship of their respective admirers, we may well realize the intensity of this notable controversy. Indeed, no more interesting contest, or, in the direction of piano composition and performance, more important one, can be found in the record of musical events. Its effects in these respects were far reaching; but of greater consequence was its results on the development of higher artistic ideals in the musicians of that day.

800.—THE FINANCIAL CIRCUMSTANCES OF THE GREAT COMPOSERS.

The recent deaths of Gounod, Tschaikowski, von Bülow and Rubinstein call to mind the great difference, in the surroundings and circumstances, between the composers of the classical period and our own times.

Bach, the greatest disciple of the contrapuntal school, died in Leipzig in 1750. He had been the recipient of a small salary as church music director. During his lifetime, appreciation for his works was limited to a section of his own country, and there it was only moderate in degree. When his widow died, ten years later, she was given a pauper's burial; yet Bach was the fountain head of all our modern music.

Händel, born the same year as Bach (1685), outlived him nine years. The most of his life was spent in England, where he was, during the latter portion, the principal musical figure. Though his operas were financial failures, his oratorios, beginning with the "Messiah" (1742), brought him renewed popularity, position and income. His lot was far more easy than that of his contemporary, Bach, though his disposition was not nearly so exemplary.

Haydn was, in common with many other musicians of his day, a sort of upper servant. His family relations were highly unpleasant, and his position was dependent on the whim of his patron prince. He was of a religious and servile nature, the latter being due largely perhaps to the custom of the times, which gave a musician, however great he might be, but little more respect than a valet or head cook. He died in 1809, with the applause caused by his oratorio of the "Creation" still in his ears. His income would to-day be deemed small by a player in a theater orchestra, and his estate was very moderate in size, and most of that was the proceeds of his English journeys.

Mozart, that gifted prodigy, that jovial good fellow, that hard-working composer, was worn out by his work and his privations when but thirty-five years old. He died in 1791. Though the greatest composer of his time, he suffered for proper financial support, and at times for sufficient nourishment. He was the victim of many conspiracies on the part of less talented musicians. He wrote his immortal operas; others profited by them. He worked; they laughed. His life was a labor to keep soul and body together and at his death he left his family without inheritance. So little was he missed that his last resting place was quickly lost sight of.

Beethoven, that rugged and self contained spirit, died in 1827. His father was a drunkard. His early home life was not the most pleasant, and even in later years he never knew the joys of a quiet home. He lived by himself and put forth the mighty children of his brain in solitude. Händel, Beethoven and Schubert form a trio of bachelor composers. Beethoven's financial circumstances were moderate, and he considered himself a poor man, though he was better situated than Mozart or Schubert in that respect.

Schubert, one of the most musical geniuses that ever lived, died in 1828, at the age of thirty-one. He was a school teacher, with hardly enough income to keep soul and body together. He was so poor that he sold the manuscripts of his songs for *tenpence,* and so unknown that he saw comparatively few of his great compositions published Dying almost alone, in great poverty,—yet before his death, sitting up and composing merry strains to bring in a mere pittance,—his life and its end were particularly pathetic.

Schumann's disposition was of that intense nature that borders on insanity; and insanity was the end of his busy life. He died in 1856, honored and beloved. His wife still lives, now (1894) seventy-five years of age, —a connecting link to the times of Beethoven, Schubert and Mendelssohn.

Chopin died in 1849, after an illness of almost ten years. He was highly honored and greatly beloved for his sweet nature. He was of a retiring disposition and seldom appeared in public. Yet the public appreciated his work even during his lifetime.

Mendelssohn had an ideal career. Surrounded by wealth, position, education, his circumstances were all that could be asked. Honored by musicians and worshiped by the people, his life is the greatest possible contrast to that of Schubert or Mozart. He died in 1847, aged thirty-nine.

Meyerbeer also was a child of favorable circumstances. Though ranking lower than that of Mendelssohn, his music obtained much popular applause, and at his death, in 1864, his funeral was such as might have been given a monarch.

The life of Richard Wagner might be divided into three epochs: the first of poverty; the second, of musical controversy and political strife; the third of rewarded success and applauded pre-eminence in the musical world. At one time he lived in a garret in Paris and did musical hack-work to keep soul and body together; at another he lived in palaces, the pet of a monarch and one of the most successful composers of musical history. The latter part of his career, which ended in 1883 was passed amid lavish and princely surroundings.

Franz Liszt, although not attaining the great pre-eminence as a composer that fell to the lot of those we have mentioned, was one of the most prominent musical figures of our century. His life reads like a dream. It is a continual ascendancy, reaching to the greatest heights of *virtuosity* and popularity. He died in 1886.

Gounod, when twenty years of age (1838) carried off the Conservatoire prize which gave him some years in Italy, for music study. On return to France, his works did not achieve immediate popularity, and even his now popular opera, "Faust," was sneered at. But becoming better understood and appreciated, he poured forth work after work which were eagerly seized by the musical public. His oratorios, "The Redemption," and "Mors et Vita" are among the best specimens of modern composition in this extended form. Applauded, flattered, appreciated, and lacking nothing in a financial way, Gounod's latter years may be compared in some slight degree with those of Wagner.

Side by side with Liszt, in the estimation of the public, stood Anton Rubinstein, and after his death, Rubinstein was the foremost figure in the pianistic world. Great as a composer, but greater as an interpreter of the works of others, Rubinstein was almost the last of the musical giants of the nineteenth century. He died in 1894, just as he was finishing his sixty-fifth year. His concert tours had brought immense sums into his coffers; but upon his discontinuance of concert giving, save for charitable purposes, his income had largely diminished, and his fortune was further decreased by the lavish expenditures at his Peterhof Villa and by his general carelessness in financial matters.

We might go on and mention the names of lesser lights. The circumstances of some of them would tend to show that even this century does not always repay genius with honor and riches. Still, the contrast between the last half century and the time that preceded it is certainly in our favor. Perhaps the twentieth century will repay all its debts to genius.

But, be that as it may, the greatest success genius achieves is in the conscious fulfilment of its high mission and not in the accumulation of riches. The possession of genius is the rarest fortune, and "Whoever fortune gives a touch, everywhere succeeds."

INDEX TO NAMES.

Reference is given to the number of the article in which the name is found. Heavy-face type indicates especial prominence of person named in article referred to.

A.

Abell, **68**
Adrian, 1
Albert, Prince, 290
Alexander, Emperor, 92
Alboni, 49, 60, 222
Amati, 174, 277
Anne, Queen, 87
Ansari, **54**
Arditi, 72, **223**
Arne, 178
Arnold, 99
Arnoldson, **182**
Arnould, **52**
Ariosti, 295
Auber, 241, 282

B.

Bach, J. S., 2, 48, 64, 127, 143, 145, 183, **207**, 221, 241, 251, 266, 273, 285, 300
Bach, Em., 241
Balfe, **6**, 41, 147
Bannister, 105
Barnum, 149, **270**
Barth, 193
Battishill, **99**
Beethoven, 16, 21, 34, 42, 48, 53, 64, 71, 80, 90, 99, 117, 134, 135, 140, 148, **150**, 154, **164**, 173, **183**, **185**, **189**, 193, 202, 205, **210**, **218**, 219, 221, **225**, **237**, 241, **250**, **254**, **262**, **271**, 272, 273, **275**, 279, 281, **282**, 285, **287**, 289, **292**, 300
Bellini, 241, 258, 282
Benedict, **223**
Benevento, 252
Beriot, 224, 241, 298
Berlioz, 4, 7, **82**, 152, 195, 241
Bettini, 11
Billington, 33, 132
Bishop, 29
Bismarck, 148
Bizet, **233**, 241
Blow, 62
Böhm, 70
Bordoni, **297**, 298
Boucher, **92**
Brahms, 144, 241
Breitkopf and Härtel, 162
Breuning, 150, 281
Bridgetower, 289
Brignoli, **208**
Britton, **105**
Bull, **14**, **17**, **116**, **165**
Buononcini, 295
Bülow, 30, 73, **85**, **128**, 144, 148, 156, **184**, 195, **212**, **228**, **239**, 284, 300
Byrd, **3**

C.

Caffarelli, 114
Campanini, 58, 120, 235
Camporese, 43
Carestini, 23
Catalini, 28, 111, 131
Catherine, Empress, 50
Cervetto, 277
Chappell & Co., 176
Charlemagne, 1
Charles II, 68
Charles IV, 92
Charles V, 290
Charles VI, 206, 290
Cherubini, 4, 138, 232, 241, 258, 274, 278
Chopin, 64, 125, 158, 241, 299, 300
Chorley, 234
Cimarosa, 16, 109, 197
Clementi, 101, 241
Coccia, 179, 282
Cooke, 170
Corelli, 63, 183, 220, 238, 241
Costa, 267
Cowen, 267
Cramer, 142, 241
Crotch, 9, 183
Cuzzoni, 23, 105, 297, 298
Czerny, 103, 158, 190, 205, 241

D.

Damrosch, 267
D'Artois, 238
David, 267, 277
Devrient, Mme., 55, 139, 188
Devrient, Edw., 2
Diabelli, 158, 189
Donizetti, 153, 258, 282
Dragonetti, 277
Ducré, 82
Dufay, 241
Dumas, 137
Duport, 281
Dussek, 252

E.

Edinburgh, Duke of, 290
Elizabeth, Queen, 25, 290
Erba, 183
Ernst, 267, 277
Esterhazy, 103, 134, 181, 266

F.

Fancelli, 58
Farinelli, 33, 83, 290
Field, 101, 115, 136
Fischer, 200
Feininger, 96
Ferdinand VI, 83
Fetis, 241
Flotow, 217
Fodor, 36, 224
Frederick, 78
Frederick the Great, 224, 290

G.

Gabriella, 45, 118, 131
Gade, 241
Garcia, 69, 81, 98
George I, 87, 201, 295
George III, 59
George IV, 293
Gerster, 13, 240
Giardini, 104
Gillott, 174
Giuglini, 227
Gluck, 16, 51, 77, 221, 241, 258, 266, 296
Goethe, 28
Goldmark, 267
Goldschmidt, 149, 270
Gounod, 176, 241, 258, 282, 291, 300
Graun, 183
Gregory, 1
Grétry, 109, 167, 258
Grisi, 106
Guarnerius, 122, 174, 245, 277

H.

Haizinger, 188, 196
Halevy, 267, 278, 282
Händel, 17, 20, 23, 32, 74, 87, 105, 119, 134, 141, 151, 155, 161, 164, 166, 175, 179, 183, 195, 201, 213, 219, 241, 252, 258, 266, 276, 282, 295, 300
Harris, Claudius, 149
Harris, Renatus, 62
Hasse, 297
Hauk, 265
Haydn, 16, 94, 97, 107, 132, 134, 135, 146, 150, 181, 185, 194, 199, 209, 221, 232, 241, 259, 266, 282, 285, 286, 288, 300
Henry VIII, 290
Hermann, 291
Herz, 130, 158
Hiller, 267
Hubey, 277
Hucbald, 241
Hummel, 103, 115, 130, 158, 183, 241
Hulsen, 30

J.

Jadassohn, 267
Jennens, 105
Joachim, 241, 267
Joseph I, 101
Joseph II, 146
Josquin, 22, 56, 183

K.

Kalkbrenner, 125, 158
Keiser, 282
Kelly, 65, 192, 238
Kiel, 230
Kreutzer, 158, 289
Kuhnau, 283
Kuhlau, 230
Kurtz, 199

L.

Lablache, 33, 75, 88, 95, 135, 222
Lachner, 241
Larivee, 253
Lassus, 241
Laulaire, 204
Lea, 249
Leoncavallo, 26, 67
Leopold I, 290
L'Estrange, 105
Lichnowsky, 281
Lind, 5, 75, 113, 121, 130, 149, 160, 224, 270
Lindley, 18
Liszt, 34, 56, 64, 84, 103, 121, 123, 128, 130, 145, 148, 158, 165, 169, 190, 205, 241, 242, 250, 269, 276, 299, 300
Lolli, 104
Louis XII, 22
Louis Philippe, 269
Lowe, 202
Lucca, 55
Ludwig, Duke, 78
Lully, 44, 62, 161, 236, 256, 258, 279

M.

Malibran, 8, 41, 55, 81, 98, 163, 215, 224, 298
Mara, 55, 124, 247
Mary, Queen of Scots, 290
Mascagni, 26, 109, 263
Mapleson, 11, 60, 108, 176
Marcellus, 19
Marie Antoinette, 238, 296
Marino, Countess of, 229
Mario, 135
Massenet, 258, 259
Matheson, 151, 241, 283
Maupin, 229, 257
Mehul, 4, 16, 51
Melba, 8
Melville, 277
Mendelssohn, 2, 35, 53, 64, 76, 90, 123, 143, 145, 153, 165, 179,

308 INDEX TO NAMES.

183, 185, 187, 223, 234, 241, 251, 267, 285, 290, 300
Mercadante, 282
Meyerbeer, 35, 150, 180, 223, 241, 258, 264, 267, 282, 300
Morell, 166
Mori, 142
Moscheles, 53, 96, 125, 225, 237, 241, 267
Moszkowski, 230
Mozart, 9, 10, 16, 40, 42, 64, 65, 97, 99, 103, 109, 121, 134, 145, 146, 150, 161, 172, 179, 183, 185, 192, 221, 228, 241, 258, 266, 268, 276, 282, 294, 300
Murska, 93, 260

N.

Nardini, 104
Napoleon, 92, 111, 126, 148, 287
Nero, 290
Neruda, 277
Nevada, 100
Nicolai, 241
Nicolini, 100
Niedermeyer, 217
Nikisch, 228
Nilsson, 8, 60, 108
Normandy, Lady, 106

O.

Ockenheim, 241
Offenbach, 267
Ottoboni, 220, 238

P.

Pacchierotti, 39
Pachmann, 12
Pacini, 282
Paderewski, 169, 208
Paesiello, 16, 50
Paine, 285

Paganini, 7, 14, 27, 79, 86, 102, 122, 130, 142, 152, 157, 174, 186, 211, 226, 241, 249, 261, 279
Palestrina, 19, 241
Palffy, 196
Paratt, 276
Pasta, 224
Patti, 31, 72, 100, 102, 177, 240
Paur, 228
Pepusch, 105
Pepys, 38
Pergolesi, 241
Persiani, 8
Philip V, 83
Piccinni, 77, 282, 296
Pixis, 158, 205
Pleyel, 241
Porpora, 46, 114, 259
Praeger, 255
Prout, 183
Purcell, 62, 241

R.

Raff, 241
Raimondi, 61
Rameau, 42, 241, 258
Reynolds, 132
Rhehazek, 165
Ricci, 282
Richter, 228
Ries, 150, 173, 218, 254, 287
Rinaldo, 48
Royer, 291
Romberg, 150
Ronconi, 66
Rosengrave, 15
Rossi, 224, 298
Rossini, 16, 29, 70, 102, 121, 133, 180, 185, 221, 236, 241, 252, 258, 279, 282, 293
Rozé, 265
Rothschild, 7, 244
Rubini, 135
Rubinstein, 228, 231, 241, 267, 300

INDEX TO NAMES.

S.

Sacchini, 16
Salieri, 196
Salomon, 59
Santley, 93
Sapellnikow, 280
Scarlatti, 15, 155, 241, 258, 282
Schascheck, 64
Schindler, 281
Schubert, 48, 57, 64, 80, 112, 158, 161, 162, 185, 195, 221, 241, 272, 300
Schmidt, 62
Schumann, 48, 159, 195, 216, 241, 246, 284, 299, 300
Seidl, 228
Shah of Persia, 108
Sheridan, 192
Sivori, 122, 211
Smart, 99
Snetzler, 214
Solon, 89
Sontag, 55, 91, 224, 298
Spohr, 101, 126, 221, 241, 244
Spontini, 109
Stainer, 206, 277
Steininger, 91
Storace, 168
Stradella, 183, 217
Stradivarius, 79, 174, 245, 277
Strunck, 63
St. Saëns, 241
Sullivan, 96
Swift, 273

T.

Tallis, 61
Talma, 126
Tamburini, 135, 243
Tarisio, 277
Tartini, 47, 195, 241
Taylor, 113
Thalberg, 130, 158, 215, 299
Thomas, Ambroise, 241, 258
Thomas, Theodore, 228
Thumb, 95

Titiens, 11, 55, 93, 108, 227
Tschaikowsky, 280, 300
Tye, 25, 198

U.

Uria, 183

V.

Verdi, 109, 133, 191, 241, 258, 263, 282
Victoria, 106, 250, 276, 290
Vidocq, 14
Vinci, 26
Viotti, 129, 238
Vivaldi, 37

W.

Wagner, 16, 82, 84, 109, 137, 146, 185, 203, 221, 228, 241, 248, 255, 258, 263, 266, 282, 285, 300
Waldstein, 150
Wales, Prince and Princess of, 219
Wales, Princess of, 290
Wallace, 110
Weber, 78, 171, 195, 221, 241. 258
Weingartner, 228
Wesley, Samuel, 99
Wesley, Charles, 99
Whitney, 84
Wieniawski, 267, 277
Wilhelmji, 277
William I, 250, 290,
William II, 290
Wuerst, 230

Z.

Zajic, 277
Zeffrini, 249
Zelter, 2, 195, 241
Zingarelli, 16, 241

www.ingramcontent.com/pod-product-compliance
Lightning Source LLC
Chambersburg PA
CBHW030809230426
43667CB00008B/1136